Geography, History, and the American Political Economy

Geography, History, and the American Political Economy

Edited by
John Heppen and Samuel M. Otterstrom

LEXINGTON BOOKS
A division of
ROWMAN & LITTLEFIELD PUBLISHERS, INC.
Lanham • Boulder • New York • Toronto • Plymouth, UK

Published by Lexington Books
A division of Rowman & Littlefield Publishers, Inc.
A wholly owned subsidiary of The Rowman & Littlefield Publishing Group, Inc.
4501 Forbes Boulevard, Suite 200, Lanham, Maryland 20706
http://www.lexingtonbooks.com

Estover Road, Plymouth PL6 7PY, United Kingdom

British Library Cataloguing in Publication Information Available

Library of Congress Cataloging-in-Publication Data

Geography, history, and the American political economy / edited by John Heppen and Samuel M. Otterstrom.
p. cm.
Includes bibliographical references and index.
ISBN 978-0-7391-2816-9 (cloth : alk. paper) — ISBN 978-0-7391-4098-7 (electronic)
1. United States—Historical geography. 2. Human geography—United States—History. 3. United States—Economic conditions. 4. Industrialization—United States—History. 5. Earle, Carville. I. Heppen, John. II. Otterstrom, Samuel.

E179.5.G464 2009
911.73—dc22 2009019067

♾™ The paper used in this publication meets the minimum requirements of American National Standard for Information Sciences—Permanence of Paper for Printed Library Materials, ANSI/NISO Z39.48-1992.

Printed in the United States of America

Contents

List of Tables and Figures

TABLES

FIGURES

Acknowledgments

We would first like to acknowledge Carville Earle for his teaching and research that has formed the basis of what we believe to be a new and exciting time for historical geography and even a new school of historical geography based on a solid theoretical foundation. This volume is dedicated to him. It is our hope that these pieces of original research inspire, as well as provide specialists and the general public alike, a greater knowledge of the fundamental interconnections among seemingly diverse times and places. We would like to thank Anne Mosher for conceptualizing the idea of this volume and Greg Veeck at Western Michigan University for helping us work out some ideas associated with this work. This book could not have come to fruition without the support of Julie Kirsch and Michael Sisskin at Lexington Books. We thank them for believing in the project and for their patience. An edited volume depends on its contributors and we express gratitude to them all for their participation, hard work and good cheer. We would also like to thank Vicki Kurtenbach, program assistant in Geography and Mapping Sciences at the University of Wisconsin River Falls, and Laurie Weisler, Natalie Lester and Millie Lewis, administrative and secretarial staff in the Brigham Young University Department of Geography, for their supreme proofreading and editing skills and clerical support. Additionally, partial financial support for this research came from a Faculty Research Grant at the University of Wisconsin River Falls.

Chapter One

Introduction: Approaching America's Geographical History

John Heppen and Samuel M. Otterstrom

This book begins with three simple questions: (1) What can theoretically guided geographic schooling offer in answering important questions of the American past? (2) What have been the geographic outcomes that have resulted from the periodic restructuring of the American political economy? (3) How can the different perspectives taken in geography and history work together in offering new interpretations of the American past—if they can work together? Regarding the latter question, Gaines Foster, the Southern historian at Louisiana State University once said to a geography graduate student under the tutelage of historical geographer Carville Earle, "[t]hat's the problem with you geographers, people vote how they feel not what they grow." That young geographer should have done a better job of explaining how the local physical geography offered farmers various agricultural possibilities within social-cultural constraints unique to their locale in addition to constraints placed on them by regional, national, and world economies. A good explanation would have been that those geographical factors at various scales played an important role in how farmers felt about political candidates, and because geography differs from place to place the resulting electoral map would have revealed political patterns that required spatial as well as social and temporal interpretations.

Foster's comment may seem unfair to some, but it does illustrate an intellectual debate between geographers and historians concerning their different perspectives on geography and history. Scholars such as Alan R. H. Baker (2003; 2007) have worked to emphasize some commonalities and the relationships between geography and history. Most recently Baker (2007) explored the usage of the terms geographical history and historical geography in order to determine ways for historians and geographers to communicate their ideas with each other more freely. In studying the terms, Baker considered how Carville Earle employed them. As Earle worked to reveal the key role of geography in explaining the past, he often referred to himself as a geographical historian who practiced geo-historical social science. This book follows Earle's belief that past geographies were instrumental in shaping histories. Here we take on the challenge issued by reviewers of Earle's *The American Way: A Geographical History of Crisis and Recovery* (2003); to apply a theoretical framework to the geographical manifestations of political and economic shifts in America's past.[1]

In this collection of essays we endeavor to illustrate the wide variety of ways that the American historical landscape has been shaped by individual forces and large-scale processes. We drew inspiration from Carville Earle. Earle's research into the American past was driven by a social scientific empiricism guided by theory. Our guiding principal is that historical geographers or geographical historians are best thought of as social scientists addressing problems of the American past using the methods and theories of geographers. Each chapter takes the challenge to apply a geographical and theoretically driven framework based on a fifty-year cycle of crisis and recovery of the American political economy to at least one fundamental issue in the historical geography of the United States. Together they provide a picture of spatial economic and political restructuring across a wide swath of American history. The questions raised also invite future empirical analysis and exploration so our evolving understanding of the geographic restructuring of the American political economy can continue to be refined.

According to Baker (2003), there have been two dominant views of interpreting the historical geography of the United States for approximately the last 30 years. Donald Meinig and Carville Earle sparred over a view of America's historical geography as order and continuity (Meinig's view) or disorder and discontinuity (Earle's view). Earle criticized Meinig's imperialistic expansionist view as being too limiting and not tackling the important big questions that have vexed students of the American past (see Earle 1992). Earle felt strongly that historical geographers, or geographical historians, were social scientists coming to terms with important questions by using an approach and method under-appreciated or dismissed by historians—a geographic, spatial, and environmental approach.

Our book reveals how the political economy of the United States has experienced cyclical reconfiguring spatial geographies. This evolution has spanned the entire period since European contact. Each succeeding generation has seen changes in settlement patterns, political systems, and economic control. Rather than a smooth trajectory this process has been one of fits and starts, where changes in the American landscape have been impacted by political and economic policies and practices both in the continent and by foreign powers during the colonial period. This volume seeks to interconnect the world of America's past using examples that span nearly three hundred years of history while ranging in geographic scale from the very local to the global. Together they illustrate the power of taking a social scientific and geographic approach in order to answer significant historical and geographic questions.

The practice of historical geography in the English-speaking world has been varied. But within that world there has been a spirited debate on the direction or focus of historical geography. Earle and Meinig represented two views or options for historical geography. Earle challenged geographers to examine the expansive nature of the American State, the continuing rise of the influence of corporate America, and the ebbs and flows and stops and starts of capitalism and how its rhythmic patterns of good times and bad times where met forcibly by the American State through alternating policy regimes. Earle believed in an empirical, practical, and, if possible, theoretically driven examination of the American Past. He also felt that there were many questions that needed to be answered or more fully answered by geographers who were social scientists.

CONCEPTUAL APPROACH AND OVERVIEW OF THE BOOK

As noted, the periodic restructuring of the American economy and society is caused by approximately fifty-year cycles of crisis and recovery (Earle 2003). The fifty-year cycles of good times and bad times run concurrent with Kondratieff waves of rising and falling wholesale prices (Kondratieff 1935). The geographic outcomes have been manifested in settlement patterns, productive and consumer activities, regional restructuring of wealth, and political regionalism. *Geography, History, and the American Political Economy* looks to answer those questions by examining the geo-historical results of the restructuring of the American political economy from local to global scales.

As Baker (2003) noted, research in the historical geography of the United States tend to be either very place specific such as Anne Mosher's *Capital's Utopia* (2004) or more broadly based. The latter category includes Meinig's four volumes on U.S. historical geography (1986; 1992; 1998; 2004) and Earle's *The American Way* (2003). Earle's goal in *The American Way* was to do what Meinig did, but in only one book with a different interpretation of American's geographical past (see Baker [2003] for more on that debate). One challenge with large sweeping works such as Meinig's and Earle's is that scholars and students of American history and geography are given either broad theoretical or non-theoretical pictures with less application to regions or places of interest. On the other side, studies looking at local regions often garner the interest of only fellow regional, temporal, or topical specialists.

Few books have offered an analysis of the historical geography of places within a larger theoretical framework. Much has been written on local and regional historical geographies, but in that body of work there have been only rare attempts to present a unified explanatory theme that explains the processes which created past and present landscapes. In contrast, even though this book's contributions are taken from variously bounded areas of space and periods of time, they are unified by one overarching conceptual theory. In this way this volume offers complementary scholarly vignettes on various places at various scales in the American past.

The contributors illustrate changes in U.S. settlement, regionalism, development, and political structure through the lens of the periodic restructuring of the American economy and society caused by approximately fifty-year cycles of crisis and recovery (Earle 2003). While the main thrust of the book centers around geographic responses to periodic cycles of crisis and recovery, the more general underlying intertwining of geography and history is emphasized. Additionally, the next chapter is a methodological and reflective discussion by Anne Mosher, who interprets Earle's geohistorical work to show its importance and relevance to American historical thought.

In summary, we take the challenge to apply a theoretically based geographical framework to the spatial manifestations of political and economic shifts in America's past. However, the structural-theoretical framework is not a straightjacket. An analogy to an almost bygone way of travel provides the best comparison. In the first half of the twentieth century, a rail journey from New York to Chicago could follow many routes, such as the New York Central's Twentieth Century Limited (made famous in the film *North by Northwest*), or the Pennsylvania Railroad's Broadway Limited, or by other trains that took you through Buffalo, Canada, Detroit, Ohio or Indiana. Regardless of specifics, you went in the same direction using the same basic method. In essence, that is the theoretical framework of this volume. The book is a journey via rail from New York to Chicago, but each rider took different trains, different railroads and had different routes, times, and accommodations. However, everyone went in the same direction traveling by the same method and stayed on the right track in their approach to their specific geographical issue. The chapters are arranged sequentially from colonial to contemporary times. They illustrate changes in U.S. settlement, development, and political structure through the lens of the periodic restructuring of the American economy and society reflected by approximately fifty-year cycles of crisis and recovery (Earle 2003). Thus, the volume is wholly grounded in theory as it offers both regional vignettes and national discourses from current to colonial times.

NOTE

1. *American Historical Review* 2004 (4) pp. 1219–1220; *Annals of the Association of American Geographers* 2004 (3) pp. 674–678; *William and Mary Quarterly* 2004 (3) pp. 556–559.

BIBLIOGRAPHY

Baker, A. H. R. 2003. *Geography and History Bridging the Divide*. (Cambridge: Cambridge University Press).

———. 2007. "Classifying Geographical History," *The Professional Geographer* 59: 344–356.

Earle, C. 1992. *Geographical Inquiry and American Historical Problems*. (Stanford: Stanford University Press).

———. 2003. *The American Way: A Geographical History of Crisis and Recovery*. (Lanham, MD: Rowman & Littlefield).

Kondratieff, N. 1935. "The Long Wave in Economic Life," *Review of Economic Statistics* 17: 105–115.

Meinig, D. W. 1986. *Atlantic America, 1492–1800*. Vol. 1, *The Shaping of America: A Geographical Perspective on 500 Years of History*. (New Haven: Yale University Press).

———. 1992. *Continental America, 1800–1867*. Vol. 2, *The Shaping of America: A Geographical Perspective on 500 Years of History*. (New Haven: Yale University Press).

———. 1998. *Transcontinental America, 1850–1915*. Vol. 3, *The Shaping of America*. (New Haven: Yale University Press).

———. 2004. *Global America, 1915–2000*. (New Haven: Yale University Press).

Mosher, A. E. 2004. *Capital's Utopia: Vandergrift, Pennsylvania, 1855–1916, Creating the North American Landscape*. (Baltimore: Johns Hopkins University Press).

Chapter Two

Earle's Theory and Conception of the Geographical History of the United States

Anne E. Mosher

Throughout his career, Carville Earle (1942–2003) showed by example how historians might use geography to reinterpret the "big historiographic issues" of American history. On more than one occasion Earle nevertheless remarked publicly that he felt that many historians tended to treat geography as a passive object, like a rather benign stage on which the drama of history unfolded—if geography was discussed at all. In contrast, Earle believed quite fervently that natural environments and cultural landscapes—as perceived by those who looked upon them, and maps—with their ability to show viewers in synoptic fashion simultaneous sets of relationships between places, actors, and resources, had the power to stir souls. Landscapes, environment and maps had sparked grand ideas, shaped the practice of everyday life, and had influenced the course of history. But to recognize how that aspect of geography—that is: *geography as an active object*—might inform historical interpretation; Earle felt that one needed something more: an understanding of *geography as a subject.* Geography is not merely the arrangement of physical landscape features and human activities over the face of the earth. It is also a perspective and a research protocol; in effect, it is a system of knowledge that includes basic spatial concepts, models, theories and analytical techniques that are part of geographical practice. This system is what Earle wanted to bring to the practice of history.

That Earle was successful is evidenced by nearly the entire body of his published professional work as well as by his teaching. His belief that others should follow suit resounded deeply with colleagues at Louisiana State University (1989–2004) in formal and informal settings. Contrary to what others at the time may have believed, they were not simply enjoying "a cold frosty one" and "just talking baseball," Carville, surrounded by department and university colleagues, students, and various interlopers, engaged in serious conversations and debates, including "visioning sessions" about a grand project to which all would contribute: the creation of a "new geographical history." Earle's *Geographical Inquiry and American Historical Problems* (1992) attempted to show what this geographical history could look like, covering—from a geographical perspective—historical topics as diverse as the identification of the basis for antebellum sectionalism (the geographies of innovation diffusion and uneven labor requirements within agriculture), and the reasons for the rise and fall of the American labor movement (the uneven geography of industrialization). He also, quite significantly, began to develop a meta-theory that linked the rhythm of American history to the various moments of geographical restructuring that had occurred in the American economy and the body politic.

Theorizing the spatio-temporal rhythm to American history became central to Earle's final book, *The American Way: A Geographical History of Crisis and Recovery* (2003). In it, he identified a deep geographical and historical structure within the ongoing development of the American nation-state. Instead of developing a chronologically progressive (*surficial)* narrative—such as the one that Donald Meinig constructs in *The Shaping of America* (Meinig 1986; 1992; 1998; 2004)—that begins with the United States as a relatively simple set of economic, political, social and spatial arrangements and ends with it being a highly complex network of physical, symbolic and transactional relationships, Earle used *The American Way* to make a geographically informed argument regarding the United States's ability to recover from economic, social and political crisis.

Core to recovery, Earle believed, were two enduring spatial logics that explained the dynamics of American geopolitics and the geography of the United States since 1789. The American Revolution ushered in two new different regimes and philosophies—Republics or Protectionist Elite regimes (PE) and Democracies or Free Trade Masses regimes (FTM). As logics, they are essentially two competing political *geosophies*; that is, "geographical ideas both true and false held by all manner of people, accounting for human desires, motives and prejudices" about what the United States was in the past, is now, and should be in the future (Wright 1947). One of these geosophies, Earle contended, conceptualizes the United States more as a Republic while the other sees it more as a Democracy.

Based on a thorough reading of American macro-political history and its attendant historiography, Earle argued that both of these geosophies have vied for political dominance in American political culture from foundation in the late-eighteenth century to the present day. They have set up an alternating and thus reoccurring pattern of contrasting public policies and spatial processes, as the country morphed in the mid-nineteenth century from an association of three "sections" (North, South, and the western frontier) into a continental nation, and then changed again in the late-twentieth century from a continental nation into transnational protector of American interests abroad. Onward, upward, and outward over time like the progressive chronologies suggest.

With startling regularity, Earle contends, the United States has shifted its worldview from one that stresses protective isolationism in foreign affairs and elitism at home (the policy regime of the Republic) to one that stresses liberalism in foreign affairs and egalitarianism at home (the policy regime of the Democracy), and back again. When in a Republican phase, government policy promotes strategies that will benefit producers, that will expand the extent of national influence into new geographical territory, and that will promote areal functional specialization. When in a Democratic phase, governmental policy promotes strategies that will benefit consumers, that will intensively develop and make useful previously acquired national territory, and that will redistribute wealth to underdeveloped regions within the country's borders (figure 2.1).

Earle's model pivots on a familiar premise: that the United States can be thought of as first, an ongoing philosophical debate, and second, as an

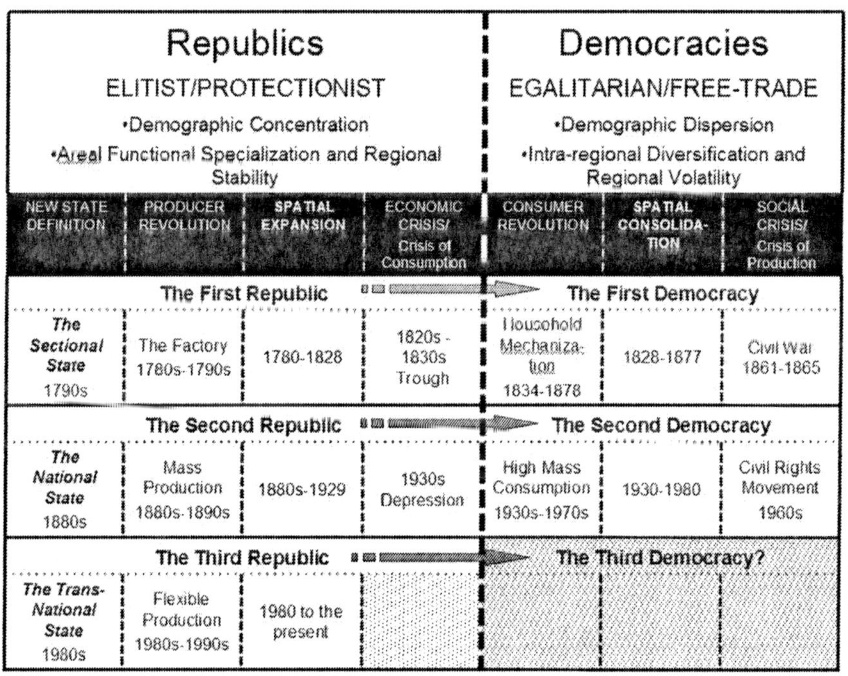

Figure 2.1. Model of the Geographical Dialectics of American Policy Regimes

institutional experiment. In a nutshell, the debate has pitted supporters of the idea that the United States functions best when it is behaving as a Republic (a unity of free peoples) against those who believe that the United States functions best when it is behaving as a Democracy (a collection of enfranchised but diverse individuals). The institutional experiment is essentially a malleable form of federalism: an enduring hierarchical operational structure that can exist as a part of, but change according to, the dialectic shifts within the philosophical debate.

To this premise, Earle adds his concern for geography. He argues that the philosophical debate as well as the institution have been influenced by: (1) geographical conditions that are specific to the North American continent, and (2) popular geosophical beliefs regarding (a) the United States' relationship to other nation-states (its place in the international realm) and (b) the United States as a place in which to live and work (the spatial organization of the domestic realm). Over time, through formal and informal political processes, geographical conditions meld with geosophical belief and are incorporated into state policies that guide the actions of the United States–as-institution and, ultimately, further shape the country's geography. Ordinances, programs, departments, and court decisions created as a part of state policy can shape places and regions and the roles they play in the broader economic, social and political system. Thus state policy exists as an intervention within a recursive relationship that interlinks political philosophy and geography (as both a mapped condition [geography as object] and as a set of spatial beliefs and practices [geography as subject]).

Earle also sees state policy as a specific kind of intervention—one that alleviates socio-economic crises which have erupted over the long-haul of American history with amazing regularity and *similarity*. He classifies these crises as being of two general types: first, crises of production that emerge when Americans have been preoccupied for a number of years with consumerism and the enactment of new definitions of citizenship instead of focusing on the creation of productive capacity; and second, crises of consumption that emerge when enacted policy fosters productive capacity but has paid less attention to Americans' ability to acquire things. Looking across American history, these crises of production and consumption seem to alternate on a forty- to sixty-year rotational basis which Earle links to the movement of the fifty- to sixty-year economic "supercycle" first identified by Nikolai Khondratieff (1935). Let us look at each of these crises and how they mesh with this supercycle and some specifics of American history.

Crises of production occur during the Kondratieff (1935) supercycle's "trough"—when prices and productivity are low. Thus far in the United States's existence, the federal state has reacted to the troughs by enacting a suite of policies (a policy regime) that will foster a business environment that is more conducive to profitable production, in which business enterprise can be reorganized, new or modified production technologies and processes can be applied, and social relations between capital and labor can be changed (Mosher 2004). This activity becomes part of a "Producer Revolution," three of which have occurred in the United States since the 1780s: the shift from household to factory production in the 1780s and 1790s, the perfection of mass production in the 1880s and 1890s and the establishment of flexible production in the 1980s and 1990s. These revolutions have helped to stimulate the supply-side of the economy and propel economic indicators upward on the upswing of the Kondratieff cycle.

Crises of consumption occur when prices and productivity are high and consumption is low. At this point in the Kondratieff cycle, the job of state policy is to foster an environment that favors the consumer, where marketing and advertising creates a better informed public and makes products more available, consumer credit replaces scarce cash, wages rise to repay debt, and a new array of regulations and services improve conditions in both the productive and reproductive spheres of labor. This activity becomes part of a "Consumer Revolution," two of which have occurred in the United States—the introduction of household mechanization between the 1830s and 1870s and the era of high mass consumption that began under FDR's New Deal in the 1930s and ended in the 1970s. These revolutions stimulated the demand-side of the economy after the profit-enhancing abilities of the production process had hit a prolonged plateau. They helped soften blows to the economy—at least temporarily—as it entered the downswing of the Kondratieff cycle.

Earle argues that during crisis, one specific side of the Republican/Democratic debate will inevitably rise to the fore to help develop a policy regime that will foster the appropriate "revolution" that will then set the country back on the road to recovery. (The proponents of the losing side of the debate do not fade away, however. They form the minority opposition that is so crucial to a true democratic process. They create the dialectical tension that Earle has chosen to embed within his model. The minority waits—in hopeful anticipation, plugging away in various geographical corners at the local and regional scales—until a change occurs in economic conditions and public sentiment propels its stalwart members back into the majority and hence, national power.

Since 1789, during crises of production the side that favors the idea of the United States as a Republic (and a geosophy that Earle calls 'Protectionist Elitist Republicanism' or Protectionist Elite regimes [PE]) has come to power. This policy regime: (1) tries to grow GDP (gross domestic product) and GNP (gross national product) through protectionist foreign policy; and (2) favors the political and economic elite through a domestic policy that sets up the overall conditions for a producer revolution. Republics have favored spatial expansion into frontier areas and demographic (population) concentration. The resulting settlement patterns results in compact settlements on the frontier. Regionally, Republics have promoted regional specialization and stability. Under Republics, regions have specialized in the economic activities where they posses a geographic advantage and so regional incomes remain stable so low-wage regions can specialize in labor-intensive activities of primary and secondary industries. In the meantime, higher income areas have remained places of high-value added manufacturing and services.

In a different manner, Democracies have promoted spatial consolidation with demographic dispersion. Frontier areas need to be consolidated with established settled areas by settling the spaces between frontier and settled areas and by instituting government sponsored transportation projects. Regionally, Democracies have brought regional diversification and regional instability. Poorer or peripheral regions have needed to diversify their economic activities in order to catch-up, thus capturing an increasing share of the national income or converging toward the national average. Additionally, producers seek to relocate to peripheral regions for lower labor costs and pro-business state and local governments. These temporal and spatial processes lead to regional income volatility.

During crises of consumption the side that favors the Democracy (a geosophy that Earle calls "egalitarian free-trade liberalism") has erected gradually a policy regime that: (1) provides economic and social opportunities for more citizens at home; and (2) attempts to pay for these policies through the externalities created by less rigidly controlled international trade, thus setting up the overall conditions for a consumer revolution.

In both cases, the policies enacted by either regime contain spatial agenda—that either put in place the infrastructural improvements, geographically targeted investment incentives, and/or program networks that will knit the country together into a tightly bound system of specialized parts (the republican policy regime) or that redistribute capital (again, often through the infrastructure and program networks) so as to lessen the disparities that exist between regions/states and to ensure equal participation of all people regardless of location (the democratic policy regime). These alternating spatial agenda have reshaped the American landscape, putting in place new elements, while at the same time creatively destroying or retrofitting older ones. Before discussing in more detail the ways in which the spatial agenda of the two policy regimes may have been articulated throughout history, however, it is first necessary to explain more fully the general geographic conditions and geosophies that Earle thinks have led to a recurring set of spatial outcomes throughout American history.

GEOSOPHIES OF PROTECTIONIST ELITIST (PE) REPUBLICANISM AND EGALITARIAN FREE-TRADE MASSES (FTM) DEMOCRACIES

In the "First Republic" (1780s–1830s), a protectionist geosophy dominated foreign policy. Britain threatened militarily and economically through the 1810s (and later in certain industries and geographical areas, such as in iron and tin production in the Great Lakes region). International borders thus mattered to the United States as it sought to control the terms of trade and delineate territorial possessions. To create a protective buffer zone, in the 1800s the American state thrust the political frontier far ahead of settlement. In the "Second Republic" (1880s–1920s), spatial expansion like this continued—through the formal and informal control of other places within the western hemisphere and Pacific Rim. Tariffs and immigration restrictions, however, made for more durable borders. In the "Third Republic" (the period since 1980), borders continue to matter but expand into the North American Free Trade Agreement and the era's policies now enable the expansion of American corporate interests overseas, not to mention the periodic deployment of troops to protect an expansive field of places that are perceived as being of strategic interest (e.g., Kuwait, Afghanistan, and Iraq).

At home, the Republican geosophy rests solidly on the idea that private property is the basis for wealth and status given the potential profit that can be derived from utilization and/or resale. Corollary to this is the notion that property ownership is not really a right, but rather a privilege that is earned through hard work, inheritance or social connection. Moreover, profit derived from property allows individuals and corporate entities to hold onto what they have and to acquire more. Thus wealth is concentrated within a narrow segment of the population. It also concentrates in specific locations, namely those that are the most accessible (e.g., peak land value intersections in cities) and where the driving sectors of the economy are found. In the First Republic this meant that population concentrated around the mercantile ports of the eastern seaboard, in the Second Republic around massive urban and suburban factories located in the industrial northeast and near corporate mining properties in the upper Midwest and West, and in the Third Republic in locations participating within the quaternary and quinary sectors—usually large metropolitan areas, primarily in regions with high amenity values such as the South and West. Remember also that the Republican geosophy incorporates the notion that all productive places are part of a larger federated whole, with each place playing a specialized role in a well-ordered, functionally interdependent economic system that consists of a dominant core region (the major population concentration) that is tethered by transportation and communication networks to a diffuse and subordinate periphery that is there either to act as a buffer against outsiders or as a supplier of natural resources and, at times, labor. Notably, traffic flows between these regions without concern for state boundaries. Based on this, Earle argues that the geographic principle of areal functional specialization becomes the policy outcome of the Republican day, that it creates relatively stable relationships between regions, but also quite distinct differences between a controlling core region and a subservient periphery.

In the "First Democracy" (1830s–1870s), a liberal free-trade geosophy dominated foreign policy and led to the internationalization of capital and labor within the United States. For example, changes in banking and foreign exchange policy allowed Europeans, particularly the British, to become heavy investors in the construction of both the short-haul railroads that began to interconnect the populated East, and the transcontinental railroad schemes intended to bring into the market's grasp the unproductive territory that had been acquired under the First Republic. Europe's hunger for American mineral resources and agricultural commodities (particularly grain, beef and cotton), also pumped millions of dollars into the regional economies of the Midwest, West and South, spurring the rapid development of resource processing, transportation, and mercantile activities—to the extent that eastern seaboard cities began to fret about the competition posed by the commodity exchanges in Chicago, San Francisco and New Orleans. Many European capitalists actually moved permanently or seasonally to the United States, aided by an open door policy toward immigration, bringing with them not only their capital, but also the business and technological know-how that ultimately transformed the textile, iron and steel, shoe, brewing and meat-packing industries. And, with the exception of the South, where the slave economy dominated for most of the period and the instability of post–Civil War Reconstruction reigned at the end, opportunities on farms and factories on the rapidly developing periphery and on the burgeoning transportation system itself attracted thousands of immigrants from northwest Europe who had been pushed out of their homelands by famine and political struggle. Such internationalization could also be seen in the "Second Democracy" (1930s–1970s), particularly after World War II, when the United States used its productive capacity to flood both domestic and foreign markets with consumer goods. This intensification of economic activity, of course, had been made possible through the spatial extension of American corporate interests abroad during the Second Republic. The country also relaxed its borders to welcome another wave of the politically dispossessed, especially from Eastern Europe, many of whom brought with them advanced training in science and technology, and to institutionalize migratory farm labor movements from Mexico into the West through the Bracero Program.

At home, the geosophy of the Democracy rested solidly on egalitarian principles—namely, that all citizens, including those outside the core and those at lower rungs on the social ladder, have a fundamental right to share in the country's prosperity—that they should have access to employment, property ownership, education, and an array of consumer goods that would improve the quality of life at home. In many ways, these principles developed in response to the elitist structures that had been emplaced during the preceding republics. Laboring people in the core and periphery alike caught glimpses of the opulent world that the American core elite had erected and compared it to the meager one in which they themselves worked and lived. Should not the Republican concerns for private property and the rational and profitable operation of the spaces of capital (the bank, the boardroom, the store, the factory office) be accompanied by a concern for the spaces of labor (the home, the field, the factory floor, the school), especially on the periphery—particularly in the South during the antebellum period, in Appalachia, the Dust Bowl region of the Midwest, the corporate farms of the West during the Great Depression of the 1930s, and in metropolitan inner-cities during the 1950s and 1960s? Such questioning (coming mainly from an alliance of core intellectuals, and from the disenfranchised in the periphery) resulted in the enactment of policy that promoted federal, state and private land sales in rural areas and suburbs, that gave rise to the articulation of a central place hierarchy that provided a diversity of goods and services right to the people (instead of them having to venture away for them), and that put some trappings of the welfare state in place. Such questioning also erupted in full-fledged social movements, calling not simply for containment of slavery within the American South as suggested by the 1820 Missouri Compromise, but also for the emancipation of African American slaves in the 1840s and 1850s, and then for the dismantling of the post-bellum apartheid segregation of African Americans and other minorities after democratic expectations had been so raised during the New Deal, during the war effort of World War II, and after military demobilizations in the 1940s and 1950s. Here, Earle argues that egalitarian principles did not easily give way to universal improvements in the quality of life enjoyed by all Americans. Instead, they actually contributed to regional instability that eventually became so untenable that it erupted in two civil wars—one sectional (the 1860s) and one urban (the 1950s and 1960s).

The two civil wars are hallmarks of the increasing role of the federal government in each of the spatial enlargement in power of the American

State in approximately 100-year cycles of one 50-year republic and one 50-year democracy. The federal government has ratcheted up its spatial scale of influence every 100 years in the cause of Civil Rights. After each two 50-year cycles there is a need to ratchet up the power of the American State in order to solve the crisis at hand. Part of the solution to the crisis has been to enlarge civic participation and integrate more people into the economy. There have been three American States: The Sectional State (1780s–1870s), the National State (1870s–1970s) and the Transnational State (1980s–2080s). In each ratcheting move, there were sectional enlargements of the power of the federal government to ensure civil and voting rights. The National State (1870s–1970s) offers an example. Reconstruction required a massive federal intervention and new constitutional amendments and court procedures to ensure civil rights for the freed slaves. The onset of the Great Depression meant that the next democracy (FTM) regime had to incorporate minorities and poorer sections of the country into the economy in order to increase aggregate demand. The Civil Rights Movement required the intervention of the federal government. The current era is the Transnational State as a global America has taken steps to ensure the civil rights of American citizens overseas. For example, during the 2000 presidential election overseas absentee ballots and the voting rights of absentee voters became an important issue (see Toobin 2001). Furthermore, American jurisdiction expanded to Iraq, Afghanistan, and Cuba in unparalleled ways such as foregoing the Geneva Convention in the treatment of enemy combatants in the name of fighting terrorism and keeping Americans and their civil liberties safe at home using the rhetoric of fighting terror over there instead of here.

In summary, Carville Earle's dialectical model provides fertile soil on which to plant and nourish numerous historical studies that can grow in their own right into productive "plants" or studies that are grounded in a unifying framework. The avenues for study and exploration are many. In this book a few examples of these seeds for discussion are shared. Each essay tests, collaborates, or challenges Earle's model of how ingrained recurring cycles have impacted the geographical history of the United States. Enjoy the journey across America's historical political economy landscape.

BIBLIOGRAPHY

Earle, C. 2003. *The American Way: A Geographical History of Crisis and Recovery.* (Lanham, MD: Rowman & Littlefield).

Kondratieff, N. 1935. "The Long Wave in Economic Life," *Review of Economic Statistics* 17: 105–115.

Meinig, D. W. 1986. *Atlantic America, 1492–1800*. Vol. 1, *The Shaping of America: A Geographical Perspective on 500 Years of History*. (New Haven: Yale University Press).

———. 1992. *Continental America, 1800–1867*. Vol. 2, *The Shaping of America: A Geographical Perspective on 500 Years of History*. (New Haven: Yale University Press).

———. 1998. *Transcontinental America, 1850–1915*. Vol. 3, *The Shaping of America*. (New Haven: Yale University Press).

———. 2004. *Global America, 1915–2000*. (New Haven: Yale University Press).

Toobin, J. 2001. *Too Close To Call*. (New York: Random House).

Wright, J. K. 1947. "Terrae Incognitae: The Place of Imagination in Geography." *Annals of the Association of American Geographers* 37, no. 1:1–15.

Chapter Three

The French in the Illinois Country, 1699–1735

Using Historical Geography to Understand European-Indian History

M. J. Morgan

In his introduction to *Geographical Inquiry and American Historical Problems*, Carville Earle writes of the "interesting angle of vision" offered by geographical inquiry, particularly those problems "stalled in historiographic traffic" (Earle 1992: 5). He advocates the investigation of the 'small zone' where he himself began, with colonies along the James River estuary in early Virginia (Earle 1979). Earle's optimal approach meshes geographical inquiry with the historian's craft: "tenacious archival research, critical evaluation of primary sources, and, above all, engagement in and resolution of historiographic controversy" (Earle 1992: 18). The result could be an integration of factors and disciplines, including demography, economics, and history, producing an evolutionary explanation for settlement puzzles.

Earle's examination of the mortality waves occurring along the James River estuary between 1607 and 1624 is groundbreaking in methodology; yet it can also be seen as a prime case study for the broader arguments he makes in *The American Way: A Geographical History of Crisis and Recovery* (2003). The ragged, painfully slow growth of English settlement in the Chesapeake brings into focus a grim disparity between anticipated returns and on-the-ground human suffering. The economic backers of the English settlements had energy and vision, driven both by dreams of New World wealth and competition for expanding empire with the Spanish and the French. These motivations were immensely powerful, resulting in ship after ship of doomed colonists arriving in Jamestown before 1624. At times, the mortality on these ships after they arrived passed fifty percent (Earle 1979). The halting growth and foundering settlements—the reality of a flawed, dangerous location—did not prove instructive for English entrepreneurs and investors. Successful English implantation in the mid-Atlantic did not occur until as late as 1675, after both Virginia and Maryland had passed a series of Town Acts to enforce settlement and town building. The financial crises occurring in the Chesapeake because of meager settlement and return were absorbed into English economic liberalism. Experimentation and risk were pre-eminent values, despite horrific errors of judgment leading to decades of mortality and Native American conflict. Tobacco fortunes later invigorated a narrative of economic revival that became amazingly tenacious, reinforced by proliferating economic networks (Earle 2003; Norton and Studnicki-Gizbert 2007).

The experience of the French in the Mid-Mississippi Valley between 1699 and 1765 is yet another story of European settlement and trial in an unexpected environment; and while the initial mission at Cahokia (1699) did not result in malarial and dysentery deaths, Seminarian priests experienced the same problem as the English ninety years earlier: French settlers simply did not emigrate to the area and build thriving towns. The highest French population, perhaps 1,000 souls, evolved sixty miles to the south of Cahokia at Kaskaskia, where alluvial flatlands along two rivers yielded rich harvests of wheat and maize. The watery, slough and marsh-filled mission lands at Cahokia did not attract French settlers. What was the effect of population disparities in the French Illinois villages? One aspect that has not been addressed is the relationship between French and Illinois Indians living near all the villages.

Carville Earle provides immediate, useful principles in the application of 'historian craft' to inquiry that is basically geographic. Of particular value are his small-scale focus and distinguishment of adjacent ecosystems. The sources he used to develop an explanation for the relentless estuarian illnesses attacking English settlers at Jamestown included Indian behaviors. In the absence of documents providing rationales for (healthful) locations of Indian villages, Earle paid attention to what Indians *did,* particularly as reported by Captain John Smith. (Smith's observations played a pivotal role in Earle's arguments concerning contaminated locales). Earle published "Environment, Disease, and Mortality in Early Virginia," at a time when scholars were debating reasons for the initial failure there. He injected a sobering, practical theory into discussions about leadership and Elizabethan values (Morgan 1975). His arguments had power because they were driven by science (the painstaking collection of disease data) but also because they were multifaceted, supported by many kinds of sources, even those that remained fragmentary. And in particular, the lives and choices of aboriginal peoples weighed into his explanations. Could these same principles assist in understanding the early Cahokia Revolt against the French, a bloodless resistance that nonetheless changed French policy?

Earle placed a keen emphasis on "resolution of historiographic controversy." However, in the historiography of French settlement in the mid–

Mississippi Valley, no controversy existed about French–Illinois Indian interaction; no probing questions had ever been asked about the early, restive experience between the French and the Cahokia Indians. Like treatments of all the French Illinois settlements, French relations with Illinois Indian subtribes have been glossed in the literature. When explanations do appear, they tend toward the familiar refrain of "tractability"—that some Indians were just more "tractable." Thus from earliest contact, the Kaskaskia are often distinguished as pastoral, pacific, and "less barbarous," while the more northern subtribes, the Cahokia and Peoria, are glossed as arch-traditional (Thwaites 1900: 231). Characterizations of tractability, unconsciously but repeatedly emphasized in the record, simplify and reduce human complexity. Like the ubiquitous phrase "Indian trouble," explanations based on tribal temperament obscure a complex, faceted history involving diverse, evolving experiences and communications among Europeans and Indians. Also considered must be French colonial policies which endorsed Catholic missionary efforts among Indians and the establishment of profitable fur trading posts while substantively ignoring agriculture. French farmers bemoaned the lack of iron farming implements available along the Mississippi, but traps and trade kettles were shipped from Paris in large numbers (Miller-Surrey 1916).

Secondly, primary sources for this period and area, even those ferreted out through "tenacious archival research" remain exasperatingly slim: the letters of Seminarian priests on the Cahokia grant, some French census data, and a few good, suggestive archaeological investigations. My study posed challenges unlike those of Earle's formidably convincing work; in Jamestown, ambitious Englishmen left many letters and the colony was a 'venture' for which commercial and mortality figures were gathered. The personal, spiritual letters of priests, collected in *The Jesuit Relations and Allied Documents,* constitute the reports of the earliest French colonial efforts in the Illinois Country. The evidence isn't so much fragmentary as opaque: Indians remain "les savages" as a collective, with virtually no delineation of gender, age, or personality beyond identification of chiefs or shamans.

Still, I wanted to know why the particular area of Cahokia, northernmost of the French riverine grants, differed so ominously in its European-Indian relationships from the remaining four French settlements. Eventually, that difference became the crux of my argument: the five French villages along a sixty-mile stretch of the Mississippi River were not all the same geographically. Differences in soils and water levels actually helped shape disparate European-Indian histories. This is most clear on the large Cahokia grant, where, in the early 1730s, the Cahokia Indians 'revolted' against the French mission. This bloodless event is the only instance of French-Illinois Indian conflict in which Frenchmen feared for their lives. At each of the other

French-Indian settlements, proximal relations were enduringly peaceful. Why was interaction so difficult on the Cahokia grant? In investigating this shadowy history, I discovered a matrix of factors connected to environment.

Cahokia, as the earliest-settled and most northern area, was also the wettest. Sailing south on the Mississippi in a hollowed-out cottonwood pirogue, a traveler at mid-eighteenth century would pass the tiny hamlet of St. Philippe, also known as St. Philippe du Grand Marais (the Great Marsh), then the settlements of Chartres and Prairie du Rocher clustered south of the great limestone Fort Chartres, and finally, eighteen miles farther down, across an expanse of rich, incredibly fertile tallgrass prairie, the busy agricultural town of Kaskaskia where French Jesuits had an expansive mission until the early 1760s. This progression of towns—as well as adjacent Indian villages—can clearly be seen on the 1755 map by Nicolas Bellin (figure 3.1). There were three Fort Chartres, constructed between 1719 and the mid-1750s. The limestone fort, the grandest and costliest in France's western North American empire, was built after the second wooden fort again rotted. All three forts were within the same two-three mile radius and supported the cluster of villages marching down the coast: St. Philippe, Chartres, Prairie du Rocher (Montague 1948; Saucier and Spineke 1969; Jelks, Ekberg, and Martin 1989). Cahokia lay above this cluster, a Seminarian concession of moist fields and heavily mesic prairies ribboned with creeks and feeder streams.

Although no one, not observers at the time nor historians of later years, has stated it directly, the fact is, as that boatman moved south along the river, he was passing lands that were becoming drier. Now this is a difficult thing to prove. There are few extant French commercial records, and they do not generally distinguish the precise location of shipments; grain floating down the Mississippi was understood as coming from "the Illinois," rather than Kaskaskia, St. Philippe, or Cahokia. In addition, the story opens in 1699, and eye-witness accounts of French religious and military swerve and change dramatically, following the vagaries of climate in that mercurial ecosystem. Complaints about "great droughts" and "periodical marshes" that appeared only after rains on the uplands are interspersed with vivid accounts of flood years in the Illinois Country (Brink, McDonough, and Company 1875; J. L. McDonough and Company 1881; Brink, McDonough, and Company 1883). Although the terms "Illinois Country" and "the Illinois" are used interchangeably by French, British, and Americans across the eighteenth century, the clearest definition of the geographic area is provided by one Lieutenant Eddington, who accompanied British Captain Thomas Stirling out to occupy Illinois in 1765: "The Country of the Illinoise is very extensive," he wrote, "comprehending all the Country on the East Side of the Mississippi from about thirty leagues above the mouth of the Ohio to a considerable distance

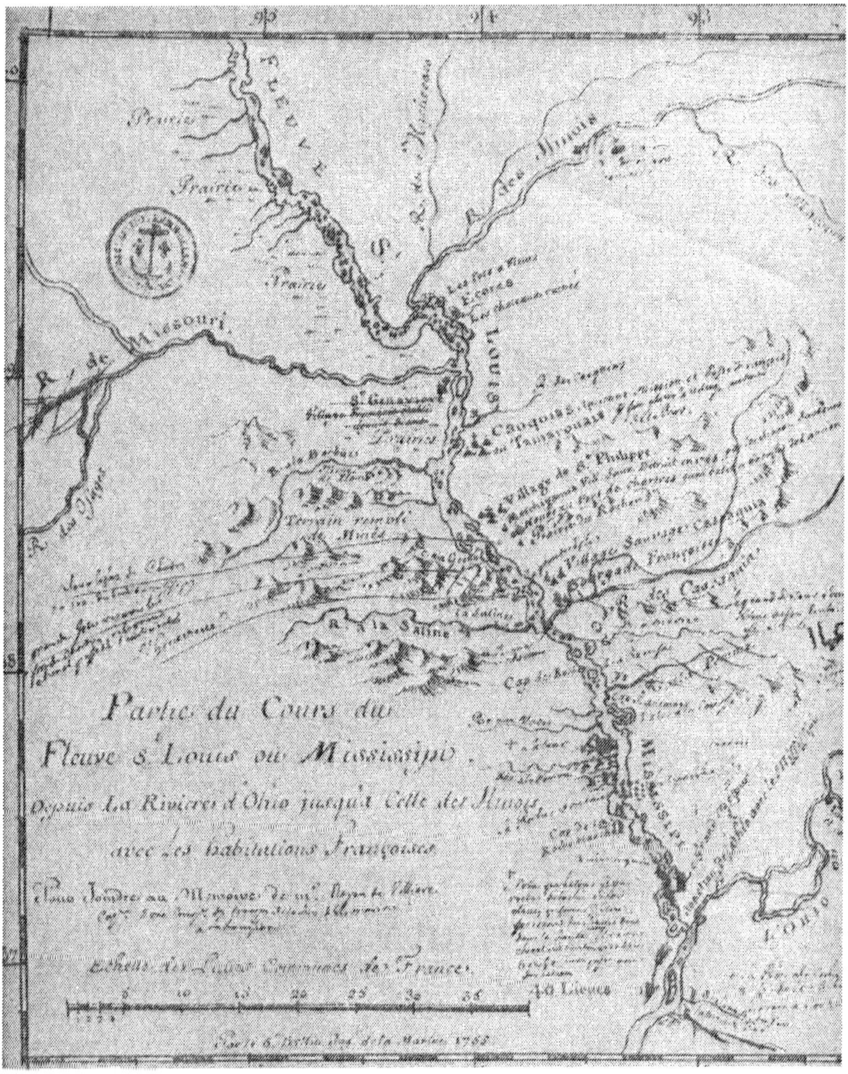

Figure 3.1. 1755 Nicolas Bellin Map

above the Illinoise River junction with the Mississippi. The name of Illinoise applies to all the Country on both sides of the Illinoise River and E. of the Mississippi almost to the bottom of Lake Michigan, the latter formerly the Illinoise Lake" (Carroon 1984: 89).

Nonetheless, despite the expansive area identified by Lieutenant Eddington, when referring to "the Illinois," even the French usually meant specifically the strip of land along the Mississippi that would become known as the American Bottom. So glossed are references to this area, and so aggregated the region, that the French settlements routinely exist in historiography that way: lumped together. Important questions remain buried in Edenic accounts of the beautiful prairie park lands. In 1698 Father Louis Hennepin inaugurated a long line of glowing impressionistic accounts of the Illinois Country by writing, "The Country beyond those Hills is so fine and pleasant that, according to the Account I have had, one might justly call it the *Delight of America*" (Thwaites 1903: 186). Such accounts also include boosterism about soil fertility. In the Illinois Country, many writers attested, it was only necessary to drive a spade in once and turn the soil loosely over. From Hennepin in the late seventeenth century to Timothy Flint in 1828, observers stressed the fecundity of Illinois soil. Even modern historians have absorbed these views. The historian of French Louisiana, Marcel Giraud, wrote in 1958, "The soil, flat and fertile, could produce crops without preliminary clearance" (Giraud 1987: 459; Le Page du Pratz 1763; Mereness 1961; Flint 1970; McCulloch and Todish 2004).

Yet it is misleading to view all the soils and soil conditions of the French settlements as the same. Earliest accounts in 1699 by the incoming French Seminarian St. Cosme describe the banks of the Mississippi "overflowing far into the woods in the spring" (Kellogg 2001: 354). Yet the description merely refers in general to lands south of the Illinois River confluence. Carl Ekberg has done the best job of addressing differences in settlement and agriculture in each of the French villages along the Mississippi, pointing out the more saturate, watery lands of the Cahokia area to the north and highlighting the wheat-growing successes of Kaskaskia to the south (Ekberg 2000). The tiny marshy village of St. Philippe, founded by the French mining engineer Phillip Renault in the early 1720s, lay north of fertile wheat lands around Fort Chartres, closer to the confluence of the Mississippi, Missouri and the Illinois Rivers. Although there are some accounts of "good wheat farms" in St. Philippe, these are not consistent references (Palm 1930b; Carroon 1984; Ekberg 2000; Brown and Dean 2003). There is consistent evidence, however, for wheat success at Kaskaskia. By 1718, a donne at the early Jesuit mission there was already experimenting with new wheat strains (Palm 1930a; Ekberg 2000). By the early 1720s, Kaskaskia was shipping rich grain harvests to New Orleans as the principal supplier in annual convoys (Miller-Surrey 1917: 288). By 1732, Kaskaskia had 14 grist mills; twenty or so miles north, St. Philippe had only two (Ekberg 2000: 266). A prodigious amount of rich, golden Illinois grain was arriving in New Orleans in French convoys, and several times in these early years, the Illinois shipments saved the fledgling, miasmic colony of New Orleans from starvation.

However, most of this French wheat was being produced at Kaskaskia, Prairie du Rocher, and Chartres. Up at Cahokia, where French Seminarian missionaries had established a mission in 1699, both settlement and grain production were halting. The best indicator of how far behind the Cahokia grant was agriculturally, in comparison to the other French settlements, is census data. These numbers do not paint a picture of thriving agriculture on the Cahokia grant.

In 1698–1699, French Catholic missionaries had descended the Illinois River into the area known today in Illinois as the Big Rivers Confluence Area. Here the Missouri and Illinois pour into the Mississippi close together, on opposite shores; other streams and creeks join the flow as well, such as Wood River, Macoupin Creek, Bay Creek, and Piasa Creek. Before drainage projects, the large Snicarte Slough ("the Sny") paralleled "the [Mississippi] river for about 25 miles upstream from the Big Rivers Area." Naturalists today describe the area as a mosaic of rivers, bottoms, bluffs, broken lands, and plains (White 2000: 1). Located only about thirty miles to the south of this riverine confluence, the Cahokia area is still part of the region. Lands directly east of the mission lay within a physical region known as the Lake Region. The terrain here indicates the presence of previous marshes, sloughs, and oxbow lakes as well as old scars (remnants) of the Mississippi channel, "known today as Goose (Cahokia) Lake, Lily Lake, Labras Lake, and Grand Marais" (Gums 1988: 9). Descriptions of the land here by journeying French in the late seventeenth and early eighteenth centuries characterize it as lush, variegated, and filled with water: "the valley between a marshy ground" (Thwaites 1903). The often-flooded Cahokia grant, occupied by French Seminarians at the Mission of the Holy Family, was "unique in the Illinois Country," holding within its 100 square miles a tiny military garrison, mission house, both French and Cahokia-Tamaroa Indian villages, and agricultural lands (Ekberg 2000: 51; Tucker 1975). These structures clustered together in the western part of the grant, nearer to the Mississippi and the island of the Holy Family Mission; however, French Cahokia land extended up to the top of the striking limestone bluffs sheltering the floodplain. Cultivated French longlots were run from the river towards these bluffs, a consistent practice of the French in the St. Lawrence River Valley, the Illinois Country, and the lower Mississippi Valley above New Orleans. Longlots were plowed from one specific land formation to another (Ekberg 2000: 60). The giant limestone cliffs, topped with scrub trees in summit profusion, provided a natural demarcation. On the most explicit map of French Cahokia, the 1735 Father Mercier map (figure 3.2), the Cahokia concession drifts from sheltering rock walls toward the Mississippi River across approximately fifty arpents (a French arpent is equal to

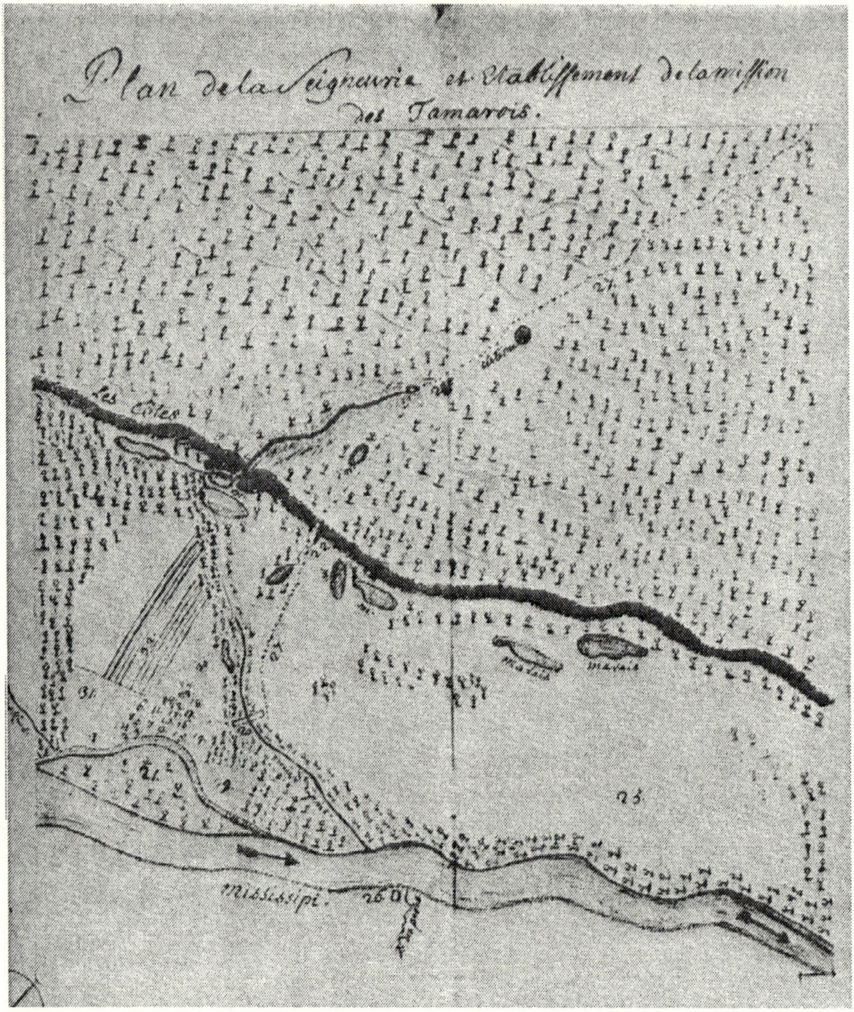

Figure 3.2. Portion of 1732 Father Mercier map Depicting the Cahokia Mission Complex

approximately .84 of an English acre). It does so in a series of bogs, marshes, and saturated wetlands. On Father Mercier's map, goose-shaped droplets dot the land, identified as "marais" (swamp). This reality is all too evident in the distribution of Cahokian commonlands and must be accounted a factor in Cahokia's small population and lesser agricultural status. A close reading of Seminarian letters and early census data makes it clear that agriculture was not developing at the rate it was farther down the French coast, especially at

Kaskaskia, located on an "alluvial plain that ultimately proved to be superb for cereal-grain production" (Ekberg 2000: 191). Father Mercier's map shows but a single band of cultivated land, ribboned arpents running roughly west-east, toward the bluffs. Across this largest French concession, occupied since 1699, the fields labeled "Domaine" touch, on their western edge, a cleared area termed by Father Mercier, "Terrain occupied by the Cahokia." The rest of the Seigneurie is a mosaic of prairie, floodplain timber, and streams. In thirty-six years of occupancy, a single cultivated area had emerged from what was likely drier prairie land.

Given the greater agricultural success of the more southern French settlements, Prairie du Rocher, Kaskaskia, and St. Genevieve across the river, Cahokia and St. Philippe become interesting as two settlements of greater commercial and trade activity (Gums 1988: 17). Both maize and wheat suffer in wet soils where the roots easily rot. The aboriginal transition to maize and tobacco-growing has been documented archaeologically as occurring up on the high ground above the American Bottom floodplain (Woods 1987; Woods and Holley 1991). The import of ground saturation for Cahokia lies in its failure to attract French settlers, and therefore, its growth as a trade rather than agricultural center. Cahokia's reputation as a trade nucleus held throughout the eighteenth century. By 1774, under the British, Cahokia was characterized as a "grand depot for Indian trade." Between 1780 and 1800, under American governance, it became known as the residence of "many north-western Indian traders" (Brink, McDonough & Company 1881: 45; McDermott 1949). In its first decades, however, French missionaries continued to promote the area as an agricultural settlement. As with all the French river colonies, there were good years for wheat and maize and bad, but French settlers were slow to arrive in Cahokia, despite a conventional interpretation that the Seminarians developed their large holdings and ministered mainly to the French settlers (Schlarman 1929: 148).

In the first thirty years of settlement, the number of French settlers at Cahokia never approached that at Kaskaskia. In 1700, there were only seven French inhabitants on this largest grant. The 1732 census lists only four French priests and helpers living at the Cahokia mission complex and three *habitants,* but it also itemizes slaves and domestic animals, both in such small numbers as to imply little growth in French population. In 1732, Kaskaskia had 102 slaves, St. Anne de Fort Chartres, 37, St. Philippe, 22, and Cahokia, 4 (Schlarman 1929: 206; Ekberg 2000: 58). This is clear evidence of a lack of agricultural growth. In 1731, the priest at the Seminarian Cahokia Mission, Father (Monsignor) Jean-Baptiste Mercier, began to purchase land from the Indians in an effort to lure French immigrants down to the Illinois Country (Walthall and Benchley 1987: 1; Schlarman 1929: 280–284). Father Mercier's letter of April 12, 1735, to the Quebec Seminary is important in that it specifically describes land and climate constraints at the Cahokia mission, including annual flux and flow of water (creating problems in the building of mills), drainage of water, location of arable land, and location of bluff forests of white walnut whose wood "is very clear." This walnut was used for the construction of the new mission house (Schlarman 1929: 288). The fact that it was timber hauled down from the bluffs suggests depletion of the wood reserves on the floodplain of the Cahokia grant, despite a low French settler population. It may reflect the need for fuel of the Cahokia-Tamaroa Indians whose village was nearby on the grant.

The Seminarians were in contact with the Cahokia and Tamaroa tribes yet still felt themselves to be isolated. Father Mercier exclaims wistfully, "If only twenty families would come down from Canada . . . more than two hundred habitants could be wonderfully placed." This view was perhaps colored by an exceptional wheat harvest that year, 1732; Mercier describes it as "3500 bundles of the best wheat in the world" (Schlarman 1929: 290). By 1743, however, he is complaining to Vaudreuil, Governor of Louisiana, "We do not grind enough grain to pay the miller" (Schlarman 1929: 284).

Father Mercier was full of plans for how the Cahokia Mission could be developed, especially in the building of mills. The granting of land in French North America carried an implicit responsibility for development, for the improvements which would lure other settlers and foster agriculture and industries that would in time repay the crown. Such responsibilities were also felt by priests, who were "nothing more than the undertakers of the settlement of a territory" (Schlarman 1929: 280). While the French Empire in North America was conceived as a scattering of tiny fur-collecting stations and settlements across a vast geographic region, the colonial policy mirrored the early English pattern of meager economic support. One historian of the lower Mississippi Valley has described how French residents at inland locales such as Arkansas Post were "left to their own designs" to survive (Usner 1992: 81; Charlevoix 1744). With only a twice-yearly riverine convoy to furnish supplies, the Cahokia priests became inventive. The 1735 letter by Fathers Mercier and Courier is interesting because their development ideas clearly focus on discussions of water and mills. The letter contains at least ten specific references to mills, the placing of mills, the problems of high and low water, the seasonal droughts:

> The *rivier du pont* [river of the bridge] also issues from a swamp and flows quite gently into the mississippi, almost directly across from the former village of the Kaskaskias. The mississippi never backwaters it to such an extent that it would not turn a mill a short distance above the place where a bridge is indicated. It is

> the cost of the dam and the lack of water in the long droughts which have kept us from building one there rather than in the hills. (Schlarman 1929: 280)

Father Mercier also compares the efforts of the Seminarians in building mills to the efforts of the Jesuits sixty miles to the south, in Kaskaskia. Priests at both establishments obviously knew what the others were doing. However, at Kaskaskia, the Kaskaskia Indians had moved two leagues north of the settlement, relocated in 1721 by the incoming French commander, Boisbriant. They lived on a prairie which became named for them (Palm 1930b: 49; Belting 1975: 58). Unless these Illinois Indians journeyed to French Kaskaskia, they were out of sight of the French residents. At Cahokia, the village of the Tamaroa was located near to both the Mission of the Holy Family (on the Isle de la Famille in the Mississippi) and the Mississippi shore; Father Mercier's 1735 letter and map clearly indicate this adjacency. In simple terms, what this meant for the French living near the mission on the Cahokia grant was daily sight of Indians. The Peoria tribe to the north frequently came to stay with the Cahokia and Tamaroa Indians; they especially did so under pressure from Fox raids (Schlarman 1929: 290; Hechenberger 1998). Historians have speculated that as the French priests acquired more land from the Illinois tribes near Cahokia, Indians reacted with hostility. The so-called Cahokia "revolt" is credited to Cahokian dissatisfaction with incursions of the French onto their hunting and agricultural grounds. This explanation—that white settlement invaded and disturbed hunting territories of Indians—so often appears in historical interpretations that it must be both questioned and expanded.

On the Cahokia grant that included much watery ground and a series of named marshes, it is likely as well that the amount of prairie was as high as fifty percent (John White, Ecological Services, personal communication, February 2004). References to prairies in letters from Seminarians, as well as the named prairies, both small and large, occurring around Fort Chartres and the Village of Chartres, support this conclusion. Father Mercier's map includes a very large southern prairie labeled "Prairie des Buttes." Thick with indigenous grasses growing as high as a man's head, obscuring and obstructing riders on horses, filled with noxious insects and a humid, choking heat in high summer, these mesic tallgrass prairies were not the home of myriad animal populations capable of providing a sustained protein base for Indian populations as high as 2000 (Zitomersky 1994: 203). Tallgrass prairies and wetlands attract small mammals and birds like rabbits, prairie chickens, squirrels, voles, and mice, most of which were hunted and consumed by both Indians and French. The roving herds of deer on the floodplain described by seventeenth century French rapidly disappeared as a food source. From the time of the permanent French settlements, a major protein source for Indians and frequently, for French themselves, came from buffalo tenderloins, carried back to villages by Indians in massive packs after days of smoking and drying on the prairie uplands (Kenton 1954: 326–327; Hauser 1973). Pork became important as well, for both Indians and European inhabitants of agricultural communities like the village of Chartres and Kaskaskia. Notarial records as early as 1724 detailing land and home sales and transfers for the village of Chartres mention hogs; in 1726 hams "of fifteen or sixteen pounds in weight" were listed as part of a selling price (Brown and Dean 2003: 359).

Although the Illinois Indians living in domiciled villages were still going on summer and winter hunts, their more permanent occupation of lands would have accelerated environmental change. Cahokia's position as a trading depot also contributed to change. The abundant waterfowl described by Hennepin and St. Cosme in 1698 were sharing the Cahokia grant not only with Indian villages experiencing many shifts of population but with a large French mission complex; the Seminarians were involved with land-clearing, mill building, and orchard-planting. Gradually across thirty years, despite the lesser French population and the lack of agriculture, the Cahokia grant became a peopled world. The impression of human activity at Cahokia is strong, conveyed by a sense of arrival, departure, of the coming and going of tribes and traders. Its location near the confluence area of Big Rivers attracted the downriver trade traffic. While there is little direct evidence of a severe decline in resident and migratory bird populations on the Cahokia grant, archaeologists who have excavated the eighteenth century French colonial Cahokia Wedge site have found a lacunae in faunal remains: very low numbers of waterfowl. "Although ducks, shorebirds, and marsh birds would have been especially abundant along the floodplain during their spring and fall migration, these species are underrepresented at the Cahokia Wedge site" (Martin 1988: 230). Additional findings from this site indicate low numbers of domestic animals in comparison with other French sites in the Illinois Country; however, trumpeter swan wing bones were represented, as well as large blue catfish (Martin 1988: 233). The lead archaeologist, Terrance J. Martin, speculates that the Cahokia French consumption pattern was more similar to Indian consumption patterns: a "selective procure[ment] of local resources on a seasonal basis in a pattern resembling Native American adaptation" (Martin 1988: 228). Questions can be raised about what this may have meant. Did the French settlers simply prefer certain sources of protein, or was the waterfowl population being affected by the mobility and trade culture around Cahokia?

The Cahokia Indians, like the Peoria to the north, had used bird populations in ritualistic and adornment practices. The trumpeter swan, for instance, becomes flightless during the molting season over the summer (Bolen 1989: 20; Johnsgard 1975). Swans can then easily be captured without need of firearms. Swansdown and swanskin, cut from a mature trumpeter swan, would furnish a delicately warm clothing layer and glorious feathers. The same can be inferred for an extinct species, the Carolina paroquet (parakeet), whose long, brilliant green feathers were seen sailing among and drooping from river trees in the American Bottom. In addition, these birds shared the habitat with snow geese, Canada geese, migrant grebes of several varieties, bitterns, herons, egrets, wood ducks, teal, mallards, widgeons, pintails, and cranes. Each bird has a distinctive call; en masse they would have produced a cacophony, particularly in the area of the Illinois River, where immense, rocky bluffs trap and magnify sound. Not all of these birds were resident throughout the year in the Big Rivers area; some were summer breeders or merely passers-through. But the Mississippi River is one of the great fly-ways of the world. As late as the year 1955, "after [at least] 75 years of intensive hunting and drastic destruction of habitat," observers counted as many as six million mallards above the Illinois River migratory corridor (Munson, Parmalee, and Yarnell 1971: 415). Just as ethnohistorical studies of the eastern and northern Woodland Indians have linked their spiritual and self-created identities to fur-bearing animals, what little is known about Illinois Indians tribes links them to this kingdom of birds (Martin 1978).

The journal of the Frenchman Deliette who encountered and lived among the Peoria before 1700 (and continued as a resident trader in the area well past 1700) is the single most authoritative source on the Illinois Indians. Most of what is known about these tribes as they were living when they met the French comes from a period of time between 1673 and 1700. Such information describes the Peoria and the Kaskaskia, dwelling then on the northern Illinois River at the Mission of the Immaculate Conception (Starved Rock). For smaller tribes such as the Cahokia, Tamaroa, and the Mechigamea, very little is known at all. Because these five tribes had become the dominant members of the Illinois Confederacy, however, and because of the geographic proximity of the Cahokia and Peoria, it is possible to use accounts of the Peoria as careful representations (Sturtevant 1978: 674).

Summer villages of the Illinois were "strung out" along the river banks and could contain many lodges; observers have counted 300 to 351 at different times before 1700. Winter lodges made use of woven cattail mats over willow frames. Summer lodges were covered with light bark sheets (elm) to admit air and light. Yet before summer camps were set up, Illinois Indians launched a month of raiding and warfare in February. It is here, in their warfare rituals, that the connection with the immense natural bird population of the Mississippi floodplain can be found. Birds were part of the rituals of war; the Illinois identified birds as emblems of supernatural power (Sturtevant 1978: 676; Hauser 1973). Warriors chose a personal bird or birds and collected their skins in a "colored reed mat" (Mereness 1961: 375). Before departing for the raid, warriors participated in night-long rituals in which the birdskins were displayed. This was to ensure the cooperation and aid of their personal bird spirits. Deliette mentions the warriors "pay[ing] homage, according to their custom, to their birds" (Mereness 1961: 376). Later, during the raid itself, "warriors gave the cries of their birds." Captives brought back to the Illinois camps sang their death chants while holding long sticks "containing the feathers of birds killed by the raiders" (Sturtevant 1961: 676–677). Thus the metaphor of the bird of prey was woven into the chronology of war raids. In addition to the role of birds, birdskins, and bird spirits in raiding and cosmology, birds were important in Indian adornment. The few representations of Illinois Indians drawn from the eighteenth century, such as the sketch shown in figure 3.3, show them brilliantly adorned with feathers, mostly waterfowl. Deliette specified that wild duck neck skin was used in making the calumet for the pipe ceremony (Mereness 1961: 391). Waterfowl populations, perhaps most legion on the Cahokia grant in the Big Rivers Confluence Area, were vital to the Illinois Indians.

Yet, by the 1730s, this lush, watery grant was almost certainly a disturbed natural habitat. Indians living adjacent to the French faced issues of deforestation (affecting firewood, nesting bird populations, and soil erosion); scarcity of small game; and possible soil exhaustion on overworked and constantly-used Indian plots (Emerson and Brown 1991: 97). Accounts of bird populations on the Mississippi River below Cahokia continued, however. In 1751 the Frenchman Bossu left a description of the St. Francis River in present-day Arkansas. "The game is so plentiful," he writes, "that when we stopped for the night on its shores [the St. Francis], it was impossible to sleep, because of the multitude of swans, cranes, geese, bustards, and ducks" (Schlarman 1929: 293). In 1765 the British commander Thomas Stirling described the Illinois Country as containing "millions of waterfowl" (Carroon 1984: 94). Stirling lists waterfowl species and even described the adornment of the calumet with waterfowl feathers. However, Stirling's destination was Fort Chartres, and there is little direct evidence that he journeyed on up to Cahokia, an additional forty miles. His log account of Cahokia contains virtually no description, merely enumerated information (Carroon 1984: 94). In general, except for strong impressions of Kaskaskia as a resplendent agricultural community, observers tended to gloss the entire Illinois Country as one environment.

However, changes in the natural habitat of the Cahokia, those that may have affected waterfowl populations, comprise only one possible factor in events leading to the Cahokia revolt of the early 1730s. The Cahokia and Peoria Indians were also proving difficult spiritual subjects. There is evidence from the letters of Father Mercier in 1732 that successful conversion

Figure 3.3. Drawing of an Illinois Indian by De Granville, circa 1701. "Capitaine de La Nation des Illinois." Collections of the New York Public Library, Astor, Lenox, and Tilden Foundations.

of the Cahokia and especially, the Peoria, was eluding priests. The Peoria, often described as "arch-traditional," in fact were perceived as impediments to the conversion of the Cahokia. In a 1732 letter to the Quebec Seminary, Father Mercier exclaims, "If only the Peoria were away from here!—they will leave this fall—we could have some hopes of doing something with several Kahos [Cahokia Indians]" (Schlarman 1929: 290). Perhaps partly because of the influence of the Peoria, by the early 1730s, relations between French settling around the Cahokia mission and the Cahokia Indians worsened. The dynamic of population must be accorded a role in escalating tensions. An important study by Joseph Zitomersky focusing on the population geography of the Illinois Indians stresses "patterns of mutually supportive relationships that existed between Indian and colonial groups" (Zitomersky 1994: 17). Zitomersky believes that Indians had a state-sanctioned role as food suppliers and that "the food producers were often the Illinois Indians themselves" (Zitomersky 1994: 19).

The ratio of Illinois Indians living on the Cahokia grant to the actual numbers of French creates questions about that food supplier role. Conventional interpretations stressing Indian hostility over invasion of traditional life ways and subsistence patterns overlook hostility created by inadequate and vacillating opportunities for trade. Where there are high and growing numbers of incoming colonists in a frontier region, the role of Indians as initial food suppliers becomes important. When the number of inhabitants is small enough to rapidly develop a self-sustaining economic world, as on the Cahokia grant, the shift in relations of power and dependence between colonists and Indians is ominous. The irritation the Cahokia felt when French pigs and cattle roamed into their fields or rooted out nests of waterfowl was perhaps exacerbated by the reality that this livestock was owned by only eleven resident Frenchmen. While studies of the effect of domestic livestock on colonist-settler relations along the seaboard have stressed hogs in particular as a "dynamic force of territorial expansion," the situation at Cahokia was complicated by demographics (Marshall 1995; Crosby 1986; Crosby 1994; Anderson 1994; Anderson 2004). The eleven Frenchmen at Cahokia must be compared to the 1,732 estimated village population for the Cahokia Indians: 1480 (Zitomersky 1994: 321). Although there would have been some French soldiers, French voyageurs and traders, and other Europeans at the Cahokia settlement from time to time, the difference between French and Indian population on this grant is notable.

All across the French and Indian settlement geography of the Mississippi and Ohio Valleys, the difference between Indian population and French population in the same area is notable. At the Fort Ouiatanon location along the Wabash River in the 1740s, for example, there may have been twenty-five resident Frenchman living next to as many as three thousand encamped Indians from different tribes. Yet no violence occurred there (Majors 1970). The escalation in troubled relations at Cahokia, leading to the "Cahokia Revolt"—a single day of Indian warfare preparation and threats—stands out in the Mid-Mississippi Valley. French colonial policy changed as a result, mandating the removal of Indians from village proximity and the creation of buffer zones.

No other Illinois tribes supported the Cahokia in their so-called revolt. The explanation for this is demographic and economic. Other Illinois tribes, bolstered by greater numbers of Europeans eager to trade for their foodstuffs, had too much to lose. In the Kaskaskia village, sixty miles to the south, Indians produced maize and wheat and could sell it to a thriving French population downriver; because of the garrison of soldiers at Fort Chartres, Indians also furnished game for the troops. Perhaps the situation at Cahokia alarmed the other Illinois subtribes: Kaskaskia chiefs even journeyed up to Cahokia to try to restore order and security between the French and the Cahokia (Palm 1930b: 71).

In May of 1733, resident priests and several inhabitants of the French village "fled at night" after a warning that the Cahokia might rise up and massacre them (Walthall and Benchley 1987: 8). The restiveness of the Cahokia and their depredations against livestock seemed harbingers of disaster. Such fears had been exacerbated by the 1729 Natchez Revolt on the lower Mississippi. In the environs of Fort Rosalie, Natchez Indians laid careful plans to entrap French settlers. Using what one historian has called "a familiar pattern of frontier exchange," the Natchez welcomed French visitors with tribute and promises of food and furs. They then massacred 145 men, 36 women, and 56 children while capturing nearly 300 black slaves in addition to some 50 French women and children (Usner 1992: 72; Kenton 1954: 439–440). The story of the Natchez Revolt has particular parallels with the French and Illinois settlement history at Cahokia. Like the declining numbers of Illinois Indians to the north, the Natchez had been decimated by contagious diseases and compressed by French land grants. From initial population estimates of perhaps 3500 before the advent of the French, the Natchez numbered barely half that, scattered among five villages (Usner 1992: 66). Father le Petit reported in 1730 that "In former times the Nation of the Natchez was very large. It counted sixty villages and eight hundred suns or Princes; now it is reduced to six little Villages and eleven Suns" (Kenton 1954: 430). And also like the Natchez, the Illinois used livestock and food-theft raids against white settlers as a prime weapon. The accounts of Indian theft at downriver missions were known; the Mississippi River was unparalleled as a conduit of information. In 1722, for instance, in a single week, the Natchez killed "eleven cattle . . .

and stole three horses, sixteen pigs, six quarts of flour, fifty quarts of corn, fifty quarts of potatoes, and forty quarts of beans" (Mississippi Provincial Archives IV 1984).

By the early 1730s, the French in Illinois had heard all about the Natchez revolt and the bloody massacre of innocent French men, women, and children. In 1733, the commandant at Fort Chartres, St. Ange, wrote to France to request additional troops, mentioning "the wrong which they [the Cahokia] have done the *habitants* [settlers] by killing their animals" (Walthall and Benchley 1987: 9). In 1732, a letter from Father Mercier refers to the "trouble we have had with them [the Cahokia]" (Walthall and Benchley 1987: 8). As a result of the bloodless Cahokia Revolt, the French insisted on the tribe removing from the French mission area. The Cahokia eventually settled near the Cahokia mounds, specifically the great terraced Monks Mound, nine miles away from the French. There the River L'Abbe mission was established for their benefit, and the French assisted the Cahokia in the plowing of fresh fields for their corn. In addition, the new Commander D'Artaguiette posted French soldiers to the small French fort at Cahokia and issued a punitive message to the Cahokia: they would receive no French presents until "they repair the wrongs which they have done" (Walthall and Benchley 1987: 10). The nine-mile corridor between French Cahokia and the Illinois tribes at the L'Abbe Mission area seems to have provided the necessary buffer zone. After this period in the 1730s, accounts of "trouble" cease. By 1752, the Cahokia were seeking French protection at Fort Chartres, hoping to avoid Fox raids. During the twenty years after their relocation, the Cahokia Indians, like the Kaskaskia to the south, became travelers and traders to French settlements. Cultural change accelerated (Brown 1979).

Because the French experience with Cahokia Indians stands out as the most tension-filled and ominous across the entire history of French occupation in the Illinois Country, it is important to seek explanations as inclusive as possible. Early French interactions with the Tamaroa, before 1700, did include some "trouble," as reported by Henri de Tonti, yet he selected the Tamaroa to be the recipients of the first French missionary efforts (Schlarman 1929: 148). For most of the next sixty-five years, the relations between the French and the Illinois Indians solidified into a strong alliance. The problems in the 1730s on the Cahokia grant stand out against that record. While investigation reveals a matrix of factors, most have to do with the original nature of the environment at Cahokia.

For the Cahokia-Tamaroa Indians, that environment was unparalleled for subsistence ecology, prolific with opportunities for aquatic harvests, outfield agriculture, nut gathering, hunting of small floodplain mammals as well as large herbivores, and a dependable resource in waterfowl, including flesh, skins, feathers, and eggs (Hauser 1973; Bareis and Porter 1984). For the French, that aquatic environment proved problematic and molded a particular kind of colonial experience. Fathers Mercier and Courier, writing from "des Tamarois" in 1735, almost casually pen the sentence: "When the waters of the Missouri and the Mississippi are very high, a great part of this island is inundated" (Schlarman 1929: 280). That island was the site of the French mission complex, the heart of the Cahokia grant. Other priests and resident French at more southern villages do discuss flooding and rarer, catastrophic floods in the years of 1725, 1748, 1772, and 1785. Yet Father Mercier's reference to inundation of the mission island is significant because of the location of arable lands: straight across from the island on the western portion of the grant, stretching eastward toward the bluffs. If the island were flooded, so were French and Indian fields. Fairly striking differences in water levels among the five French settlements did clearly result in distinct histories. The kind of presumptive thinking Carville Earle termed "aggregate regionalism" has not been limited to eastern geographies.

Illinois is now known as the prairie state; yet the natural, watery fluctuations of her internal Grand Prairie have been vigorously subdued with drainage tiles, ditching, fencing, and plowing. This process began with the entrance of American settlers after the Revolution and dramatically accelerated with the advent of the steel plow in the 1840s. So coated with virile corn is the state today that it is easy to forget the once dynamic environmental diversity, especially the aquatic bottomlands. There, the abundance and variety of native floodplain plants developed as a result of alluvial flooding, of having to spread into disturbed and marginal habitats. To combat annual, relentless inundation with mud, these varieties compensated through the production of immense amounts of seed (King 1994: 29). The preference of migrating waterfowl for the Mississippi flyway, those varied and colorful species with which the Cahokia had become spiritually aligned, was built in part around copious, heavily laden seedheads. Stands of common arrowhead or smartweed fed the "millions of waterfowl" described so consistently by observers along the Mississippi. Relationships among plants, animals, birds, and Indians—an "exchange" ecosystem depending on water—were inexorably altered when Europeans arrived (Zawacki 1969; Nelson, Redmond, and Sparks 1994).

That alteration produced initially, perhaps, a significant sense of unease and loss among the Cahokia Indians. And that sense of loss occurred on many levels, not only because of erosion of hunting grounds. Journeying into the world of historic Cahokia Indians reveals the complexity of human beings whose cosmology, living, trade relations, and warfare practices were webbed into a riverine habitat. Environmental change sent shock waves, minor at first, but intensifying, through all aspects of Cahokian life; and those changes were not accompanied, initially, by rich opportunities for trade with Europeans. There were just too few resident French in the Cahokia area.

French colonists' failure to arrive was tied directly to problematic, inundated soils and poor harvests. Inexperienced Seminarians were forced to survive under a neglectful French economic policy focused much more on fur harvesting than on agricultural settlement. Because of the success of wheat farming farther down the Mississippi, the story of watery Cahokia has been obscured. A much more faceted narrative can be discerned when inquiry includes both history and environmental geography, when the evolution of a particular small settlement is clarified. The humid bottomlands of the Mississippi in western Illinois are replete with microhistories that deserve a closer scrutiny. In this case, small-scale investigation reveals as well as resolves problems of history.

BIBLIOGRAPHY

Anderson, Virginia DeJohn. 1994. "King Philip's herds: Indians, colonists, and the problems of livestock in early New England," *The William & Mary Quarterly*, 3rd Ser. 51, no.4.

———. 2000. *Creatures of Empire: How Domestic Animals Transformed Early America.* (New York: Oxford University Press).

Bareis, C. J., and Porter, J. W. 1984. *American Bottom Archaeology: A Summary of the FAI-270 Project Contribution to the Culture History of the Mississippi River Valley.* (Urbana: University of Illinois Press).

Belting, N. 1975. *Kaskaskia under the French Regime.* (New Orleans: Polyanthos).

Bolen, H. D. 1989. *The Birds of Illinois.* (Bloomington: Indiana University Press).

Brink, McDonough, and Company. 1875. *An Illustrated Historical Map of Monroe County, Illinois.*

———. 1881. *History of St. Clair County, Illinois.*

Brown, M. K. 1979. *Cultural Transformations among the Illinois: An Application of a Systems Model.* (East Lansing: Michigan State University Press).

Brown, M. K., and Dean, L.C. 2003. *The Village of Chartres in Colonial Illinois, 1720–1765.* (Ville Platte, Louisiana: Provincial Press).

Carroon, R., ed. 1984. *Broadswords and Bayonets: The Journals of the expedition under the command of Captain Thomas Stirling of the 42nd regiment of Foot, Royal Highland Regiment (The Black Watch) to occupy Fort Chartres in the Illinois Country, August 1765 to January 1766.* (Illinois: The Society of Colonial Wars in the State of Illinois).

Charlevoix. 1744. *Journal D'Un Voyage Fait Par Ordre Du Roi Dans L'Amerique Septentriole.* (Paris, France).

Crosby, A. 1986. *Ecological Imperialism: The Biological Expansion of Europe, 900–1900.* Cambridge: Cambridge University Press.

———. 1994. *Germs, Seeds, and Animals: Studies in Ecological History*. New York: M. E. Sharpe.

Earle, C. 1979. *Environment, disease, and mortality in early Virginia: The Chesapeake in the Seventeenth Century*. Chapel Hill: University of North Carolina.

———. 1992. *The practice of historical geography: Geographic Inquiry and American Historical Problems*. Stanford: Stanford University Press.

———. 2003. *The American Way: A Geographical History of Crisis and Recovery*. Lanham, MD: Rowman & Littlefield.

Ekberg. C. 2000. *French Roots in the Illinois Country: The Mississippi Frontier in Colonial Times*. Urbana: The University of Illinois Press.

Emerson, T. E., and Brown, J. A. 1991. "The late prehistory and protohistory of Illinois," in *Calumet & Fleur-de-Lys: Archaeology of French and Indian Contact in the Midcontinent*, ed. John A. Walthall and Thomas E. Emerson. Washington, DC: Smithsonian Institution Press.

Flint, T. 1970. *A Condensed Geography and History of the Western States, or the Mississippi Valley, Vol. II*. Gainesville, FL: Scholars' Facsimiles and Reprints.

Giraud, M. 1987. *A History of French Louisiana, II, Years of Transition, 1715–1717*, trans. Brian Pearce. Baton Rouge: Louisiana State University Press.

Gums, B. 1988. *Archaeology at French Colonial Cahokia*. Springfield: Illinois Historic Preservation Agency.

Hauser, R. 1973. The ethnohistory of the Illinois Indian tribe. Unpublished doctoral dissertation. Northern Illinois University. Copy at Illinois Historical Survey.

J. L. McDonough and Company. 1883. *The Combined Histories of Randolph, Monroe, and Perry County, Illinois*.

Jelks, E., Ekberg, C., and Martin, T. 1989. *Excavations at the Laurens Site: Probable location of Fort de Chartres*. (Springfield: Illinois Historic Preservation Agency).

Johnsgard, P. 1975. *Waterfowl of North America*. (Bloomington: Indiana University Press).

Kellogg, L. P. 2001. *Early Narratives of the Northwest, 1634–1699*. (New York: Charles Scribner's Sons).

Kenton, E., ed. 1927. *The Indians of North America*. (New York: Harcourt, Brace).

King, F. B. 1984. Plants, People, and Paleoecology: Biotic Communities and Aboriginal Plant Usage in Illinois. Scientific Papers, Vol. XX. (Springfield: Illinois State Museum).

McCulloch, I., and Todish, T., eds. 2004. *Through So Many Dangers: The Memoirs and Adventures of Robert Kirk, Late of the Royal Highland Regiment*. (New York: Purple Mountain Press).

McDermott, J. F., ed. 1949. *Old Cahokia: A Narrative and Documents Illustrating the First Century of Its History*. (St. Louis: The St. Louis Historical Documents Foundation).

Majors, H. M. 1970. *Fort Ouitanon and the Wabash River 1700–1824*, (privately published manuscript, Seattle, Washington. Copy at the Lilly Library, Bloomington, Indiana).

Marshall, J. M. M. 1995. "A melancholy people: Anglo-Indian relations in early Warwick, Rhode Island 1642—1675," *The New England Quarterly* 8, no 3.

Martin, C. 1978. *Keepers of the Game: Indian Relations and the Fur Trade.* (Berkeley: University of California Press).

Martin, T. J. 1988. "Animal remains from the Cahokia Wedge Site," in *Archaeology at French Colonial Cahokia*, edited by Bonnie L. Gums. (Springfield: Illinois Historic Preservation Agency).

Mereness, N. D., ed. 1961. *Travels in the American Colonies.* (New York: Antiquarian Press).

Miller-Surrey, N. M. 1916. *The Commerce of Louisiana during the French Regime: 1699–1763.* (New York: Columbia University Press).

Mississippi Provincial Archives, Vol. IV and V. *French Dominion.* (Baton Rouge: Louisiana State University Press, 1927).

Montague, E. J. 1948. The *History of Randolph County, Illinois, Including Old Kaskaskia Island* (1859), ed. Elisabeth Pinkerton Leighty. Sparta, Illinois.

Morgan, E. S. 1975. "The Jamestown fiasco," in *American Slavery, American Freedom: The Ordeal of Colonial Virginia.* (New York: W.W. Norton Company).

Munson, P. J., Parmalee, P. W., and Yarnell, R. A. 1971. "Subsistence ecology of Scovill, a terminal middle woodland village," *American Antiquities*, 36: no 4.

Nelson, J. T., Redmond, A., and Sparks, R. E. 1994. "Impacts of settlement on floodplain vegetation at the confluence of the Illinois and Mississippi Rivers," *Transactions of the Illinois State Academy of Science*, 87: no 3 and 4.

Norton, M., and Studnicki-Gizbert, D. 2007. "The Multinational Commodification of Tobacco, 1492–1650: An Iberian Perspective," in *The Atlantic World and Virginia, 1550–1624*, edited by Peter C. Mancall. (Chapel Hill: University of North Carolina Press).

Le Page du Pratz. 1763. *A History of Louisiana, or of the Western Parts of Virginia and Carolina: Containing a Description of the Countries that lye on both Sides of the River Mississippi: With An Account of the Settlements, Inhabitants, Soil, Climate, and Products, 2.* (London: T. Becket and P. A. De Hondt).

Palm. M. B. 1930a. "The first Illinois wheat," *Mid-America* 13.

———. 1930b. *The Jesuit Missions of the Illinois Country 1673–1763.* (Cleveland, OH: Saint Louis University).

Saucier, W. J., and Spineke, K. W. 1969. "Francois Saucier, engineer of Fort de Chartres, Illinois," in *Frenchmen and French Ways in the Mississippi Valley*, edited by John Francis McDermott. (Urbana: University of Illinois Press).

Schlarman, J. H. 1929. *From Quebec to New Orleans: The Story of the French in America.* (Belleville, Illinois: Beuchler Publishing Company).

Sturtevant, W. C. 1978. *Handbook of North American Indians.* (Washington, DC: Smithsonian Institution).

Thwaites, R. G., ed. 1900. *The Jesuit Relations and Allied Documents*, 66. (Cleveland: Burrow Brothers Company).

———. 1903. *Father Louis Hennepin: A New Discovery of a Vast Country in America*, 1. (Chicago: A. C. McClurg & Company).

Tucker, S. J. 1942, 1975. *Indian Villages of the Illinois Country*, 2. (Scientific Papers, Illinois State Museum, Part I: Atlas).

Usner, D. J. 1992. *Indians, Settlers and Slaves in a Frontier Exchange Economy: The Lower Mississippi Valley before 1783.* (Chapel Hill: University of North Carolina Press).

Walthall, J. A., and Benchley, E. D. 1987. *The River L'Abbe Mission: A French Colonial Church for the Cahokia Illini at Monk's Mound.* (Springfield, IL: Illinois Historic Preservation Agency).

White, J. 2000. *Big Rivers Area Assessment: Early Accounts of the Ecology of the Big Rivers Area*, 5. (Springfield: Illinois Department of Natural Resources).

Woods, W. I. 1987. "Maize agriculture and the late prehistoric: a characterization of settlement location strategies." in *Emergent Horticultural Economies of the Eastern Woodlands*, edited by William F. Keegan, Center for Archaeological Investigations. (Occasional Paper No. 7. Southern Illinois University).

Woods, W. I., and Holley, G. R. 1991. "Upland Mississippian settlement in the American Bottom region" in *Cahokia and the Hinterlands: Middle Mississippian Cultures of the Midwest*, edited by Thomas E. Emerson and R. Barry Lewis. (Urbana: University of Illinois Press).

Zawacki, A. A. 1969. *Early Vegetation of the Lower Illinois Valley: A Study of the Distribution of Floral Resources with Reference to Prehistoric Cultural-Ecological Adaptations.* (Springfield, Illinois).

Zitomersky, J. 1994. *French-Americans–Native Americans in Eighteenth-Century French Colonial Louisiana: The Population Geography of the Illinois Indians, 1670s–1760s.* (Sweden: Lund University Press).

Chapter Four

Economic Diversity, Industrialization, and Urbanization in Early-Nineteenth-Century Connecticut

Kristen N. Keegan

Carville Earle (2003) has described the period 1820–1840 as a time of significant change in many dimensions of the United States' economy, geography, and society. The year 1828 marks the approximate transition point between two eras in his periodization of U.S. history: the First Republic (1780s–1828) and the First Democracy (1828–1877). The new federal policies of the 1830s led to more urban growth in already-settled areas, while tariff reductions and other policies led to economic volatility and diversification. These changes were not instantaneous, many of them having substantial effect only after 1840 in most places. This research examines the changes in Connecticut's economic structure at the municipal level between 1820 and 1840 within this larger economic context. Those changes reflect Connecticut's position among the states in the northeastern region that formed the chief locus of the new trends of industrialization and urbanization that were, according to Earle, encouraged by the political economy of the period. The chapter explores three topics related to this period of urban growth and economic development: (a) the sectoral makeup of Connecticut's municipalities in each of the years 1820, 1830, and 1840; (b) the relationship between municipal population and sectoral composition; and (c) how both of these conditions changed over the study period. The research also considers whether the findings are consistent with Earle's characterization of the period 1828–1840 as being one of urban growth, economic diversification, and economic volatility within long-settled areas like Connecticut. The theoretical perspective employed here regards the ability of a place to attract and hold both a growing population and an increasingly diverse economic base to be a useful indicator of its economic viability. While the success, or failure, of individual places is not a stated component of Earle's model, it can be considered a measure of the influence of the trends he describes, and this study finds that the changes at the municipality level in Connecticut during the 1820–1840 period are consistent with the model.

Over the course of the nineteenth century, the state of Connecticut changed from a rural agricultural landscape to an urban industrial society. However, this process was not uniform across the state. Among the state's more than 100 municipalities, a select few became booming cities, others remained quiet rural backwaters, while still others developed industrial villages that over time displayed greater or lesser degrees of impermanence. The present study considers whether the future success, in terms of continuing population growth, of these municipalities can be predicted from economic data of the early part of the century, when the sorting process was just beginning. The study uses the Herfindahl index of diversification, which measures the level of dominance or equality among members of set. Such a diversity index yields information on whether a given local economy is dominated by the primary (agricultural and/or resource extraction), secondary (manufacturing), or tertiary (services) sector, and thus illuminates the process of economic transition from rural-agricultural to urban-industrial. Economic studies of this time period in the United States are difficult, because reliable economic data for it are scarce; in addition, most of what is available omits the tertiary sector. The present study uses a data source that has been overlooked by most scholars: a valuation of each municipality's residents' property, collected for state tax purposes. Although these data are not perfectly suited to the present purpose, they are an improvement over what has been generally used, as they make possible a more complete picture of the municipalities' sectoral composition.

BACKGROUND

A study that directly examines economic development and diversity in the context of the United States in the early nineteenth century is that of Diane Lindstrom (1978), who considered the role of economic diversity in the economic growth of the Philadelphia region between 1810 and 1850, using that state's Grand List data, among other sources. She found that while the rural hinterland dominated the agricultural sector, the urban center came to specialize in, yet did not completely dominate, the secondary sector. Her study's attention to the tertiary sector, however, focused on external trade, while this chapter considers that sector more locally, simply as part of Connecticut municipalities' economic diversity. Other efforts to explain the growth of urban places have focused on a variety of specific factors. A particularly important study by James Vance (1970) argued for the importance of commerce, and specifically long-distance wholesale trade, as a key factor in the development of new urban places. He intended his mercantile model to be a supplement to Christaller's traditional central place theory, which suggested that urban places develop as a result of local economic interactions (de Souza 1990); Vance believed this was not a sufficient explanation. Vance's model is particularly appropriate for colonized areas like British North America, where two-way commercial links to Britain and other colonies were important to the location and survival of many towns and cities. By the early nineteenth century, Connecticut had been settled for almost two centuries and was no longer "colonial," but the fading imprint of the earliest settlement patterns still remained on the landscape. A problem with applying Vance's and Christaller's models to specific places is a lack of data on tertiary economic activities, particularly before the twentieth century. Even secondary sector data can be difficult to find. One partial answer to this difficulty has been to focus on the transportation network, which tends to link central places with one another and facilitates both local and extra-local trade. Edward K. Muller (1976; 1977) proposed that "nodality," the level of connectedness of a place in the transportation network, can be substituted for centrality in explaining the growth of urban places. Working from a study of the Ohio Valley between 1800 and 1860 and then generalizing from there, Muller argued that changes in transportation technology, which tended to change routes, led to resorting of central places, with some places growing and some losing population. The importance of the transportation network cannot be overlooked, but neither should it be overemphasized. The historical record indicates that for every place that benefited from a change such as construction of a railroad, there were others that received no such benefit. The present research omits the transportation network in order to isolate the influence of the base economy on historical development. Interestingly, in the state of Connecticut the first significant rail line (a thirty-six-mile link between Hartford and New Haven only) was not opened until 1838/1839; a second important line, serving Norwich and the northeastern mill towns, opened in 1840 (Turner and Jacobus 1989). Given this late development, it appears that it was the existence of these thriving mercantile and industrial centers that attracted the railroads to them.

Numerous studies have shown a connection between population size and the number of central place functions, typically tertiary-sector activities of various kinds (King 1984). These are not necessarily or even largely the wholesaling activities on which Vance focused. In addition, aside from Vance, the literature does not make it clear whether this correlation is driven by the population or by the central place functions themselves. Even if, as Allan Pred (1980) has demonstrated for the United States in the period 1840 to 1860, the larger cities captured more of the increasing population than the smaller ones, it is still difficult to say whether this was due to their size or to their economic composition. The empirical evidence examined here seems to suggest that an initial advantage in size and tertiary activity kept Connecticut's largest places in or near the lead in population, while the relationship between industrial activity and population size is negligible. This is consistent with LeBlanc's (1969) finding that before about 1850, industrial location in New England had not begun the process of agglomeration that characterized the latter half of the century. This chapter supports LeBlanc's conclusion that early industrial development was fairly ubiquitous across the landscape, and thus bore little relationship to the size of the places where it was located.

August Lösch's expansion of Christaller's central place theory, however, describes central places as nodes of production, directly linking industrial activity to central place theory (de Souza 1990). Pred (1966; 1980) stated that Lösch's version of central place theory encompasses industrialization as a consequence of the appearance of urban markets, and further that after 1840, secondary functions gradually displaced tertiary functions as the economic engines of the major urban centers. The present research indicates that these theories are at best only partly correct with respect to the emerging industrial economy of early nineteenth century Connecticut. Central place research has tended to focus on mature urban systems, rather than embryonic ones (see Otterstrom 2007); nor have historic studies other than Lindstrom's (1978) attempted to consider the relationship between economic structure and urban growth. As an immature urban system, Connecticut was in the midst of a sorting process that eventually would lead to a stable hierarchy—and still far from an ideal place to apply central place models. Thus, the general model of American economic geography proposed by Earle (2003) provides a better explanation. At the scale of the whole United States, his periodization places the 1820–1840 time period of this study between eras, and at the beginning of a period of economic change and volatility at the regional level. To a certain extent, this study shows, these changes also can be discerned at the local scale of Connecticut municipalities' growth and economic diversification.

DEFINITIONS AND DATA

The unusual nature of Connecticut's geographic organization requires some explanation, as does the characteristics and limitations of the economic data to be utilized here. From its beginnings, Connecticut's fundamental unit of organization has been the corporate entity known as the "town," which encompasses the territory and most of the functions commonly associated with counties in other parts of the United States. As of 1820, there were also five incorporated cities, with a sixth added in 1836, each of which had previously been part of a town. For statistical purposes, however, the state continued to treat the town and city as identical units, so that data for the city and town of Hartford, for example, were always combined. Hence, the more general term "municipalities" will be used as a collective reference to these entities throughout this chapter. In addition, during the early nineteenth century the number of municipalities was continually changing, as new towns broke off from old ones or were formed by joining parts of several towns into a new one. In 1820, there were 121 municipalities, with 130 in 1830, and 139 in 1840. This makes direct comparisons between these panel years (such as shift-share analysis, for example) too problematic to attempt here.

Throughout much of its history, including the study period, the State of Connecticut required the collection of information about the property of its citizens, in order to fairly apportion the burden of taxes on that property for the support of the state government. These data were collected annually by officials for each municipality and compiled into ledgers by the Office of the Comptroller, and were referred to as the Connecticut Grand List (Connecticut State Archives, Record Group 8, Item 76, Vols. 1–6). Lindstrom (1978) used data from the Pennsylvania Grand List in her study.

The Grand List contains numerous categories of data that can be assigned to the standard economic sectors of agriculture, manufacturing, and services (or primary, secondary, and tertiary). Although the simple term "services" for all kinds of tertiary activity seems impractically broad by modern standards, it reflects the broadness and vagueness of the state legislature's understanding of the activities they were trying to tax at the time. In particular, the elements that are here assigned to each sector are:

Agriculture	Land + Cattle
Manufacturing	Mills + Distilleries + Manufactories
Services	Stores + Assessments

Such categorization is inevitably imperfect, but it is known that the assessed values were, with the exception of "assessments," the selling value of the property, and thus reflected the varying uses to which it was put. For example, an acre of plowed and planted land would be worth more than an acre of woodland. For a manufactory (the early nineteenth-century word for "factory"), store, and so on, the assessed value would include its property, inventory, and income. The category "assessments" is an exception and a practical problem. Short for "faculty assessments," this category captured, for tax purposes, the income of persons whose work included little physical plant—services such as attorneys, doctors, and the like (Jones 1896; Connecticut 1835). This category is not exactly "property," therefore, but it does help to fill out the tertiary sector and for that reason is retained.

I transcribed the Grand List data for 1820, 1830, and 1840 from the original documents. The historical population data used for this study was compiled by the Map and Geographic Information Center (1996).

HISTORICAL CONTEXT

At the beginning of the nineteenth century, Connecticut, like the rest of southern New England, had an agricultural economy leavened by a few commercial centers located near navigable waters and by some small, largely home or shop-based manufacturing enterprises. Although machine-driven textile manufacturing had been introduced to the region by 1790, as late as 1810 the technology was still immature and the total number of facilities in the entire region was probably less than 125. Connecticut also had notable iron-making facilities, primarily in the northwestern corner of the state, a modest hat export industry located mainly in the inland part of the state's southwestern corner, and another of shoes based in a quartet of towns in different parts of the state. As of 1810, the impact of these facilities on the population of the towns in which they were located was negligible at best (Bidwell 1915). During the decades up to 1840, the Grand List reported the number of manufactories in the state rising from 672 (1820) to 1,466 (1830) to 2,005 (1840).

The box plots in figure 4.1 and the statistics in table 4.1 and table 4.2 show how the overall populations of the towns responded to these economic changes. The box plots of the 1820, 1830, and 1840 data show very little change in the populations of the majority of the towns. In each year, the population distribution was clearly skewed towards the smaller end of the scale, with three-quarters of the towns having populations of less than 3,000 persons. The uppermost quartile ended below 5,000 in each of the three study years, while the outlying and extreme cases rose ever higher. The statistics in table 4.1 expand the date range to 1810–1850 in order to provide a larger historical context for the population changes. The slight shifts from year to year are more clearly visible in this table: the minimum population fell by 231 between 1820 and 1850, while the mean population shifted up and down by a maximum of 211 persons. The maximum population, in contrast, reflects a near tripling of the size of the largest town, while the state's total population rose by a little over 100,000—but half of that growth occurred between 1840 and 1850. The statistics associated with

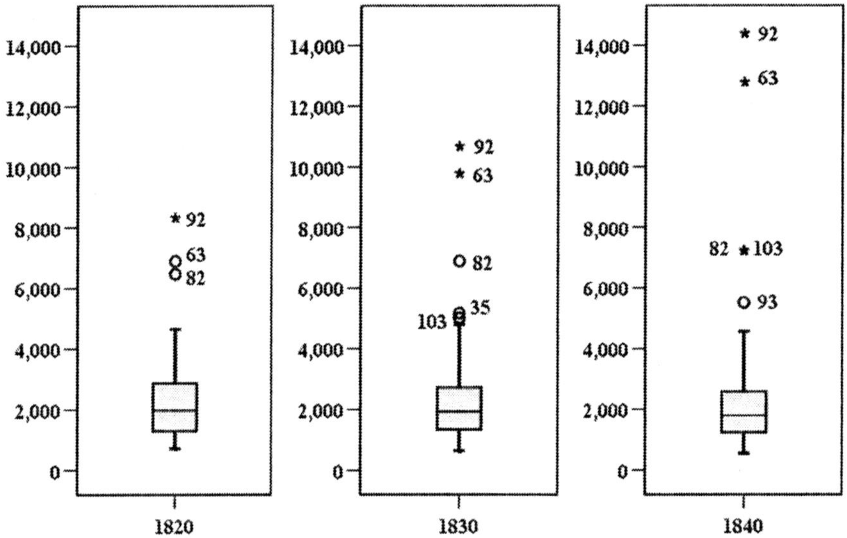

Figure 4.1. Boxplots of Town Population, 1820–1840. The outliers (o) and extreme cases (*) are Hartford (63), Middletown (82), New Haven (92), New London (93), Norwich (103), and Saybrook/Deep River (35). *Source:* Map and Geographic Information Centr, 1996.

Table 4.1. Population Statistics

Year	*N*	*Minimum*	*Maximum*	*Mean*	*Total*
1810	119	700	6,967	2,201.19	261,942
1820	121	731	8,327	2,238.50	270,859
1830	130	651	10,678	2,289.82	297,677
1840	139	548	14,390	2,230.78	310,078
1850	149	500	20,345	2,441.83	363,833

Table 4.2. Population Boxplot Statistics

Year	*Q1*	*Q2*	*Q3*	*IRQ*	*Q4*
1810	1,344.00	1,963	2,748.00	1,404.00	4,639
1820	1,308.25	1,991	2,877.50	1,569.25	4,664
1830	1,338.75	1,936	2,749.75	1,411.00	4,805
1840	1,232.00	1,791	2,599.00	1,367.00	4,570
1850	1,298.00	1,848	2,660.50	1,362.50	4,651

the box plots, in table 4.2, show a similar overall stability: the first quartile (Q1), second quartile or median (Q2), third quartile (Q3), and interquartile range (IRQ) changed by less than 200 persons between 1810 and 1850, and most often by much less than that.

Thus, during this larger period the overall population changes in Connecticut towns reflected a concentration of population in a few places, with most of the state showing population stability. This was true even during the population jump between 1840 and 1850. These trends are consistent with Pred's (1980) finding that the largest cities across the nation captured most of the population growth between 1840 and 1860, suggesting that this pattern holds at both the macro and micro scales of analysis. Similarly, Earle's (2003) periodization scheme describes this time period as the start of an era of consolidation of population within existing settled areas. During the earliest decades of the nineteenth century, so much of Connecticut's excess population emigrated to the newly settled areas on the frontier that in 1817 the governor expressed the need to provide incentives to keep people from moving away (Van Dusen 1961). The statistics just described show that there was some delay in Connecticut's response to the larger trends described by Earle. At the same time, however, what growth there was flowed primarily to a few large places. I will now address the relationship between these population trends and the economic structure of the Connecticut towns.

METHODOLOGY

Connecticut's nineteenth century transition from a rural agricultural society to an urban industrial society was, at the municipality level, a geographically varied process. A diversity index is a useful tool for highlighting local trends when examining the relationships among population size and different types of economic activity. The Herfindahl index was chosen for its mathematical simplicity and ease of interpretation. This index, sometimes known as the Hirschman index, was developed by economists to measure the level of concentration within industries, but is easily adaptable to the larger question of sectoral diversity. Where the original index would refer to individual firms and their shares of a market, I substituted the three economic sectors and their shares of the "economy" as represented by the Grand List data. Thus, where s_i is a sector's proportion of the economy of a given town i (out of n towns), I calculated

$$H = \sum_{i=1}^{n} (s_i)^2 \qquad \text{for all } s \tag{3.1}$$

The summary value *H* represents the level of concentration (or diversity) in the system. This value will always be less than 1, with lower numbers representing lower concentration or higher diversity, and by squaring the proportions the difference between larger and smaller values is emphasized (see, *e.g.*, Schmalensee 1977). This makes both general trends and the more extreme values stand out. In addition, both the summary values and the squared proportions are useful for understanding the level of economic diversity in Connecticut's municipalities during the study period.[1]

The base sectoral data for each study year was attached to a GIS shapefile of the towns in that year, and the Herfindahl index calculations were performed using that program's calculate functions. The historic town boundary files were created by William F. Keegan and lightly edited by this author. In addition, the Spearman rank correlation coefficient was used to measure the level of correlation between population and the economic variables. A nonparametric measure was used because none of the data in this study displayed a normal probability distribution.

ANALYSIS

The results of the Herfindahl index and Spearman's correlation coefficient calculations were quite consistent across the three study years. This summary of the results makes some attempts to place them in historical context, while leaving a more detailed discussion to the following section. Broadly speaking, however, the results show an increasing level of economic diversity and non-frontier population growth across the study period, consistent with Earle's (2003) proposed model. In each year, this discussion deals with only the municipalities that had the lowest Herfindahl index results and/or the highest population. The Herfindahl index cutoff points for discussion vary from year to year, as rising levels of secondary sector activity led to increased diversity, and lower index scores. The map in figure 4.2 shows the locations of these low index value towns in the years 1820, 1830, and 1840, with the cities labeled.

Results for 1820

For this year the vast majority of the state's 121 municipalities had Herfindahl index numbers of 0.9 or greater, with the agricultural sector overwhelmingly dominant in all these cases. Only eleven municipalities had a Herfindahl index value of less than 0.9; in fact, the lowest value of all was only 0.4428. The

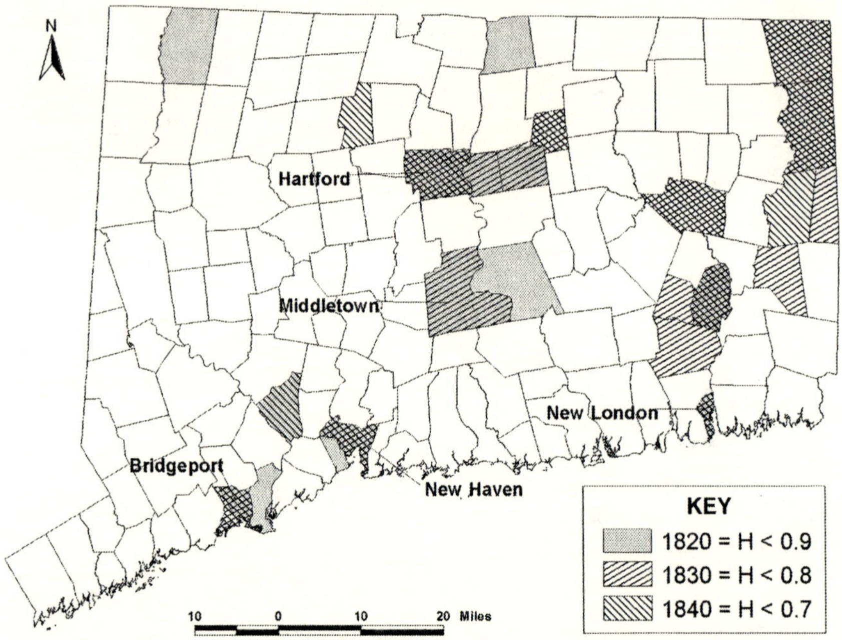

Figure 4.2. Map of Low Herfindahl Index Numbers in 1820, 1830, and 1840.

index values, squared sector proportions, and populations are presented in table 4.3, sorted by Herfindahl value from the lowest (most diversified) to the highest (least diversified). The table also includes the towns with populations greater than the third quartile boundary of 2,877.5, as shown in table 4.2; the existing city-containing places are marked with an asterisk. All five of the cities were contained in the set of eleven municipalities with index values less than 0.9. Examination of this table reveals several points of interest. First, the source of the overall high level of concentration was the agricultural sector, which was the largest component in all cases. Second, in six of the eleven cases the tertiary component was larger than the secondary component, and five of those cases were the incorporated cities; the sixth, Stratford, would later subdivide to provide territory for the town and city of Bridgeport. Third, three of the four least diverse municipalities in this group of eleven had tertiary values of zero, while the fourth had a tertiary value of 0.0001; but all eleven had secondary values of at least 0.0009, which was not the case for many of the other towns with more than 2,877.5 inhabitants.

The latter characteristic of the data should not be over-interpreted, because the category "mills" included essential rural facilities such as grist mills and sawmills, and every town had at least one of these according to this data set. In contrast, 51 of the state's 121 municipalities had no manufactories, and 59

Table 4.3. 1820 Data Summary

Town	*H Index*	*Primary*	*Secondary*	*Tertiary*	*Population*
New London*	0.4428	0.2551	0.0045	0.1832	3,330
New Haven*	0.4915	0.3868	0.0036	0.1011	8,327
Hartford*	0.6082	0.5577	0.0009	0.0496	6,901
Norwich*	0.6568	0.6344	0.0054	0.0170	3,634
Canaan	0.7960	0.7859	0.0099	0.0002	2,332
Stratford	0.8061	0.7998	0.0011	0.0052	3,438
Middletown*	0.8529	0.8496	0.0009	0.0024	6,479
East Hartford	0.8760	0.8723	0.0037	0.0000	3,373
Chatham	0.8793	0.8760	0.0033	0.0000	3,159
Derby	0.8829	0.8802	0.0026	0.0001	2,088
Enfield	0.8918	0.8892	0.0026	0.0000	2,065
East Windsor	0.9078	0.9058	0.0020	0.0000	3,400
Norwalk	0.9082	0.9070	0.0007	0.0005	3,004
Newtown	0.9281	0.9269	0.0012	0.0000	2,879
Saybrook	0.9299	0.9293	0.0004	0.0002	4,165
Farmington	0.9303	0.9293	0.0010	0.0000	3,042
Fairfield	0.9317	0.9311	0.0005	0.0001	4,151
Stamford	0.9346	0.9337	0.0009	0.0000	3,284
Litchfield	0.9406	0.9401	0.0004	0.0001	4,610
Glastonbury	0.9428	0.9423	0.0005	0.0000	3,114
Windsor	0.9451	0.9444	0.0007	0.0000	3,008
Granby	0.9456	0.9449	0.0007	0.0000	3,012
Wethersfield	0.9523	0.9520	0.0002	0.0001	3,825
New Milford	0.9579	0.9575	0.0004	0.0000	3,830
Thompson	0.9583	0.9579	0.0004	0.0000	2,928
Danbury	0.9602	0.9599	0.0003	0.0000	3,873
Woodstock	0.9638	0.9635	0.0003	0.0000	3,017
Mansfield	0.9647	0.9645	0.0002	0.0000	2,993
Stonington	0.9661	0.9660	0.0000	0.0001	3,056
Groton	0.9662	0.9661	0.0000	0.0001	4,664
Lyme	0.9697	0.9695	0.0002	0.0000	4,069
Greenwich	0.9877	0.9877	0.0000	0.0000	3,790
Guilford	0.9916	0.9916	0.0000	0.0000	4,131

This table is sorted by Herfindahl Index value and contains the data for towns where (a) $H < 0.9$, or (b) Population $> 2{,}877.5$ (the third quartile boundary). Towns marked with * include incorporated cities.

had no distilleries. Only thirteen, however, had no stores, and only one had no reported faculty assessment value. Finally, in the entire state only six municipalities had a tertiary component greater than 0.0005; all of the six were in the group of eleven most diverse municipalities, and in fact were the same six that had a higher tertiary values than secondary values. In 1820, then, the state of Connecticut was still overwhelmingly rural, and only a tiny fraction of its municipalities had a significant level of tertiary economic activity, while most of them had some secondary activity.

The next step was to determine whether there is any statistical relationship between population and the composition of the municipalities' economies; more specifically, whether the Herfindahl index values and population are positively correlated. According to a Spearman's rank correlation coefficient test, the two variables are *negatively* correlated, with a coefficient of –0.310 (the one-tailed significance of the result is 0.000 at $\alpha = 0.01$). The base data themselves confirm that the municipalities with the lowest Herfindahl index scores are not necessarily the largest in population. While New Haven, Hartford, and Middletown—three city-containing municipalities listed in table 4.1—were the three largest in population as of 1820, the other eight of the eleven with low index values were smaller in population than many other less-diverse municipalities, as table 4.3 shows. Indeed, three towns were in the lower half of municipalities in number of inhabitants. Norwich was only the thirteenth largest municipality in the state, while New London was the seventeenth largest. Canaan, with the highest secondary-sector squared proportion in the group, was just the forty-sixth largest. Some of this can be explained by the physical size of the municipalities; New London, for example, was and is one of the smallest in the state, and so its economy did not include as much of a rural segment as others, such as Hartford and New Haven. The case of Canaan's high dependence on the secondary sector can probably be explained by iron industry activities there, which focused on geographically localized resources (in fact, the dollar value of Canaan's twenty-two manufactories was the highest dollar value in the state, while that of its agricultural sector ranked near the middle). Overall, however, these results indicate that in 1820, the effects of localized economic development had not reached a point at which the population of industrial and commercial places was normally higher than that of agricultural places.

At this point, however, a caveat is necessary. Although the summary Herfindahl statistic is not positively correlated with population size, the level of tertiary economic activity in this data set is so correlated. The Spearman's test yields a correlation coefficient of 0.399 (significance of 0.000) when applied to population and the squared proportion of tertiary activity. An additional test substituted the dollar value of the tertiary activity, because for many towns the proportion was zero out to four decimal places; this test found an equally significant correlation coefficient of 0.685. Interestingly, testing the correlation between population and proportion of secondary activity also finds positive correlation, albeit with a coefficient of 0.211 that is only significant at the 0.05 level rather than 0.01; however, substituting the dollar value for the proportion yields a correlation coefficient of 0.606 (significant at 0.01). Secondary and tertiary are also positively correlated with each other, at a level of 0.281 (significant at 0.01). Finally, combining the dollar values of secondary and tertiary activities yields a correlation coefficient of those two with population of 0.842 (significant at 0.01).

The source of the negative correlation between the Herfindahl index values and the population values must be the primary sector, the proportion of which is negatively correlated with population; the coefficient is –0.309, significant at 0.01. Given the very rural nature of Connecticut's economy in 1820, this reflects the high proportion of the population and its resources that were engaged in agricultural work rather than commercial or industrial activities. On the other hand, most of these correlation coefficients are not convincingly high. Recalling that a coefficient of 1 or –1 indicates complete positive or negative correlation, and 0 indicates an absence of correlation, it is clear that the coefficients given above do not show very strong correlation in either direction. This is true in all the panel years, so that these results cannot be considered strong conclusive evidence of correlation between diversity and population size. The much higher correlations of the dollar values with population are of interest, but this information does not address the overall structure of the towns' economies and its relationship with population growth.

In summary, the 1820 analysis found that of the 121 municipalities in existence that year, 110 had Herfindahl index scores of 0.9 or greater, with their economies dominated by the primary sector. The eleven cases with lower scores, and hence more diversity, displayed varying sources for their diversity. Some had a mix of secondary and tertiary activity, and the less diverse towns of the group skewed toward the secondary rather than tertiary sector. A positive statistical relationship between population and economic diversity could be found only by omitting the overwhelmingly dominant primary sector from the analysis. At this early stage of the industrialization-urbanization process, the influence of tertiary and secondary activity on overall population trends was not significant enough to counter the influence of the primary sector. This is a pattern that Earle (2003) might predict for a First Republic regime (expected to end as of 1828), with only a few places showing signs of economic diversification.

Results for 1830

Ten years later, the state's overall economic diversity had increased noticeably. Thirty-six of 130 municipalities had Herfindahl index values of less than 0.9, over three times the number in the previous decade. Table 4.4 provides the statistics for the sixteen towns that had index values of less than 0.8, together with those with populations greater than 2,749.75 (the third quartile boundary). These low index value towns are also depicted in figure 4.2. The

Table 4.4. 1830 Data Summary

Town	*H Index*	*Primary*	*Secondary*	*Tertiary*	*Population*
New London*	0.4076	0.1924	0.0123	0.2029	4,356
Norwich*	0.4165	0.3228	0.0404	0.0533	5,179
New Haven*	0.4226	0.1862	0.0082	0.2282	10,678
Hartford*	0.4875	0.3739	0.0031	0.1105	9,789
Bridgeport	0.5131	0.4473	0.0084	0.0574	2,800
Windham	0.6450	0.6021	0.0426	0.0003	2,812
Killingly	0.6671	0.6257	0.0414	0.0000	3,257
Thompson	0.6820	0.6485	0.0334	0.0001	3,380
Griswold	0.7283	0.7034	0.0249	0.0000	2,212
Middletown*	0.7401	0.7294	0.0047	0.0060	6,892
Bozrah	0.7554	0.7365	0.0189	0.0000	1,079
Manchester	0.7796	0.7647	0.0149	0.0000	1,576
Sterling	0.7840	0.7688	0.0152	0.0000	1,240
Vernon	0.7858	0.7716	0.0142	0.0000	1,164
East Hartford	0.7886	0.7753	0.0133	0.0000	2,237
Montville	0.7965	0.7840	0.0125	0.0000	1,972
Norwalk	0.8430	0.8393	0.0026	0.0011	3,792
Glastonbury	0.8485	0.8427	0.0058	0.0000	2,980
Waterbury	0.8845	0.8815	0.0029	0.0001	3,070
Saybrook	0.9034	0.9021	0.0009	0.0004	5,018
Haddam	0.9045	0.9027	0.0017	0.0001	3,025
East Windsor	0.9152	0.9135	0.0017	0.0000	3,536
Danbury	0.9225	0.9214	0.0010	0.0001	4,311
Stamford	0.9234	0.9223	0.0011	0.0000	3,707
Stonington	0.9235	0.9227	0.0004	0.0004	3,401
Newtown	0.9244	0.9233	0.0011	0.0000	3,096
Litchfield	0.9250	0.9242	0.0005	0.0003	4,456
Woodstock	0.9261	0.9248	0.0013	0.0000	2,917
Chatham	0.9280	0.9270	0.0009	0.0001	3,646
Berlin	0.9318	0.9310	0.0007	0.0001	3,037
Windsor	0.9368	0.9359	0.0009	0.0000	3,220
Groton	0.9411	0.9405	0.0005	0.0001	4,805
Fairfield	0.9445	0.9441	0.0002	0.0002	4,226
Lyme	0.9469	0.9464	0.0004	0.0001	4,092
New Milford	0.9558	0.9554	0.0004	0.0000	3,979
Greenwich	0.9561	0.9558	0.0003	0.0000	3,801
Weston	0.9568	0.9563	0.0005	0.0000	2,997
North Stonington	0.9605	0.9602	0.0003	0.0000	2,840
Wethersfield	0.9649	0.9647	0.0001	0.0001	3,853

This table is sorted by Herfindahl Index value and contains the data for towns where (a) $H < 0.8$, or (b) Population > 2,749.75 (the third quartile boundary). Towns marked with * include incorporated cities.

table omits seventeen towns with Herfindahl index values between 0.8 and 0.8999, but whose population was less than the third quartile boundary.

Sixteen municipalities had index values of less than 0.8 including four that were below 0.4: the large cities of New London, New Haven, Hartford, and Norwich. The fifth largest city, Middletown, was among these sixteen diverse cities, but as before, it lagged behind the others. Bridgeport, created out of Stratford and Fairfield as of 1821 but still not a city, was the fifth most diverse with a Herfindahl index value of 0.5131. This latter case illustrates the influence of geography on the economic structure of the time; Bridgeport's territory included the least rural parts of two towns (without that urban section, Stratford was only the sixty-second most diverse town of the 130 in 1830), while New Haven had shed part of its rural territory as part of the new town of Oxford (ninety-ninth most diverse). This jurisdictional separation of rural and urbanizing areas was itself an outgrowth of the economic and physical changes in the latter places.

Comparing table 4.3 and table 4.4 reveals both similarities and differences between 1820 and 1830. First, in 1830 the most diverse municipalities still had the highest level of tertiary activity, but in this year there were also two municipalities that had *more* tertiary than primary activity, an important change. Of these, New London had a very small physical area, as was noted above, but Norwich did not. Second, except for the town and city of Middletown, the remaining municipalities' relatively high diversity is explained by a strong level of secondary activity, though in no case was secondary activity the largest sector of the economy. In addition, of the six non-city municipalities in the low-diversity group of 1820, at least five had been surpassed in diversity by others in the 1830 list (although if one counts Bridgeport as if it were Stratford, that would be only four out of six). This was due to their increased proportions of secondary activity, which was in some cases higher than that present in the cities, as was the case in 1820. In summary, the only reliable indicator of continuously high diversity between 1820 and 1830 was a high level of tertiary activity in the first study year.

The results of the Spearman's rank correlation coefficient tests are similar to those for 1820. The Herfindahl index *(H)* values still were negatively correlated with population, with a coefficient of –0.369 (with one-tailed significance at the 0.001 level). The tertiary sector was positively correlated with population, with a coefficient of 0.466; the secondary sector was positively correlated at 0.297; and the primary sector was negatively correlated at –0.368 (all with one-tailed significance at the 0.001 level). Notwithstanding the positive correlations between population and the tertiary and secondary sectors, it was still the case in 1830 that many of the municipalities with the greatest economic diversity were smaller in population than numerous

Table 4.5. 1830 Dollar Values (in thousands)

Town	Total	Primary	Secondary	Tertiary
New London	5,579.19	2,447.25	618.67	2,513.27
Norwich	21,576.40	12,258.60	4,338.33	4,979.47
New Haven	19,004.79	8,200.40	1,726.00	9,078.39
Hartford	50,479.41	30,867.98	2,828.33	16,783.09
Bridgeport	8,720.21	5,831.85	800.00	2,088.36
Windham	18,226.20	14,143.00	3,760.43	322.76
Killingly	18,825.74	14,891.62	3,828.33	105.79
Thompson	23,795.11	19,161.52	4,350.77	282.83
Griswold	12,751.27	10,694.28	2,013.33	43.66
Middletown	39,223.13	33,498.07	2,683.50	3,041.56

less-diverse municipalities. For example, Windham, with the sixth lowest *H* index as shown in table 4.4, was only the thirty-first largest town in population; Killingly was the twenty-first largest; Thompson the twentieth largest; Bridgeport the thirty-second largest; and Griswold the fifty-fourth largest.

Table 4.5 shows the dollar value (in thousands) of the sectors as reported by the Grand List for the ten towns with the lowest Herfindahl index values, including the five towns with the lower populations. These dollar values show that by the standards of the time these smaller towns had large amounts of secondary or, in the case of Bridgeport, tertiary-related property. These were comparable to, or in some cases greater than, the amounts reported for the larger cities, and far higher than those listed for many towns with greater populations. The proportional information in table 4.4 shows the same ratios of activity by sectors. Nonetheless, as with the 1820 data, a series of Spearman tests for correlation between population and dollar values also finds higher correlations: 0.635 for the secondary sector, 0.684 for the tertiary sector, and 0.684 for the combined sectors (all significant at 0.01). The research question, however, is whether diversity as measured by the Herfindahl index appears related to population growth, and the Spearman test found a slightly higher negative correlation between the index values and population of 1830 than it did for the 1820. Thus, it still cannot be said that any clear relationship between diversity and population size existed in 1830. This year was very early in Earle's First Democracy regime and in the industrialization process, so the effect of the new political economy cycle cannot be expected to be great at that time.

Results for 1840

Economic diversity across the state continued to increase, so that by 1840 there were fifty-eight municipalities with Herfindahl index values of less than 0.9, which comprised about 42 percent of the 139 municipalities. Table 4.6 lists all the twelve municipalities with Herfindahl index values of less than 0.7, and all those with a population above the third quartile boundary of 2,599, sorted by Herfindahl index value. This omits eighteen towns with index values between 0.7 and 0.8999, all with populations less than the third

Table 4.6. 1840 Data Summary

Town	*H Index*	*Primary*	*Secondary*	*Tertiary*	*Population*
New London*	0.3771	0.1579	0.0270	0.1922	5,519
Norwich*	0.3780	0.2460	0.0408	0.0912	7,239
New Haven*	0.3797	0.1840	0.0248	0.1709	14,390
Bridgeport*	0.4514	0.3564	0.0141	0.0809	4,570
Hartford*	0.4578	0.3122	0.0043	0.1413	12,793
Canton	0.5533	0.4519	0.1013	0.0001	1,736
Vernon	0.5682	0.4798	0.0883	0.0001	1,430
Thompson	0.5931	0.5232	0.0697	0.0002	3,535
Killingly	0.6079	0.5408	0.0671	0.0000	3,685
Windham	0.6167	0.5637	0.0526	0.0004	3,382
Plainfield	0.6584	0.6131	0.0453	0.0000	2,383
Derby	0.6720	0.6425	0.0287	0.0008	2,851
Middletown*	0.7172	0.7042	0.0074	0.0056	7,210
Glastonbury	0.7599	0.7415	0.0184	0.0000	3,077
Waterbury	0.7676	0.7568	0.0099	0.0009	3,668
Enfield	0.8143	0.8051	0.0092	0.0000	2,648
Norwalk	0.8151	0.8100	0.0023	0.0028	3,863
East Haddam	0.8261	0.8196	0.0063	0.0002	2,620
East Windsor	0.8463	0.8405	0.0057	0.0001	3,600
Saybrook	0.8540	0.8509	0.0021	0.0010	3,417
Berlin	0.8548	0.8509	0.0036	0.0003	3,411
Ashford	0.8589	0.8540	0.0049	0.0000	2,651
Stonington	0.8723	0.8701	0.0012	0.0010	3,898
Danbury	0.8961	0.8942	0.0017	0.0002	4,504
Woodstock	0.8962	0.8936	0.0026	0.0000	3,053
Stamford	0.9108	0.9097	0.0008	0.0003	3,516
Chatham	0.9210	0.9200	0.0009	0.0001	3,413
Litchfield	0.9241	0.9234	0.0004	0.0003	4,038
Granby	0.9277	0.9268	0.0009	0.0000	2,611
Suffield	0.9298	0.9288	0.0010	0.0000	2,669
Groton	0.9331	0.9322	0.0000	0.0009	2,963
Lyme	0.9368	0.9363	0.0002	0.0003	2,856
Newtown	0.9396	0.9389	0.0007	0.0000	3,189
New Milford	0.9472	0.9467	0.0004	0.0001	3,974
Greenwich	0.9527	0.9523	0.0004	0.0000	3,921
Wethersfield	0.9570	0.9567	0.0002	0.0001	3,824
Fairfield	0.9627	0.9625	0.0001	0.0001	3,654

This table is sorted by Herfindahl Index value and contains the data for towns where (a) $H > 0.7$, or (b) Population > 2,599 (the third quartile boundary). Towns marked with * include incorporated cities.

quartile boundary. The first point to notice is that between 1830 and 1840 the city and town of Middletown fell further down the list of most diverse places; in this year, it held thirteenth place with a value of 0.7172, only a little less than in 1830. The other five city-containing municipalities (Bridgeport became a city in 1836) were the five most diverse places in the state. They were also five of the six largest in population (the sixth being Middletown). After those six, however, there were many municipalities that were larger in population yet less economically diverse than the others listed in table 4.6, which is consistent with the results from previous years. In addition, of the ten non-city municipalities at the top of the 1830 list (excluding Bridgeport), only four are found at the top of the 1840 list. This is not to say that they had become substantially less diverse; in fact, each of them still had Herfindahl index values close to their previous numbers, and were still among the twenty most diverse. They simply had been surpassed in diversity by other municipalities, rather than maintaining their lead.

The Spearman's rank correlation calculations yield results similar to those in previous years. The correlation between Herfindahl index values and population was negative, with a coefficient of –0.454, even larger than in 1830. That between population and tertiary sector activity was a positive 0.454; between population and secondary was 0.366; and between population and primary, –0.453. Correlations using the dollar values for the sectors against the population again yielded stronger positive coefficients for the secondary sector (0.623), the tertiary sector (0.717), and the combined secondary and tertiary (0.693) (all significant at .01). As of 1840, then, Connecticut municipalities displayed a statistically significant negative correlation between population and economic diversity as measured by the Herfindahl index, as they did in 1820 and 1830. Statistically significant and moderately strong correlations between population and the other two sectors also appeared. The overall 1840 economy was still dominated by the agricultural sector, and membership in the category of most diverse towns did change substantially from the preceding decade; but the presence of significant secondary activity in 1820 or 1830 did not at all guarantee a town's continued ownership of high diversity or a significant increase in population. Only the municipalities with a strong lead in the tertiary sector—and not all of those—retained both high population and low diversity index scores. But the many changes in municipalities' diversity and population rank, combined with the very strong increase in certain places' population and the overall increase in secondary sector activity, suggest support for Earle's First Democracy model within the context of the pre-existing municipal hierarchy.

CONCLUSION

Looking forward to the population figures for 1900, there is even less reason to regard early economic diversity as a predictor of long-term population growth for places that did not show strong tertiary performance from the earliest date. Among the municipalities that existed in both 1840 and 1900 (that is, omitting the twenty-nine new municipalities that appeared during that time period), five of the ten largest in population in 1900 were also city-containing municipalities in 1840 (all of them but Middletown, which was the eleventh largest). The other five, however, were new entries, which had not appeared on the 1840 or earlier most-diverse groups shown in the tables. It is true that of the seven non-city places in the most diverse group in table 4.6 (1840), three were still among the twenty largest places in 1900, and two more among the thirty largest; but in 1840, Waterbury (the fourth-largest municipality in the state in 1900) was only the fifteenth largest and had a Herfindahl index value of 0.7676; Meriden (the fifth-largest in 1900) was the sixty-fourth largest in 1840, with a Herfindahl index value of 0.8066. The dynamic nature of the development process is made clear by these details. The only clear indicator of long-term population growth is the tertiary sector, and not only does that apply to only a small number of municipalities, but the progress of Middletown shows that it is not an universally applicable principle. But Earle's theory does not require that the First Democracy phase of the American political economy result in successful businesses or places, only that the economic and geographic landscape would be distinctly altered. That is certainly the case in Connecticut in the period between 1820 and 1840, as this analysis shows.

The urbanization process is generally held to be a part of the industrialization process. At the same time, central place theory holds that places attract population through the presence of central place functions, which are usually considered service or tertiary sector activities (King 1984). Therefore, it was expected that some link would be found among economic diversity involving both of these sectors, industrialization, and population growth. With regard to the places that became major cities and those that remained very rural, there clearly is such a link, especially with respect to the tertiary sector. The results are far less conclusive with respect to the mid-level places, probably reflecting the influence of random and external factors on the local development process. Overall, the resulting economic structure appears to be partly consistent with central place theory, with a group of persistent large places with high levels of tertiary activity, and a rural hinterland. It is not, however, a static system, but one in which a middle group of places with a substantial secondary sector component displays high variability with respect to most variables. The clear connection between tertiary activity and population size in such a dynamic context seems more consistent with Vance's (1970) mercantile model, which itself has ties to central place theory.

The preceding analysis clearly suggests a strong relationship between a high level of tertiary activity and population size between 1820 and 1840 and well into the period beyond that time. From a theoretical perspective, however, this relationship is inconclusive, as this analysis cannot suggest that the level of tertiary activity caused the higher population; it is just as likely that the high population encouraged the growth of the tertiary sector. Perhaps, however, this kind of feedback loop should be expected, as Pred's (1980) analysis suggested. But it does not explain why particular places in Connecticut were more successful than others in terms of population growth. Vance's mercantile model offers a possible explanation: each of the municipalities with the highest tertiary values in 1820 and forward was an early-established river or sea port that presumably established long-distance trade relationships. Still, if all that is required to sustain such growth is an initial advantage, then more complex economic theory can add little to our understanding of these historical and geographic trends.

The converse of this small set of advantaged municipalities is the large set of places that remained extremely rural, with minimal secondary and tertiary activity. Many of them clearly lacked the advantages of location and timing of the largest municipalities. Yet, as the brief discussion of the 1900 population figures suggests, a few of these places did eventually become large urban cities despite their slow start. The available data are not sufficient to suggest whether this was due to shifts in wholesaling activity, as Vance might have it, or increases in the manufacturing base, as promoters of industry then and now would have it. If the latter, then these rural places must have moved first into the third group identified in this study, which consists of places that did develop an early industrial base but did not have a substantial tertiary component. Even across this twenty-year study period, these places were extremely variable in population growth, overall diversity, and level of secondary activity. This instability is indicative of the sorting process identified by LeBlanc and predicted by Earle's model of the changing political economy. In this process, localized resources such as water power, and random factors such as the existence of energetic local entrepreneurs and the availability of capital combined with external factors such as market trends, inventions, and transportation together both created and destroyed industrial capacity across New England. Muller (1977) also suggested a sorting process in terms of city size that was affected by changing transportation technology across the United States over time. These ideas and this study's early nineteenth century data suggest that the volatility of the industrializing system was substantial and that the ultimate results of the process are difficult, if not impossible, to predict except in a few unusual cases.

These research results are also consistent with Earle's expectation of increasing population growth behind the frontier, which consolidated population in pre-existing places, and also the parallel trend of specialization, as the state and region turned more and more to secondary sector economic activity. At the municipal scale dealt with here, these trends caused a few places to become population outliers with an increasing tilt toward secondary or tertiary activity, while others remained at the opposite extreme of almost exclusively primary activity, and an intermediate group is captured by these statistics in the midst of unpredictable change. The First Democracy period extended to 1877, according to Earle, so this study only captures the beginning of the specialization/consolidation process. However, it may be that both economic historians and development planners need to accept the existence of random chance as well as external factors, including Earle's political economy model, in the development of modern economies and urban systems. It is true that such an understanding will complicate efforts to foster economic development in both post-industrial and industrializing societies. Still, acceptance of the risk of failure may lead to a clearer understanding of both historic and future economic development, and ultimately to a higher rate of success.

NOTE

1. The study used the dollar value of the properties as they were reported in the Grand List, primarily because the units reported in the various categories ranged from acres of land to cows to factories, and the faculty assessments had no reported units at all. Dollar values provided the only common unit of measurement among these categories. In addition, facilities such as factories and distilleries were often operated seasonally, which would be reflected in their assessed value but not, of course, in their numeration. The values in the different panel years have not been adjusted for inflation, as the study does not attempt direct comparison of dollar values between different years.

BIBLIOGRAPHY

Bidwell, Percy Wells. 1916. "Rural Economy in New England at the Beginning of the Nineteenth Century," *Transactions of the Connecticut Academy of Arts and Sciences* 20. (New Haven, CT: The Academy, 1999).

Connecticut, State of. 1835. *The Public Statute Laws of the State of Connecticut.* (Hartford, CT: John B. Eldredge).

De Souza, Anthony R. 1990. *A Geography of World Economy.* (Columbus, OH: Merrill Publishing Group).

Earle, Carville. 2003. *The American Way: A Geographical History of Crisis and Recovery.* (Lanham, MD: Rowman & Littlefield Publishers).

Jones, Frederick Robinson. 1896. "History of Taxation in Connecticut, 1636–1776," *Johns Hopkins University Studies in Historical and Political Science,* 14, no. 8. (Baltimore: The Johns Hopkins Press).

King, Leslie J. 1984. *Central Place Theory.* (Beverly Hills, CA: Sage Publications).

LeBlanc, Robert G. 1969. *Location of Manufacturing in New England in the Nineteenth Century.* Geography Publications at Dartmouth No. 7. (Hanover, NH: Center for the Study of Social Change, Dartmouth College).

Lindstrom, Diane. 1978. *Economic Development in the Philadelphia Region, 1810–1850.* (New York: Columbia University Press).

Map and Geographic Information Center. 1996b. "Historic Population Counts for the Towns of Connecticut from 1774–1990." *Storrs, CT: Map and Geographic Information Center,* <http://magic.lib.uconn.edu/cgi-bin/MAGIC_DBsearch3.pl?Geography=37800&Loc=0000>.

Muller, Edward K. 1976. "Selective Urban Growth in the Middle Ohio Valley, 1800–1860," *Geographical Review* 66, no. 2 (April 1976): 178–199.

———. 1977. "Regional Urbanization and the Selective Growth of Towns in North American Regions." *Journal of Historical Geography* 3, no. 1: 21–39.

Otterstrom, Samuel M. 2007. "Rapid Settlement Diffusion: The Development of the Semi-Peripheral Region North of San Francisco, California: 1850–1880." *Historical Geography* 35: 241–268.

Pred, Allan. 1966. *The Spatial Dynamics of U.S Urban-Industrial Growth, 1800–1914: Interpretive and Theoretical Essays.* (Cambridge, MA: MIT Press).

———. 1980 *Urban Growth and City-Systems in the United States, 1840–1860.* Harvard Studies in Urban History. (Cambridge, MA: Harvard University Press).

Schmalensee, Richard. 1977. "Using the H-Index of Concentration with Published Data," *The Review of Economics and Statistics* 59, no. 2: 186–193.

Turner, G. M., and M. W. Jacobus. 1989 *Connecticut Railroads: An Illustrated History.* (Hartford, CT: Connecticut Historical Society).

Van Dusen, Albert E. 1961. *Connecticut.* (NY: Random House).

Vance, James E., Jr. 1970. *The Merchant's World: The Geography of Wholesaling.* (Englewood Cliffs, NJ: Prentice-Hall, Inc).

Chapter Five

The Structural Transformation of the Antebellum Red River Valley Settlement Systems in Louisiana

Keumsoo Hong

In his masterpiece, *The Information Age* (1996), Manuel Castells captures one of the most significant historical changes in our time, the rise of the network society. He claims that a technological revolution centered on information is reshaping the material basis of societies. Indeed, a network-based social structure has become a powerful instrument for the suppression of space and the annihilation of time. The astonishing development of an information society has been, by all means, revolutionary. A similar sea change occurred with far-reaching consequences more than a century ago on the American landscape. Increased literacy levels, the development of advanced printing technology, and widespread circulation of printed materials helped feed an information-consuming American public and fostered a nineteenth-century communication revolution. Further, as Gouldner (1982) identifies a profound interconnection between the communication revolution and the proliferation of ideologies, these revolutionary developments in information technology brought about a fundamental change in the American way of life and the structure of *mentalité*.

In most traditional societies, as social historians have elaborated, news was distributed through a variety of information nodes such as markets, churches, schools, taverns, alehouses, coffeehouses, salons and courthouses.[1] The information or *mis*information was transmitted by context-laden face-to-face conversations. In the course of time, the advent of print communication accelerated the rhythm of everyday life, transforming traditional place-bound societies into time- and information-bound ones. The rearrangement of public places as an arena for consuming mass-produced printed materials, the diversification of knowledge-dissemination mediums, and the expansion of information fields all aided to enlarge the public sphere and to expedite the civilizing process (Thrift 1985: 394; Gregory 1987: 130–31).

In politics, the increased density and frequency of information exchange facilitated the formation of a collective identity and a new sense of nationhood. The Americanization that occurred in the area of the Louisiana Purchase in 1803 offers a case in point. The spread of English throughout the former Francophone region alone constituted one of the most potent assertions of centralized power. In this fashion, "the effective penetration of the tentacles of government," to quote Brayshay and his colleagues (1998: 268), "was critically dependent upon access to rapid and reliable communications."

Incorporating U.S. post offices as a main subject matter, this study seeks to address what Hillis (1998) laments as the "invisibility of communications in geography." While the theoretical, conceptual and methodological improvements achieved by Walter Christaller have helped to explain the spatial principles regulating the functions, sizes, numbers, hierarchies, and spacing of settlements, and while Pred's (1971; 1973; 1980) seminal inquiries into pre-electronic communication have disclosed the impact of specialized economic information on the growth of U.S. city systems, little has been done to deal with institutional aspects in tracing the evolutionary path of a regional settlement system. Historical geography has incorporated two important leitmotifs regarding the issues of settlement: *evolution* and *system*. The evolutionary, or transformative, theme is instrumental in looking at the pattern and process relationship as it places the time factor in a central position. The systemic approach, on the other hand, has been effective in drawing a broader picture. It views the whole as more than the sum of its parts.

In this essay I attempt to present a constructive way of interpreting the periodic transformation of settlement systems in the Red River Valley of Louisiana using post offices as proxy. Being a nexus of information networks, a post office proves to be a useful tool in linking the two methodological perspectives of evolution and system. Some researchers pay attention to changing postal rates from a stepped structure to a flat one in order to buttress their case for a reconfiguration of regional structures driven by time-space convergence. Others stress the critical role of postal services in connection with the growth of urban central places. This paper sets out to add one more scheme to the literature, post office as an indicator of the evolution of settlement systems. Specifically I am concerned with the transformation of the antebellum urban and rural postal settlements in the Red River Valley of northwest Louisiana. I will pursue this based on the solid intellectual legacies of Skinner's regional systems and Earle's dialectical progression of historical geographies (Skinner 1986; 1988; Earle 2003).

Skinnerian regional systems offer a fertile ground for the test of theories of changing geographical patterns, historical processes and social conditions. His model pays special attention to the basic building block of a river basin, as it constitutes an integral unit of regionalization and plays a mundane function as skeleton of transportation networks. Skinner's regional systems evolve within internally differentiated and externally interdependent river basins. Significantly, the model stresses the four-fold structures of inner core, outer core, inner periphery, and outer periphery in a river valley. Here the core refers to lowland riverine areas featuring efficient transportation, intensive agriculture, high productivity, fertile land, higher wages, elevated prices of land and goods, easy accessibility to credit, dense population, developed infrastructure, complex occupation structure, and early urbanization, industrialization, commercialization and politicization. The periphery, on the other hand, indicates highland backcountry based on a semi-autarkic economy (Skinner 1986; 1988). In Skinner's thesis, regions and subregions differ from one another not only in resource endowments, but also in the timing and nature of their respective economic and sociopolitical development processes. Regional divergence occurs as these places respond to exogenous shocks, with some areas exhibiting a better capacity to absorb those unforeseen influences. Skinner provides a fitting illustration when he contrasts peripheral subregions that are subject to short-term shocks of epidemics, drought, flooding, harvest failure and rebellion with core regions that are better positioned to deal with minor shocks yet still vulnerable to sustained major ones caused by technological innovation, productivity change, economic depression, and demographic shifts (Skinner 1977: 18; 1985: 287).

In furthering Skinner's theorem and in decoding the causality of the structural change of regional geographies, Earle's perspectives are particularly helpful. In a nutshell, Earle's picture of American past and geographical changes collides with Meinig's grand rhetorical model of "continuous" (re)shaping which is specified in *The Shaping of America* series. Meinig's (1986: xv) thesis assumes that the United States has made gigantic strides with a continually changing geographic character, structure and system. As far as Earle is concerned, however, this is an "exceptionally refined example of a high Tory interpretation of the American geographical past." By this critique he disputes a historical geography that advances with "a measured and dignified sense of order and decorum," insisting instead that capitalist ideology leaves room for marked "discontinuity" (Earle 1999: 12). Earle thinks the spasmodic fluctuation of capitalist parameters denotes irregular or semi-regular geographical changes. Therefore, what matters most to him in the explication of geographical changes in the extremely volatile capitalist regime are *timing*, *rate* and *driving forces* (Earle 1978). He carries his dialectic logic to articulate surveys of geohistorical changes in All Hallow's Parish, American South and the United States. What makes Earle's (1975; 1992; 2003) inquiries special is the way in which the boom and bust cycles of economies and alternating political ideologies are intertwined with geographical changes. Based on this reasoning, he artfully reconstructs the rhythmic transformation of local, regional, sectional and national geographies of the United States.

Led to believe that Louisiana's geographical past has been influenced by periodically alternating regimes of economy and politics, I will capture in the remaining pages the trajectory of the dialectical transformation of settlement systems of the Red River Valley which, I think, is reflected partly by the changing spatial distribution and hierarchical organization of postal service centers. This chapter begins by discussing the history of U.S. postal service. This sets the stage for the detailed elaboration of the agenda of the regional geography associated with the growth of post offices in the Red River Valley. The geohistorical synopsis of the evolution of the antebellum postal settlement systems in the region is dealt with next, for which a variety of primary and secondary literature and statistics are employed and analyzed with particular reference to timing and rate of these changes. Following the review, interpretation and analysis, I conclude with retrospection about the significance of Earle's dialectic model of geohistorical social science.

THE ANTEBELLUM U.S. POSTAL SERVICE: A BRIEF SKETCH

During the colonial period, letters and news were transmitted haphazardly. Colonists entrusted mails and official messages to public officers, travelers, merchants, captains of private vessels, and other informal messengers. As were in the Virginia "tobacco posts" where each plantation owner carried out the duty of passing news on to the next plantation, official messages were circulated by neighborly arrangement (Blount 1976: 370–71). By the eve of the American Revolution, the British had used postal services as revenue-generating monopoly industries, their functions ranging from the transmission of letters and printed materials to the transportation of travelers and baggage.

In the early nation-building stages, information services were vital for the U.S. federal government to manage frontier affairs, consolidate central power and tie the country together. In other words, the development of postal system was inextricably linked to the progress of the nation (Bowen 1851: 5). Because of the need for a powerful institution to carry out such a critical national project, the federal government had, since 1782, laid postal service under its own control and management. Then in 1789, the U.S. Constitution ceded power to Congress to establish post offices and postal roads wherever it deemed conducive to the general interest and the development of the nation (*De Bow's Review* 5 [1848]: 156).

An act of 1792 gave a Postmaster-General the right to appoint regional postmasters. Steamboat alleys were declared postal routes by 1813, and the same occurred for railroads twenty-five years later. Prior to the introduction of these faster modes of transportation, mails were transported by stages and horses on contract (*Table of Post Offices* 1817: 87). An 1845 Law extended this contract system to be applicable not only to stagecoaches but also to steamboats and railroads. To ensure celerity, certainty, and security, fines were imposed upon those who delayed mail delivery and damaged the mail. The postage stamp made its first appearance with the act of March 1847 (*Statistical Abstract* 1930: 351).

Although it was not always profitable, U.S. postal service achieved remarkable progress during the period between 1790 and 1860. The number of post offices per 10,000 persons increased constantly, from 0.19 in 1790 to 9.06 in 1860 (see table 5.1). Overland postal roads increased by over 238,000 miles during the same period, growing from 1,875 miles to 240,594 miles. This amounted to an annual increase of some 3,410 miles. Railroads and steamboat lines added mileage, speeded up mail delivery, and enhanced regularity.

The development of U.S. postal services resulted in the adjustment of postage rates. The Act of 1792 set the rate at 6 cents for a single-page letter traveling up to 30 miles. Thereafter, this base rate increased as follows: from 30 to 60 miles, 8 cents; from 60 to 100 miles, 10 cents; from 100 to 150 miles, 12 cents; from 150 to 200 miles, 15 cents; from 200 to 250 miles, 17 cents; from 250 to 350 miles, 20 cents; from 350 to 450 miles, 22 cents; and more than 450 miles, 25 cents (Gullinan 1968: 249). By 1845 the American transportation revolution helped to dramatically compress this postage structure from nine classes to just two. Now, customer could send a single letter up to 300 miles for only 5 cents; more than 300 miles, 10 cents. Moreover, the costs for a 300-mile letter fell by 75 percent from 20 cents to 5 cents. An act of 1851 eased the burden of distance even further by imposing a charge of only 3 cents for the circulation of a single letter within the bound of 3,000 miles.

Embedded in all histories and geographies, communication systems are destined to control time and space in due course. Further, communication intrinsically carries geopolitical ramifications, as it has helped political powers to control territory, to project military power, to defend citizens, and to facilitate expansion of sphere of influence. This explains the reason why territorial states tried first and foremost to put communication systems under control in their pursuit of hegemony (Hugill 1999: 1–23). As has been seen, the same was true of the United States. Although it was not until the institution of the user-friendly public telegraph line and the opening of transatlantic telephone cable that the United States came to realize a hegemonic dominance

Table 5.1. Progress of the U.S. Post Offices, 1790–1860

Year	#, P.O.	*P.O./10,000 Persons*	*Post Road (Miles)*	*Railroad (Miles)*	*Steamboat (Miles)*	*Postage (Revenue)*	*Transport Cost*	*Other Expenditures*[a]	*Net Revenue*
1790	75	0.19	1,875			$ 37,934	$ 22,081	$ 10,058	$ 5,795
1795	453		13,207			160,629	75,359	42,533	42,737
1800	903	1.70	20,817			280,804	128,644	85,348	66,812
1805	1,558		31,076			421,373	239,635	137,730	44,008
1810	2,300	3.18	36,406			551,684	327,966	168,003	55,715
1815	3,000		43,966			1,043,065	487,779	260,342	294,944
1820	4,500	4.67	73,492			1,111,927	782,425	378,501	–48,999
1825	5,677		94,052			1,306,525	785,646	443,397	77,482
1830	8,450	6.57	115,176			1,919,300	1,272,156	686,953	–39,809
1835	10,770		112,774	1,098		3,152,376	1,553,222	1,031,886	567,268
1840	13,458	7.88	155,739	2,818		4,543,522	3,213,043	1,505,193	–174,714
1845	14,183		143,940	4,633		4,289,842	2,898,630	1,422,102	–30,890
1850	18,417	7.94	178,672	9,021	10,826	5,499,985	2,965,786	2,247,167	287,032
1855	24,410		227,908	18,333		6,642,136	5,345,238	4,623,104	–3,326,206
1860	28,498	9.06	240,594	27,129	14,976	8,518,067	8,808,710	10,361,900	–10,652,543

Note: [a] Other expenditures include compensation to postmasters and incidental expenses. Mileage of railroads and steamboat lines refer to that used as postal routes.

in telecommunications, during the antebellum period the U.S. postal service was indispensable for the service of enlightened information consumers and for the consolidation of the sectional system. When it comes to the South, post offices played a critical role in mediating political messages for justifying its "peculiar institution" among landed plantation capitalists.

This peculiar situation included geographies of exclusion that were deeply rooted in the Red River Valley societies, while the social distribution of information was more or less egalitarian for the elite and free population in the Red River Valley. Provided that any stock of information and knowledge is differentially distributed according to gender, age, and race of social groups as well as geography (Thrift 1985: 369), a large number of servile people in the region must have been excluded by the antebellum Southern culture that prohibited slaves from participating in long-distance communication. Even those who had learned to write were legally barred from owning pens, ink and paper and were required to have a pass in order to leave the plantation. Furthermore, postmasters simply refused to mail letters for slaves without written instructions from their masters (Northup 1968: 175). Although some slaves challenged these stringent controls and participated in the making and consumption of news that played a significant role in conveying local, national and international information as well as private messages to neighboring communities, it took almost one more century for the subaltern to draw unswerving constitutional support for the civil right of communication in the United States.

POST OFFICES IN THE ANTEBELLUM RED RIVER VALLEY

The Red River Valley as a region has distinctive historical and geographical features. Founded as a French colonial district in 1714, the river basin initially constituted a geopolitical marchland between two competing European powers—France and Spain. Almost half a century later in 1763 the French ceded sovereignty over the region to the Spanish colonial government. Even after the United States' Louisiana Purchase in 1803, this frontier region remained strategically important in its new role as a gateway to Spain's Texas territory.

The Red River Valley relied on staple crops and a slave labor system for its economic viability as other parts of the antebellum Lower South did. With its fertile soils and relatively benign climate, the region became part of the Cotton Belt by the 1830s and, following successful experimentation with sugarcane in the mid-1840s, defined the northern limit of sugar country. The valley's development was hindered by the so-called Great Raft, the huge logjams that blocked navigation on the Red River and governed the pace, rate and direction of the settlement process.[2] With the clearance of the logjams downriver from Shreveport in 1836, the valley opened a new chapter in its history. The removal of the raft liberated large acres of fertile land, attracted many English-speaking immigrants to this place, and set the stage for the Americanization of this Francophone enclave. The valley, established as the Natchitoches District under the French, grew to comprise eleven parishes on the eve of the American Civil War (figure 5.1).

The origin of post offices in the Red River Valley can be traced back to St. Jean Baptiste des Natchitoches which was established in 1717 as a French colonial fort.[3] Although not a post office by designation, the garrison town nonetheless performed *de facto* functions of the name.[4] It was only after the 1803 Louisiana Purchase that the Red River post offices became institutionalized

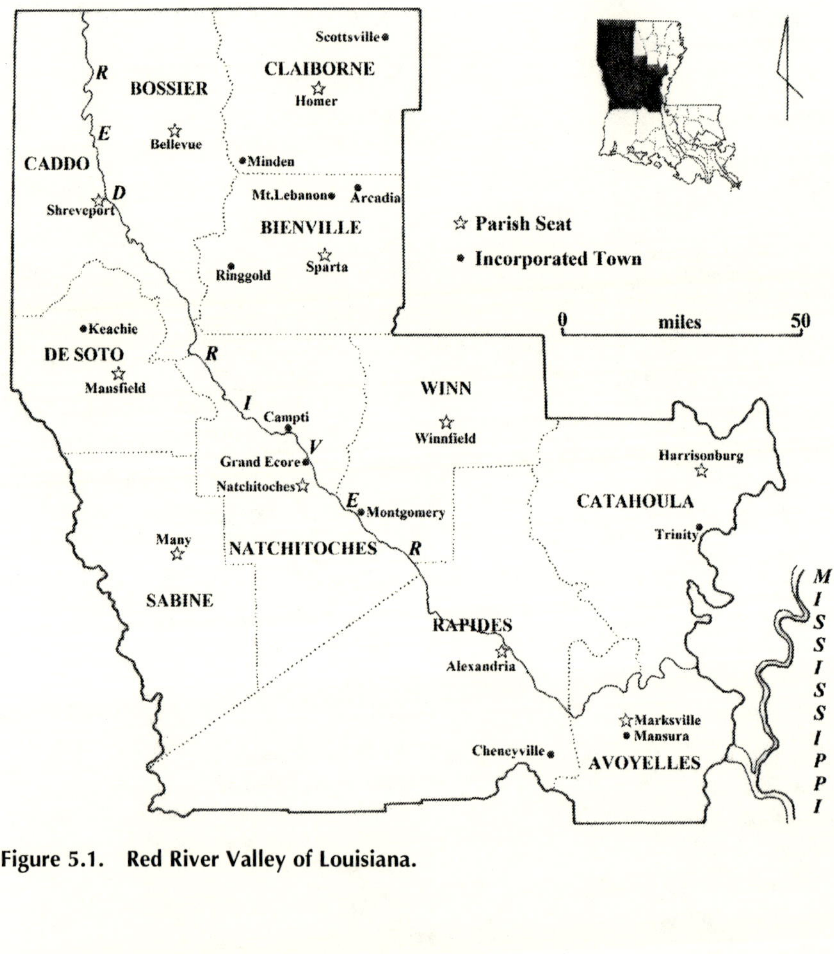

Figure 5.1. Red River Valley of Louisiana.

agents of the information services. At the outset, special agents stationed at New Orleans took care of the arrangement of mail delivery for the newly purchased territory. Mail sorted there moved northwest by coach. In April 1841, steamboats began transporting mail as often as river conditions allowed.[5]

The steamboat mail packets delivered private letters, commercial correspondence, and political news at an accelerated speed. It was the steamer *Meteor* for example that brought Shreveport news of the 1848 revolution in France and the consequent decline in cotton price amid the turmoil.[6] Around this time, national news was transmitted from Washington through Richmond and Mobile to New Orleans on 1,726 miles of telegraphic line (*DeBow's Review* 8 [1850]: 289). The news thus collected was distributed throughout the region via steamers and coaches, and the decreasing time gap in information exchange brought fundamental changes in the behavior and attitude of the Red River people. The news of moderate demand in the Liverpool cotton market, for example, led planters and merchants to hold the cotton stocks for the future, instead of selling them at low prices as they usually did before.[7]

In order to enhance the efficiency of the mail delivery process, a regional distributing office was established at Natchitoches in the mid-1840s. The distribution center was relocated to Grand Ecore in 1851, and then finally to Alexandria in 1855. These regional communication centers handled mail for both eastern Texas and the Red River Valley (Dorr 1938: 1160). Postmasters in these distributing centers sorted letters, newspapers, and magazines by route, and entrusted the delivery of the mail to local contractors (Bowen 1851: 10–11).[8] Mail contractors, in addition to delivering letters and newspapers, carried passengers and freight between places designated by Congress for a transportation fee based on road conditions and the weight and volume of the freight. The mail contract was a franchise that could be sold or bought out.

Generally speaking, post offices in the Red River Valley opened most days from 9 a.m. to 1 p.m. and from 2 to 5 p.m. On Sundays, the hours of operation lasted from 9 to 10 a.m. and from 2 to 3 p.m.[9] Some in the backcountry offered services only thrice weekly, while those located in towns did so for 6 or 7 days a week. The latter handled mail arriving at and departing from the office every two, three or four days for the various directions. For instance, the mailing schedule for the Mt. Lebanon office in Bienville Parish was set in the following manner:

> *Southern*, via Alexandria (arrives Tuesday and Saturday at 6 p.m.; departs Monday and Thursday at 6 a.m.), *Northern*, via Homer (arrives Wednesday and Sunday 6 p.m.; departs Wednesday and Sunday at 6 a.m.), *Western*, via Shreveport and Minden (arrives Wednesday, Friday and Saturday at 1 a.m.; departs Tuesday, Thursday and Saturday at 11 p.m.), *Eastern*, via Monroe (arrives

Tuesday, Thursday and Saturday at 11 p.m.; departs Wednesday, Friday and Sunday at 1 a.m.). H. Gibbs, P.M. August 9, 1855 (*Louisiana Baptist*, Mount Lebanon, February 21, 1856).

To the extent that a communication system connects important centers of social, economic and administrative activities (Falk & Abler 1985: 22), so the rapid expansion of post offices in this valley represented the multiplication of central places over space and time. Post offices in the context of the Red River Valley functioned as what Skinner (1977: 216) calls the "command posts" that served to articulate and integrate human activity. Just as the establishment of towns preceded the breaking of soil in the West, as Wade (1959) declares, post offices represented the settlement system spearheads of northwest Louisiana. In that sense, the Red River Valley in its nascent stage was what I would call a postal frontier parallel in geographical significance to Wade's urban frontier. Although the building of some prominent post offices was just a concomitant part of early urban development, many others were established ahead of the towns themselves.

The general trend in the expansion of Red River Valley postal service between 1805 and 1861 was of steady growth (see table 5.2). In that period, the number of post offices in the region multiplied from 3 to 128. The increase came as a direct response to the growth of population, the spread of settlement along the frontier, the expansion of cotton and sugar production, the annexation of Texas, and the spoils system of political patronage associated with Jacksonian democracy. Red River Valley post offices numbered more than 30 in 1841, 40 in 1843, 70 in 1851, and 100 in 1857. Besides this numerical increase, quality of postal services as measured by the number of post offices per 10,000 people also showed steady improvement, from 0.40 in 1811 to 0.89 in 1861.

The fortunes of the Red River Valley post offices displayed either instantaneous or lagged association with the movement of cotton prices that modulated the pace of the settlement process in this region. Increasing demand for the staple crop and subsequent hikes in unit prices awakened agrarian capitalists' natural inclinations to invest in new cotton fields along with supporting rural community and post office building while business was good. This relationship between cotton price and post office numbers is shown in figure 5.2. Average cotton prices reached their highest point in the mid-1810s and then fell from their peak after Napoleon's defeat in 1815 through to the late 1820s. Another period of elevated prices in the 1830s was followed by a decline in the 1840s, before cotton recovered somewhat in the 1850s.

The most dramatic developments in the region's staple economy, settlements, and post offices occurred in the 1830s. In contrast, during the first two decades of the 1800s settlers in the Red River Valley were engrossed in

Table 5.2. Post Offices in the Antebellum Red River Valley of Louisiana

Year	*Natch 1805*[a]	*Rapid 1805*	*Avoy 1807*	*Catah 1808*	*Claib 1828*	*Cadd 1838*	*DeSo 1843*	*Sabin 1843*	*Boss 1843*	*Bien 1848*	*Winn 1852*	*RRV*	*PO/ 10000*[b]
1805	1	1		1								3	
1808	1	1		1								3	
1811	1	1		1								3	0.40
1816	1	1	1	1								4	
1817	2	2	1	1								6	
1819	2	1	1	1								5	
1821	2	4	1	1								8	0.44
1822	2	4	1	1								8	
1823	3	4	1									8	
1825	2	4	1	1								8	
1827	2	3	1	1	1							8	
1828	3	3	1	1	1							9	
1829	5	3	1	1	1							11	
1831	6	3	1	1	2							13	0.56
1833	5	3	1	2	2							13	
1835	5	3	1	2	2							13	
1836	4	2	1	2	2							11	
1837	5	4	4	3	2							18	
1839	5	4	6	1	4							20	

(*continued*)

Table 5.2. *(continued)*

Year	*Natch 1805*[a]	*Rapid 1805*	*Avoy 1807*	*Catah 1808*	*Claib 1828*	*Cadd 1838*	*DeSo 1843*	*Sabin 1843*	*Boss 1843*	*Bien 1848*	*Winn 1852*	*RRV*	*PO/ 10000*[b]
1841	8	5	6	3	7	3						32	0.62
1842	8	5	7	2	9	4						35	
1843	9	6	6	4	9	5	1	1				41	
1845	8	4	7	6	8	5	3	2				43	
1846	6	4	7	4	7	5	4	2	1			40	
1847	6	6	7	4	8	5	4	3	4			47	
1849	6	7	10	7	6	5	5	4	3	5		58	
1851	9	9	7	7	10	5	7	5	7	8		74	0.83
1853	6	8	9	6	12	4	10	7	9	8	3	82	
1854	4	8	8	10	14	4	9	6	9	9	6	87	
1855	7	9	7	10	13	5	9	7	7	10	7	91	
1857	6	11	7	9	15	8	10	7	10	10	9	102	
1859	7	12	7	11	19	10	10	10	12	12	10	120	
1861	8	13	7	13	19	11	12	12	10	12	11	128	0.89
±[c]	7	12	6	12	18	8	11	11	9	7	8	125	0.49

Notes: RRV(Red River Valley); [a]year of the establishment of a Parish, [b]post offices per 10,000 persons, [c]net increase of post offices. For the calculation of the number of post offices per 10,000 persons, population data are drawn from decennial censuses which enumerate the number of people as of June 1 in each decennial year.

Sources: List of Post Offices in the United States (1805, 1808, 1855, 1857, 1859); *Table of Post Offices in the United States* (1811, 1817, 1819, 1825, 1836, 1837, 1842, 1846, 1851); *Register of Officers and Agents, in the Service of the United States* (1816, 1821, 1822, 1823, 1827, 1828, 1829, 1831, 1833, 1835, 1839, 1841, 1843, 1845, 1847, 1849, 1861); *Rode's U.S. Post Office Directory and Postal Guide* (1853); *The U.S. Post Office Directory and Postal Guide* (1854).

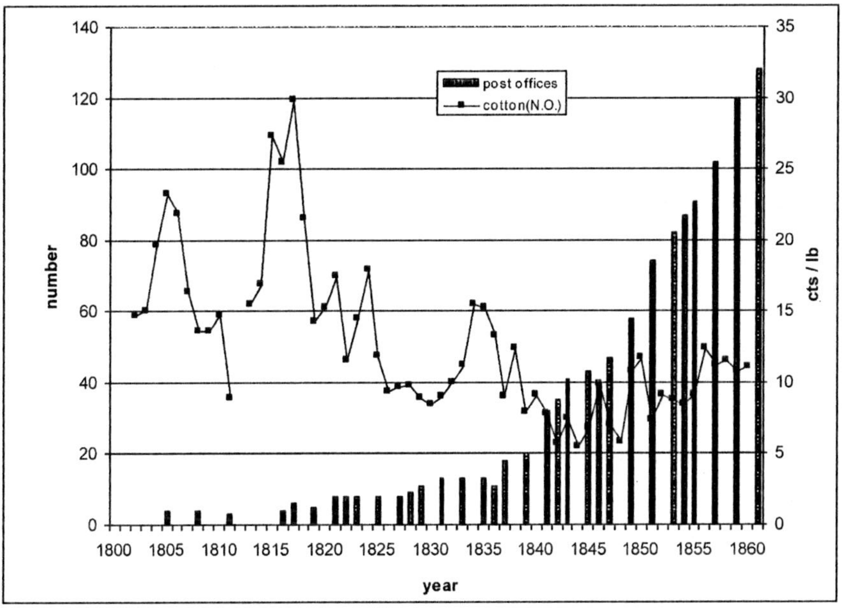

Figure 5.2. Weighted Yearly Average Prices of Short-Staple Cotton at New Orleans and the Growth of Red River Valley Post Offices.

experimenting with cotton in response to very high prices. But settlers were sparse and the expansion of post offices proceeded slowly. At the end of the 1820s only eleven post offices were in operation. In the 1830s the Red River Valley underwent a significant transformation from a primitive diversified regional economy to a large-scale specialized cotton production region. The booming decade pushed market production steadily farther into northwest Louisiana and planters' reckless rushes for profit maximization ushered in settlement expansion. Cheap and plentiful land was available in the Red River Valley, which kept the landed local elite from managing their land as a permanent investment. This became a chief reason for land abuse. Meanwhile, the rural hinterlands began to specialize, benefiting from the comparative locational advantage of producing the staple for the mills in the emerging megalopolis on the Atlantic seaboard and in the European core because of the region's good accessibility.

In the second place, the removal of logjams on the river opened a vast amount of land for the cultivation of crops and new stretches of the river for navigation (Humphreys 1984: 73). Additionally, steady urbanization including the establishment of the Town of Shreve's Company (later renamed Shreveport) created booming labor markets for immigrants as well as natives.[10] As a result, population in the Red River Valley exploded in the 1830s by an unprecedented 120 percent from 23,251 to 51,314, and the number of post offices increased by 146 percent from 13 in 1831 to 32 in 1841.[11]

Toward the end of the boom of the 1830s, however, the Red River Valley was forced to confront the inevitable downturn ahead. As the demand and price of raw cotton fell in the northwest European core, the impacts rippled through daily life in the cotton fields and along the levees of the Red River. To make matters worse, regional cotton production decreased because of soil erosion from exploitative cultivation and natural disasters such as drought, flooding, killing frost, and worms that ate their way through a large part of the crop (Champomier 1844–1861; Mills 1977: 221–22; Hong 2004). In the depressed cotton economy of the 1840s, planters, farmers, field laborers, slaves, and merchants suffered altogether. Fortunately, the successful experiment with sugarcane in Avoyelles and Rapides parishes in the mid-1840s was a great relief to the Red River people, as it helped to cushion the economic shock.

Thanks to the introduction of the alternative cash crop of sugar, the initiation of a new agrarian regime of diversification, sustained population growth and Jacksonian patronage the number of Red River Valley post offices more than doubled from 32 in 1841 to 74 in 1851. As a matter of fact, this decade saw the most significant improvement in terms of the number of post offices per 10,000 people of any decade (see table 5.3).

The slower pace of expansion during the economic recovery of the 1850s suggests that the spatial organization of the information fields in the Red River Valley had entered a consolidation phase. In this decade, growth rates in population (62.7 percent) and post offices (73 percent) were the lowest of the late antebellum period. The slowing trend becomes more prominent when it comes to the number of post offices per 10,000 inhabitants. That figure only registered a modest increase of 7.2 percent during that decade.

A close observation of the lists of post offices highlights several geographical patterns. First, the earliest post offices in each parish tended to be located

Table 5.3. Statistical Comparison of the Progress of Population and Post Offices

Statistics	*1811*	*1821*	*1831*	*1841*	*1851*	*1861*
Population[a]	7,443	18,363	23,251	51,314	88,641	144,209
Increase Rate		146.7%	26.6%	120.7%	72.7%	62.7%
No. of P.O.	3	8	13	32	74	128
Increase Rate		166%	62.5%	146.2%	131.3%	73.0%
P.O. / 10000	4.0	4.4	5.6	6.2	8.3	8.9
Increase Rate		10%	27.3%	10.7%	33.9%	7.2%

Note: [a]Population data are drawn from federal censuses which registered the mid-year number of people in 1810, 1820, 1830, 1840, 1850, and 1860.

at parish seats. This political and legal centrality virtually guaranteed the continuity and growth of postal towns such as Marksville, Harrisonburg, Alexandria, Natchitoches, Many, Mansfield, Shreveport, Bellevue, and Winnfield. Other post offices, however, exhibited a high degree of instability. Numerous post offices on the federal lists were established, terminated, reinstalled, relocated, and renamed. To a large extent, the viability of local post offices was a function of the fortune of the communities that they served.

Transshipment points, inland crossroads, and other stopping places along the overland roads and waterways provided ideal locations for post offices. Names of post offices provide clues to the location: Pleasant Hill, Simm's Port, Logansport, Burr's Ferry, Kirk's Ferry, Parham's Landing, Bossier Point, Harf's Bluff, Connell's Cross Roads, and Long Street, to name a few. Country stores also provided postal services as evidenced by such post office names as Davis' Store, Cook's Store, Red Store, and Sentell's Store. The shopkeeper-*cum*-postmasters had locked mailboxes, containing pigeonholes which carried the names of patrons. These stores, besides managing the exchange of local products and dry goods, served as information and communication centers. Red Store of Rapides Parish is a good example. This store located at a crossroad housed a tavern and a post office. It functioned as a social center where news was dispensed, goods bought and sold, money loaned and repaid, and horses refreshed (Barber 1967: 91, 94).

Postal routes proved vital for shaping the information system as much as post offices (figure 5.3). They consisted of public and special roads, steamboat lines, railroads, and navigable canals (Bowen 1851: 21). Typically, high-order centers of political, administrative, and economic functions were central nodes within this pre-electronic information network. Prior to the diffusion of the magnetic telegraph, communication was a subset of transportation; hence a place's connectivity and accessibility within a transportation network were fundamental determinants of the place's centrality in the information web. Post offices at the administrative, legal and commercial centers usually served as nodes of incoming and outgoing transportation lines (table 5.4). The Red River was, without doubt, an artery of the region's postal routes. Post offices in towns along the Red River drew many overland branch lines, too. In 1850, Alexandria had seven route links entering into the city; Shreveport had five and Natchitoches-Grand Ecore seven. Away from the river, Harrisonburg had five links, and the other inland parish seats of Homer, Mansfield, Many and Bellevue had four connecting routes, respectively.

Regional differences in those route links are significant, for they determined the size and importance of the postal service centers. Weaving a net of post offices, these communication routes brought in generous exchanges

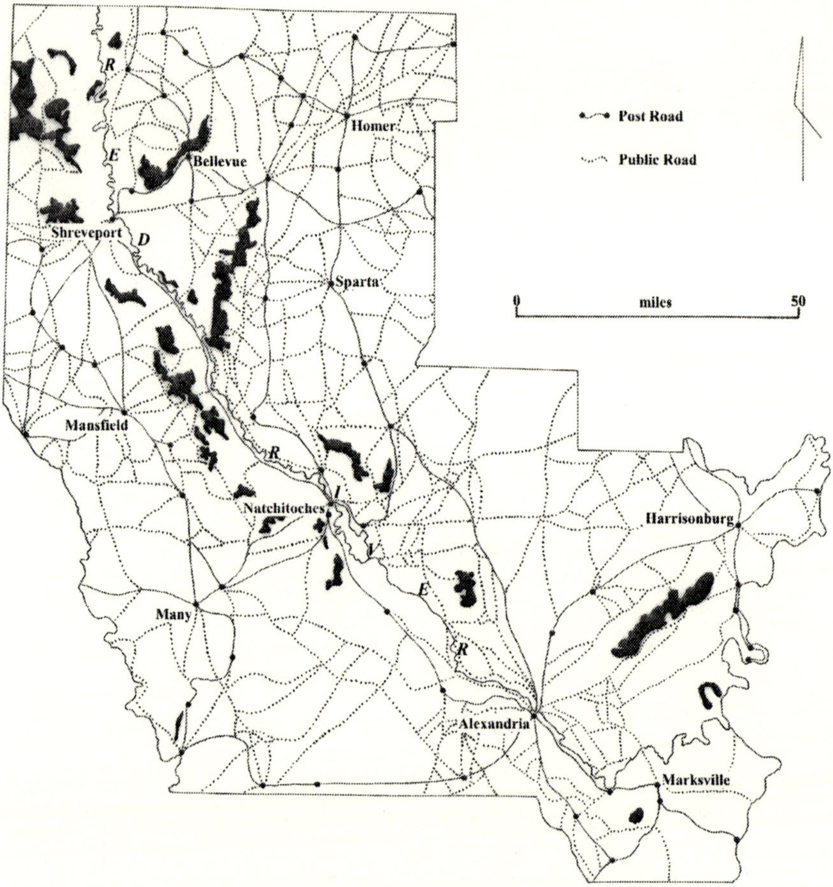

Figure 5.3. Post Roads of the Red River Valley, 1850

of information. Cheaper, quicker and more frequent communication lines meant a strengthening of the importance of the service centers—what Christaller (1966: 18) terms centrality, which means the relative importance of a place with regard to the region surrounding it or the degree to which the town exercises central functions. As a rule, a good communication route system permits low postal fares and displays a high potential for information exchange. Larger centers of postal services such as Alexandria, Natchitoches, and Shreveport, therefore, tended to have more routes than other minor ones, serving as pivots of hierarchical ordering and structuring regional information field.

Table 5.4. Qualitative Features of the Red River Valley Post Offices, 1851

Post Office	*Parish*	*#, p- road*[a]	*t-p.o.*[b]	*c.h.,p.o.*[c]	*m-service/week*	*x-state p.o.*[d]	*Pop. Wm*[e]	*Rank*[f]
Natchitoches	Natch	3	x	x	2	x	1,261	1
Alexandria	Rapid	3	x	x	9	x	672	2
Shreveport	Cadd	7	x	x	8	x	1,728	3
Minden	Claib	7	x	x	7	x	533	4
Mansfield	DeSo	8	x	x	9	x		5
Greenwood	Cadd	5	x		5	x		6
Cheneyville	Rapid	1						7
Harrisonburg	Catah	6	x	x	10	x	326	8
Trinity	Catah	2	x		1		500	9
Mt. Lebanon	Claib	2	x		1		360	10
Holmesville	Avoy	2	x		1			11
Cloutiersville	Natch	1						12
Many	Sabin	4	x	x	2			13
Cotile	Rapid	1						14
Pineville	Boss	1						15
Blossom Hill	Cadd	1						16

(*continued*)

Table 5.4. *(continued)*

Post Office	*Parish*	*#, p- road*[a]	*t-p.o.*[b]	*c.h.,p.o.*[c]	*m-service/week*	*x-state p.o.*[d]	*Pop. Wm*[e]	*Rank*[f]
Athens	Claib	3	x	x	2	x		17
Pleasant Hill	DeSo	1						18
Keachie	DeSo	2	x		1			19
Fort Jesup	Sabin	2	x		3			20
Campti	Natch	1						21
Huddleston	Rapid	1						22
Bellevue	Boss	3	x	x	2			23
Quay	Claib	2	x		1			24
Marksville	Avoy	2	x	x	1			25
Logansport	DeSo	2	x		1			26
Bayou Rouge	Avoy	1						27
Simm's Port	Avoy	1						28
Grand Cane	DeSo	1						29
Allen's Sett.	Claib	1						30

Notes: [a]number of postal roads passing through the office, [b]terminal post office which located at the start or end of a postal road, [c]post office at the parish seat, [d]cross-state post office which linked Louisiana to other adjacent states, i.e., Mississippi, Texas or Arkansas, [e] the White male population, [f] ranked by the amount of postmasters' annual commissions in the year 1849 (for actual values, see Table 5.4).

Sources: Eli Bowen, *The United States Post-Office Guide* (New York: D. Appleton & Co., 1851; reprint, New York: Arno Press, 1976); *Register of Officers and Agents* (1849).

POST OFFICES AS AN INDICATOR OF THE EVOLUTION OF SETTLEMENT SYSTEMS: EVIDENCE AND INTERPRETATION

A system is defined as an accumulation of interdependent units. The relationships among the interconnected subsystems are simultaneously spatio-temporal and causal. In this sense, systems analysis offers an integrated framework for the examination of geographical change driven by certain causal factors (Miller 1965a: 202; Langton 1972: 170). It is generally recognized that systems analysis places emphasis on continual energy inputs and hierarchical differentiation of subsystems, and that a self-organizing open system increases order by decreasing entropy (Chorley 1964: 50; Curry 1964: 145). In this study, the quantity of inbound and outbound information exchanged through the medium of post offices embodies energy input, and the hierarchical rank-size distribution of postal service centers is the key representation of the spatial order that developed in the region. Both sets of data are vital to understanding the evolutionary path of the Red River Valley settlement system.

In applying a systemic approach to the study of settlement, the first logical step is to define mutually interacting, functionally related variables, which should be in measurable or definable states (Hagen 1961: 145). This study uses postmasters' commissions as an indicator of the volume of information flows to trace the transformation of postal settlement systems.[12] Postmasters were compensated by commissions on the postage collected (*Register of Officers and Agents* 1816: 70). In 1850, for instance, they were entitled to the following rates: 40 percent on the first $100, 33.3 percent on the next $300, 30 percent on the next $2000, and 12.5 percent on the postage exceeding $2400 (table 5.5). For the postage of newspapers and magazines, a 50-percent commission was allowed (Bowen 1851: 39). The net compensation after deducting the expenses, however, could in no case exceed $2000 per annum, or $500 per quarter (*Register of Officers and Agents* 1822: 120).

Data on commissions are available for eleven separate years. After grouping the post offices by parish, I summed the amount of commissions and

Table 5.5. Rate of Commission on Letter Postage in Selected Years

Year	*Less than $100*	*$100–$400*	*$400–$2400*	*Over $2400*
1850	40%	33.3%	30%	12.5%
1854	50%	40%	35%	15%
1854 (July)	60%	50%	40%	15%
1857	60%	50%	40%	15%

Sources: Eli Bowen, *The United States Post-Office Guide* (New York: D. Appleton & Co., 1851), 39; *The U.S. Post Office Directory and Postal Guide* (1854); *List of Post Offices in the United States* (1857).

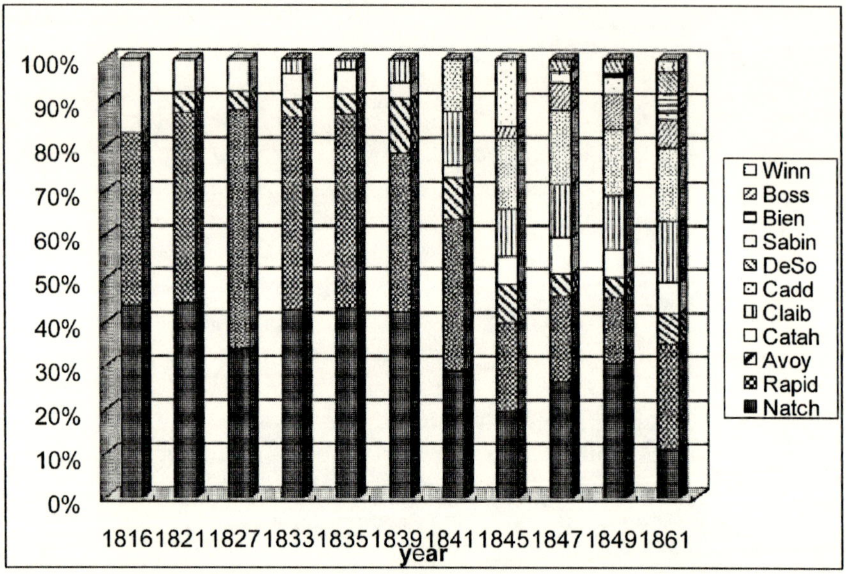

Figure 5.4. Share of Postal Services Reflected on Postmasters' Commissions.

generated a diagram which allows intra-regional and temporal comparisons of the share of information services among parishes (figure 5.4). The diagram demonstrates that Rapides and Natchitoches parishes together account for more than 75 percent of the mail-delivery services through 1839. Their dominant position, however, weakened over time as new parishes were created. Six years later (1845) and through 1861, no parish accounted for more than 20 percent of compensation to postmasters. All this reflects parish creations, noticeably in the 1840s. Not even the rise of Shreveport of Caddo Parish, with its key role in cotton exports and its sphere of influence reaching far beyond the state border into northeast Texas, had much of an impact on the distribution of postmasters' commissions.

The basic rank-size rule defines that a regional settlement system, when ordered according to the size of individual subsystem, has a characteristic distribution which reflects the social and economic parameters of the system (Dziewonski 1972: 75). To put this theorem to the test, graphs are constructed on a log-log chart that shows the rank-size distribution of postmasters' commissions. Out of the eleven curves thus created, I present five—those pertaining to the years of 1816, 1827, 1839, 1849 and 1861—for purposes of making 10-year comparisons (table 5.6 and figure 5.5). Note that the rank-size curves move upward to the right in accompaniment with the transition of the y-intercept. The slopes of the curves flatten over time, which implies

Table 5.6. List of Postmasters' Commissions

Rk	1861		1849		1839		1827		1816	
1	Alexandria	$1500.00	Natchitoches	$1174.61	Natchitoches	$653. 64	Alexandria	$384.34	Natchitoches	$129.96
2	Shreveport	1090.62	Alexandria	459.70	Alexandria	596.32	Natchitoches	252.35	Alexandria	116.66
3	Natchitoches	599.27	Shreveport	385.55	Fort Jesup	214.52	Harrisonburg	58.71	Catahoula	49.48
4	Homer	317.65	Minden	298.39	Cheneyville	169.52	Cheneyville	51.69	Avoyelles[a]	
5	Minden	297.28	Mansfield	199.23	Marksville	134.68	Marksville	35.52		
6	Mansfield	251.00	Greenwood	198.39	Harrisonburg	76.80	Cloutiersville	12.91		
7	Harrisonburg	228.59	Cheneyville	127.07	Holmesville	51.60	Allen's Sett.	11.47		
8	Trinity	171.34	Harrisonburg	120.16	Overton	49.52	Cotile	7.72		
9	Marksville	168.55	Trinity	115.65	Cloutiersville	46.20				
10	Mt. Lebanon	141.09	Mt. Lebanon	90.02	Borodino	44.00				
11	Evergreen	118.77	Holmesville	67.74	Cotile	40.04				
12	Coushatta Ch.	108.64	Cloutiersville	60.69	Campti	35.36				
13	Keachie	107.31	Many	55.91	Russellville	31.20				
14	Cheneyville	99.76	Cotile	53.64	Plaisance	21.84				
15	Winnfield	91.53	Pineville	52.74	Mt. Lebanon	21.80				
16	Collinsburg	89.89	Blossom Hill	51.97	Bayou Rouge	21.08				
17	Cotile	88.74	Athens	44.58	Negreet	19.40				
18	Ringgold	82.75	Pleasant Hill	44.01	Allen's Sett.	18.84				
19	Arcadia	81.24	Keachie	43.25	Bordeaux	17.08				
20	Greenwood	76.81	Fort Jesup	40.66	B.Rouge Pierre	15.08				
21	Bellevue	76.30	Campti	39.24	Bushly Creek	5.96				
22	Campti	67.77	Huddleston	37.68						
23	Lecompte	66.40	Bellevue	37.34						
24	Morauville	60.49	Quay	37.07						
25	Cloutiersville	59.73	Marksville	35.25						
26	Simmsport	59.42	Logansport	33.25						
27	Sparta	57.08	Bayou Rouge	27.35						
28	Sicily Island	54.91	Simm's Port	26.27						
29	Sentell's Store	52.79	Grand Cane	25.56						

(continued)

Table 5.6. *(continued)*

Rk	*1861*		*1849*		*1839*		*1827*		*1816*	
30	Holmesville	50.85	Allen's Sett.	25.26						
31	Haynesville	47.68	Willow Chute	24.34						
32	Pleasant Hill	47.13	Burr's Ferry	22.69						
33	Plainville	45.88	Flat Lick	21.12						
34	Athens	44.55	Coushatta Chute	20.32						
35	Big Bend	43.76	Parham's Land.	19.54						
36	Mansura	41.37	Red Land	18.54						
37	Wh.S. Springs	37.75	Negreet	18.06						
38	Spring Ridge	36.50	Big Bend	17.64						
39	Lisbon	36.41	Black Lake	16.91						
40	Rocky Mount	35.44	Saline	13.58						
41	Scottsville	32.33	Grand Ecore	13.05						
42	Lamothe	31.66	Cooksville	11.59						
43	Kingston	31.57	Hinestone	11.69						
44	Bethany	29.89	Walnut Creek	11.22						
45	Gordon	27.10	Hap Hazard	10.59						
46	Cotton Valley	26.56	Wh.Sulp.Springs	9.31						
47	Forest Grove	26.18	Mansura	9.05						
48	Wheeling	23.75	Big Creek	7.17						
49	Logansport	23.64	Bushley Creek	6.26						
50	Huddleston	23.57	Ringgold	5.73						
Ex[b]	78 Other P.O.s	801.66	8 Other P.O.s	27.25						
σ		176.39		171.70		183.20		139.47		43.14

Notes: [a]Since the post office of Avoyelles had not been established a year, no accounts was rendered. [b]number of unlisted post offices and the sum of their commissions. Rk rank, σ standard deviation.
Source: Register of Officers and Agents in the Service of the United States (1816, 1827, 1839, 1849 and 1861).

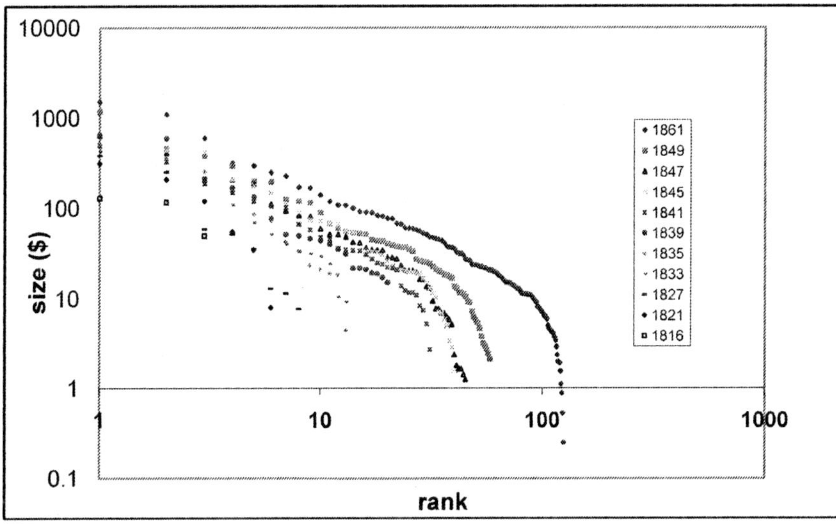

Figure 5.5. Rank-Size Distribution of Postmasters' Commissions, 1816–1861

that the pace and pattern of these changes were largely governed by middle and small-sized post offices as mediated by the three high-ranking regional information centers of Natchitoches, Alexandria, and Shreveport.

These trends indicate that the settlement system as represented by post office commissions (mail-flow volume) was growing in size and density and was becoming more diversified with the addition of new strata in the hierarchies. Standard deviations (σ) of the commission generally increase toward the end of the antebellum era: 1816 (43.1), 1827 (139.5), 1839 (183.2), 1849 (171.7), and 1861 (176.4). This suggests that postal settlements in earlier periods were more similar in size and function, whereas those coming later had more variable class intervals. Indeed, six hierarchies are identified on the 1839 log-log curve—the year that has the greatest value of standard deviation.

These graphical representations of the region's expanding settlement system are projected onto a series of maps in order to reveal the historical geographical trends (figure 5.6). Each post office is ordered hierarchically based on the size of commissions. As the maps illustrate, post offices were confined to the Red River Corridor in the early stage of settlement (1816). The riverine post offices at Natchitoches, Grand Ecore, and Alexandria played, in sequence, the role of the distributing offices in the region and formed the hearth of the communications system from which branch offices would later spread out. By 1827, Alexandria had displaced Natchitoches from the top of the postal hierarchy and the system added five new post offices—all southeast of

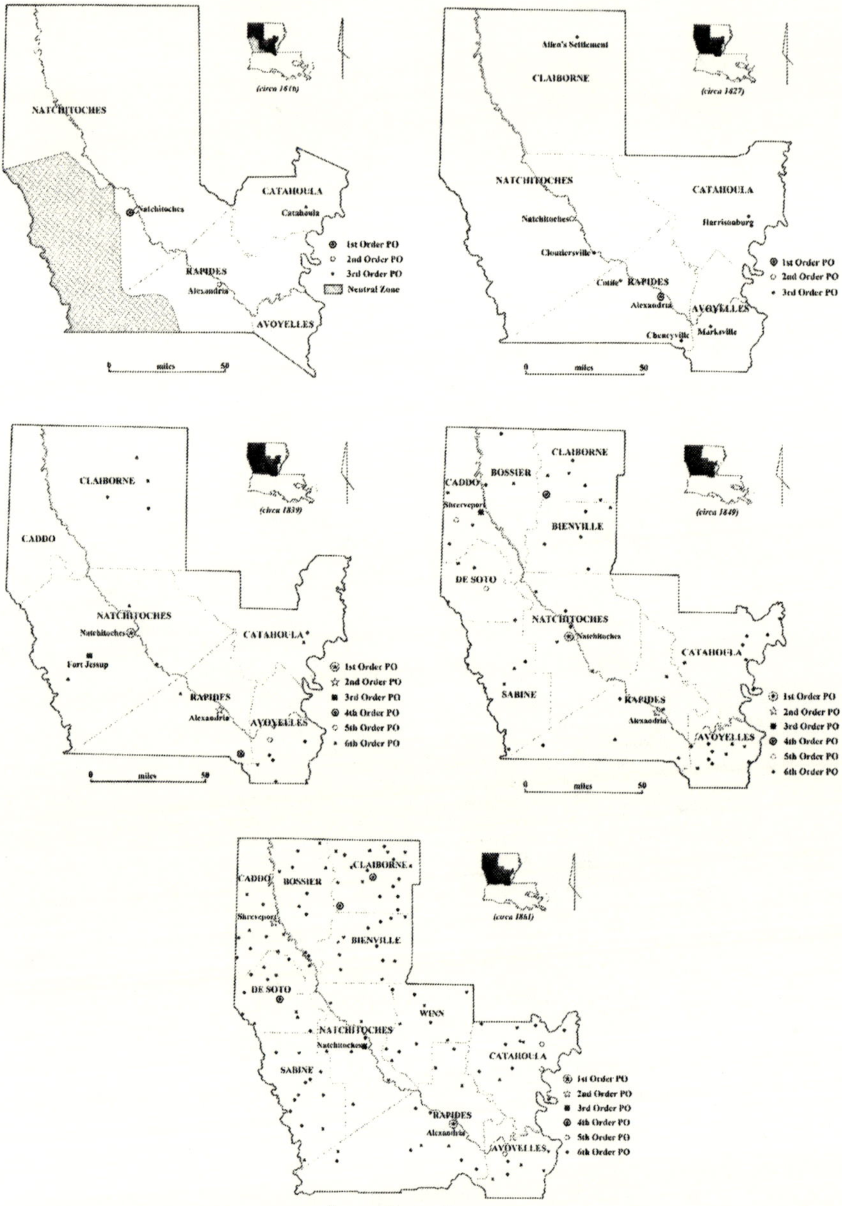

Figure 5.6. Spatial Organization of Information Fields in the Red River Valley, 1816–1861.

Natchitoches. The expansion of the system proceeded apace in the 1830s, as post offices increased from 8 in 1827 to 20 in 1839. Moreover, Natchitoches won back the lead from Alexandria—a lead it held for the next decade.

In the 1830s and 1840s, the valley's postal system gradually expanded away from the river and into the interior rural areas, partitioning the region into a hierarchy of postal nodal points and their information fields. This survey suggests that the number of post offices increased rapidly during the 1840s (from 20 in 1839 to 58 in 1849) and most of the newly opened offices were lower-order centers. Concurrently, some post offices established earlier had closed or failed to appear on later lists. Post office mortality was modest in the 1840s. Of 20 post offices established as of 1839, only 4 were disestablished by 1849; at the same time, 37 post offices were established—a net gain of 33. Post office openings and closures were numerous in the 1850s. Of 58 post offices in 1849, 13 had been disestablished by 1861; while 82 new post offices opened—a net gain of 69 (table 5.7).

Meanwhile, post offices moved up and down the hierarchical ladder and at variable rates; some rose faster than the average, others remained static, and still others actually declined in relative importance. Volatility, as it was, characterized the 1830s. In that decade, only one post office of Natchitoches moved upward, while seven others including the first-ranking Alexandria fell to lower status. This unstable regime was replaced by a consolidation phase during the next two decades. In the 1840s, 14 out of 58 post offices (24.1 percent) retained their hierarchical status and 40 of 128 (31.3 percent) were stable in the 1850s.

Generally speaking, and consistent with Jacksonian democratic principles, post offices were distributed in an egalitarian manner, that is, new post offices were equally distributed in the valley. None of the valley's eleven parishes in 1861 has fewer than 7 post offices or more than 19, and eight of the parishes had between 10 and 13. Areas to the north and east of the river reported 71 post offices while areas south and west reported 57. Note, however, that the three largest post offices in the region as of 1861 (Alexandria, Shreveport, and Natchitoches) were all located on the south side (right bank) of the Red River. As it turns out, this distribution pattern embodies a Skinnerian scheme of lowland core and upland periphery.[13] Most high-ranking post offices concentrated on the Red River corridor; while sixth-ranking small ones packed the outskirts of the region (see figures 5.1 and 5.6). Exceptionally, three fourth-ranking post offices (Mansfield in De Soto Parish and Minden and Homer in Claiborne Parish) were located at inland nodal points. Traditionally, these post offices played the role of what Skinner terms outer core, linking northwestern Louisiana to Texas and Arkansas.

Table 5.7. Hierarchical Shifts of the Red River Valley Post Offices

	1816–1827					*1827–1839*					*1839–1849*					*1849–1861*				
H[a]	*R*	*S*	*F*	*Ds*	*E*	*R*	*S*	*F*	*Ds*	*E*	*R*	*S*	*F*	*Ds*	*E*	*R*	*S*	*F*	*Ds*	*E*
1st			1					1				1						1		
2nd	1					1						1				1				
3rd		2			4			6		1			1		1	1				
4th													1		1		1			1
5th													1		2		1	1		
6th										12		12		4	37	3	38		13	82

Notes: [a]hierarchy, R rise from, S stable, F fall from, Ds discarded, E newly established.

Source: Register of Officers and Agents in the Service of the United States, 1816–1861.

CONCLUSION

Historical geography uses historical data to reconstruct the geographies of past societies. During the last few decades, efforts have been made to incorporate hypotheses, models, and other analytical tools. As Jakle (1971: 1084) predicts, historical geographers are "no longer content to study spatial relationship in its static sense but are focusing increasingly on spatial change through time." The most prominent figures associated with this adventurous foray into geohistorical social science might be G.W. Skinner and Carville Earle. Borrowing a theoretical insight from Skinner's core-periphery regional structure and Earle's dialectic geohistorical perspectives, I have so far tried to add systemic and evolutionary tint to the spatial organization of pre-electronic communication systems. Laying special focus on timing and rate, this study specifically traced the evolutionary path of settlement systems in the temporal and regional context of antebellum Red River Valley using post offices—what Meinig (1993: 250) characterizes as "the base level of a nascent hierarchy of central places"—and postmasters' commissions as proxy for the volume of information flows.

Prior to the American Civil War, post offices served as nascent functional centers in the frontier region. Based on the assumption that the hierarchical system of postal settlements is a function of the extent of information exchanged, the chapter followed the periodic changes in the contours of the structures of the Red River Valley urban and rural settlements. An input or output of people and information forces the variables beyond the range of stability, initiating a reconfiguration in the number, size, position, direction, pattern, order and density of subsystems over time and space. In an evolutionary system, the general directions of change include an increase in the number of components, an increase in the size, range, complexity, and integration of the system, a reorganization of relationships among subsystems, and an increase in the amounts of information (Miller 1965a: 224; 1965b: 372).

The development of the Red River Valley postal system gives credence to the evolutionary trends just mentioned. First, the information system of the antebellum Red River Valley expanded in terms of size and density. Second, the growth of the system was driven by the addition of small- and mid-sized post office communities with the mediation of high-ranking postal towns on the Red River. Third, inland parish seats, interior nodal points, and other places of administrative, commercial and transportation importance functioned as intermediate centers in the hierarchical diffusion of information. Fourth, by 1861, post office locations and postmasters' commissions were fairly evenly distributed across the Red River Valley, albeit with slight biases in favor of the upper valley over the lower and the left bank of the river over the right. That said, all of the dominant centers in the region's postal system—Natchitoches, Alexandria, and Shreveport—occupied the southern side or right bank of the Red River.

With those encouraging findings, this study bear outs what Skinner and Earle so elegantly visualize in their models. Skinnerian theorem turns out to have relevance to the core-periphery distinction in the distribution and size of post offices in the region. Historical evidence shows postal settlements thin out and become smaller as one moves outward from the riverine core areas. Further, statistics, graphs and rank-size curve identify Earle's dialectical episodes accompanying the evolution of settlement systems in the Red River Valley. Antebellum Louisiana, following Earle's (2003) paradigm, seems to have passed through the scaled-down version of "Republican regime" of spatial expansion and demographic concentration with an elitist geography of regional stability and specialization prior to 1830 and the "Democracy regime" of spatial consolidation and demographic dispersion with an egalitarian geography of regional volatility and diversification posterior to the year. Earlier, the postal settlement increased in number and size. The transformation process then accompanied the hierarchical fragmentation of postal settlement and periodic rearrangement of the configuration of settlement structure. Combined together, the earlier expansion phase of postal settlement was replaced by the consolidation regime during and after the 1840s. The infilling process was backed by sustained population growth and Jacksonian patronage. Importantly, the discontinuous shaping of regional geography in the Red River Valley was propelled by the contentious interplay between specialization and diversification. The alternating regimes were to a great extent tied to the crisis from cotton monoculture and the recovery by adopting environmentally sound agrarian wisdom of crop rotation combining corn, cotton and cowpea.

In all, this chapter shows that the antebellum Red River Valley was a region representing an internally differentiated, interdependent and integrated Skinnerian type system. Given that the region was on the ladder of "nested hierarchy" building from the local to the global, the pace, timing and rate of periodic evolutionary path were set not only by region-specific endogenous factors but at the same time by exogenous parameters of prices of staple crops and alternating ideological regimes. In this respect, Earle's vision of periodic structures, dialectical dynamics, and series of spatial reconstructions is of vital importance to our quest of more fully explaining the intricately varied historical geography of the United States.

NOTES

1. Social, economic, and political implications of the flows of gossip, rumor, advertisements, and news mediated by these institutional nodes appear in E. P. Thompson's (1971) diagnosis on markets, Peter Clark's (1983) monograph on alehouses, Lawrence Klein's (1997) essay on coffeehouse civility, and Frank Owsley's (1982) sketch of antebellum churches and district courts.

2. A brief description of the raft can be found in *De Bow's Review* 19 (1855): 437–38: "The Red River raft was an accumulation of trees, logs, and drift, extending over the surface of the river from bank to bank, and for miles in extent, so close and compact as to be walked over without wetting the feet. Broom-straw, willow and other small bushes are growing out of the rich alluvial earth that covers the logs, so that it presents the appearance of an old worn-out field that has been abandoned to grow up again." The clearance started in 1833 by the U.S. engineers led by Captain Henry Miller Shreve. His team removed 70 miles of logjam for the first year and the partial completion of the task led to the establishment of Shreveport in 1836. The logjam was pulled out at the end of nineteenth century.

3. The fort was founded by St. Dennis who was dispatched to find a commercial outlet and check the advance of the Spaniards from the west. As it turned out, Natchitoches was the first European settlement established in the present-day Louisiana. The French fort was a square palisade, which functioned as a barrier against the Spanish force. The 1722 census reported that roughly 87 people lived in the garrison including 14 men, 10 women, 10 children, 20 Black slaves, 8 Indian slaves, and 25 Natchitoches Indians (Mills 1981: 3–4).

4. Writing in 1812, Amos Stoddard talked about the connection between military post and postal services: "The road we have traced out is the great thoroughfare between Red River and the city of Mexico. . . . The Spaniards, at all the villages and at nearly all the rivers on this route, have established small military posts, composed of 8 or 10 men each, not merely as guards of security but to facilitate the passage of public letters and dispatches, which are carried with as much expedition between the Sabine and the most distant provinces, as in any part of the United States. All these posts are provided with mules. As soon as the mail arrives at one post, it is hastened by a fresh mule and rider to the next, and so on; it travels night and day, and is seldom obstructed, or even retarded, by the weather" (p.197).

5. The *Red River Whig*, an official weekly newspaper of the town of Alexandria, reported that the first mail delivered under this arrangement was received on Monday evening on April 26, 1841 (*Red River Whig*, Alexandria, Saturday, May 1, 1841).

6. *Shreveport Journal*, Shreveport, Monday, April 3, 1848.

7. *Southern Advocate and Catahoula Register*, Trinity, Saturday, October 22, 1853.

8. The Contract Office of the Post Office Department chose mail contractors from applications submitted to it. The terms of contract varied from one place to another

and from one mail line to another. As an example, *The Villager*, an official weekly of Avoyelles Parish, announced a new contract for conveying the mail for 4 years in the following places: 94 miles from Red River Landing to Alexandria, daily; 6 miles from Simmsport to Big Bend, once a week; 30 miles from Simmsport to Moreauville, once a week; and 24 miles from Holmesville to Moreauville, three times a week (*The Villager*, February 20, 1858).

9. *Red River Whig*, Alexandria, Saturday, November 21, 1840; *The Bossier Banner*, Bellevue, March 9, 1860.

10. The peopling of the Red River Valley was driven not only by the presence of cheap and fertile land, the rapid expansion of cotton, the clearance of logjams, the relocation of Indian tribes, and the loose enforcement of public-land laws, but also by such push factors as soil exhaustion and limited labor market in the Old South (see Gray 1933: 896–900).

11. U.S. Census Office, *Population of the U.S., The 5th (1830) and 6th (1840) Censuses* (Washington, DC: Government Printing Office).

12. *Postal settlement* used in this essay is defined as hamlets, plantations, villages, towns, cities, and other settlement units which had post offices in their bounds.

13. For more on the central ideas of G. William Skinner's regional system, see his, "The Structure of Chinese History," *Journal of Asian Studies* 44 (1985): 271–92; "Regional Systems in Nineteenth-Century France," Precis (1986); "Nobi as a Regional System," Paper prepared for the Second Workshop of the Nobi Regional Project, Aichiken Sangyo Boekikan, Nagoya, 6–10 January 1988.

BIBLIOGRAPHY

Abler, R. F. 1971. "Distance, Intercommunications, and Geography." *Proceedings of the Association of American Geographers* 3: 1–4.

Barber, P. K. 1967. *Historic Cotile.* (Baptist Message Press).

Blount, W. M. 1976. "U.S. Postal Service." *Dictionary of American History* 5, (New York: Charles Scribner's Sons): 370–374.

Bowen, E. 1976. *The United States Post-Office Guide.* (New York: D. Appleton & Co., 1851; reprint, New York: Arno Press).

Brayshay, M., P., Harrison, and B. Chalkley. 1998. "Knowledge, Nationhood and Governance: The Speed of the Royal Post in Early–Modern England." *Journal of Historical Geography* 24: 265–88.

Bruchey, S. 1967. *Cotton and the Growth of the American Economy: 1790–1860.* (New York: Harcourt, Brace & World).

Castells, M. 1996. *The Information Age: Economy, Society and Culture.* vol. 1: *The Rise of the Network Society.* (Blackwell).

Champomier, P. A. 1844–1861. *Statement of the Sugar Crop of Louisiana.* (New Orleans: Cook and Young).

Chorley, R. J. 1964. "Geomorphology and General Systems Theory." *General Systems* 9: 45–55.

Christaller, W. 1966. *Central Places in Southern Germany*, translated by C. W. Baskin. (Englewood Cliffs: Prentice-Hall).
Clark, P. 1983. *The English Alehouse: A Social History, 1200–1830.* (London: Longman).
Curry, L. 1964. "The Random Spatial Economy: An explanation in settlement theory." *Annals of the Association of American Geographers* 54: 138–46.
Dorr, J. W. 1938[1860]. "A Tourist's Description of Louisiana in 1860." *Louisiana Historical Quarterly* 21: 1110–14.
Dziewonski, K. 1972. "General Theory of Rank-Size Distributions in Regional Settlement Systems: Reappraisal and reformulation of the rank-size rule." *Papers of the Regional Science Association* 29: 73–86.
Earle, C. V. 1975. *The Evolution of a Tidewater Settlement System: All Hallow's Parish, Maryland, 1650–1783.* (University of Chicago, Department of Geography Research Paper, No. 170).
———. 1978. "Comments on the Continuous Shaping of America." *American Historical Review* 83: 1206–9.
———. 1992. *Geographical Inquiry and American Historical Problems.* (Stanford, CA: Stanford University Press).
———. 1999. "Continuity or discontinuity—that is the question! The Shaping of America in the gilded age and progressive era." *Journal of Historical Geography* 25, no. 1: 12–16.
———. 2003. *The American Way: A Geographical History of Crisis and Recovery.* (Lanham, MD: Rowman & Littlefield).
Falk, T., and R. Abler. 1985. "Intercommunications Technologies: The Development of Postal Services in Sweden." *Geografiska Annaler* 67B: 21–28.
Gouldner, A. W. 1982. *The Dialectic of Ideology and Technology.* (New York: Oxford University Press).
Gray, L. C. 1958 [1933]. *History of Agriculture in the Southern United States to 1860.* (Gloucester, MA: Peter Smith).
Gregory, D. 1987. "The Friction of Distance? Information Circulation and the Mails in Early Nineteenth-Century England." *Journal of Historical Geography* 13: 130–54.
Gullinan, G. 1968. "Appendix A: Summary of the Most Important Laws Concerning Postage Rates." *The Post Office Department:* 249–251. (New York: Frederick A. Praeger).
Hagen, E. E. 1961. "Analytical Models in the Study of Social Systems." *American Journal of Sociology* 67: 144–51.
Hillis, K. 1998. "On the margins: The invisibility of communications in geography." *Progress in Human Geography* 22: 543–66.
Hong, K. 2004. "An Ecological Reflection on the Food Self-Sufficiency Debate of the Antebellum American South." *Journal of the Korean Geographical Society* 39, no.2: 171–94.
Hugill, P. J. 1999. *Global Communications since 1844: Geopolitics and Technology.* (Baltimore: Johns Hopkins University Press).

Humphreys, H. D. 1984. "The "Great Raft" of the Red River" in *North Louisiana*, edited by B. H. Gilley, pp. 73–91. (Ruston, LA: McGinty Trust Fund).

Jakle, J. A. 1971. "Time, Space, and the Geographic Past: A prospectus for historical Geography." *American Historical Review* 76: 1084–1103.

Jannell, D. G. 1969. "Spatial Reorganization: A model and concept." *Annals of the Association of American Geographers* 59: 348–64.

Klein, L. E. 1997. "Coffeehouse Civility, 1660–1714: An Aspect of Post-Courtly Culture in England." *Huntington Library Quarterly* 59: 31–51.

Langton, J. 1972. "Potentialities and Problems of Adopting a Systems Approach to the Study of Change in Human Geography." *Progress in Geography* 4: 125–79.

Leech, D. D. T. 1879. *The Post Office Department of the United States of America.* (Washington, DC: Judd & Detweiler).

Meinig, D. W. 1986. *The Shaping of America: A Geographical Perspective on 500 Years of History*, vol. 1 *Atlantic America, 1492–1800.* (New Haven: Yale University Press).

———. 1992. *The Shaping of America: A Geographical Perspective on 500 Years of History*, vol. 2 *Continental America, 1800–1867.* (New Haven: Yale University Press).

———. 1998. *The Shaping of America: A Geographical Perspective on 500 Years of History*, vol. 3 *Transcontinental America, 1850–1915.* (New Haven: Yale University Press).

Mills, G. B. 1977. *The Forgotten People: Cane River's Creoles of Color.* (Baton Rouge: Louisiana State University Press).

Mills, E. S. 1981. *Natchitoches Colonials: Censuses, military rolls, and tax lists, 1722–1803.* (Chicago: Adams Press).

Miller, J. 1965a. "Living Systems: Basic concepts." *Behavioral Science* 10: 193–237.

———. 1965b. "Living System: Structure and process." *Behavioral Science* 10: 337–79.

Norman, N. P. 1942. "The Red River of the South." *Louisiana Historical Quarterly* 25: 397–535.

Northup, Solomon. 1968. *Twelve Years a Slave: Narrative of Solomon Northup.* (Auburn: Derby and Miller, 1853; reprint, Baton Rouge: Louisiana State University Press).

Owsley, F. L. 1982. *Plain Folk of the Old South.* (Baton Rouge: Louisiana State University Press).

Pred, A. 1971. "Urban Systems Development and the Long-Distance Flow of Information through Preelectronic U.S. Newspapers." *Economic Geography* 47: 498–524.

———. 1973. *Urban Growth and the Circulation of Information: The United States System of Cities, 1790–1840.* (Cambridge, MA: Harvard University Press).

———. 1980. *Urban Growth and City-Systems in the United States, 1840–1860.* (Cambridge, MA: Harvard University Press).

Preston, R. E. 1991. "Central Place Theory and the Canadian Urban System" in *Canadian Cities in Transition*, edited by T. Bunting and P. Filion, pp. 148–77. (Toronto: Oxford University Press).

Register of Officers and Agents in the Service of the United States, 1816, 1827, 1839, 1849, and 1861.

Skinner, G. W. 1977. "Regional Urbanization in Nineteenth-Century China" in *The City in Late Imperial China*, edited by G. W. Skinner, pp. 211–49. (Stanford, CA: Stanford University Press).

———. 1985. "The Structure of Chinese History." *Journal of Asian Studies* 44: 271–92.

———. 1986. "Regional Systems in Nineteenth-Century France." (A precis. September, 1986).

———. 1988. "Nobi as a Regional System." (paper prepared for the Second Workshop of the Nobi Regional Project, Aichiken Sangyo Boekikan, Nagoya, January 6–10).

Stoddard, A. 1812. *Sketches, Historical and Descriptive of Louisiana*. (Philadelphia: Mathew Carey).

Statistical Abstracts

Thompson, E. P. 1971. "The Moral Economy of the English Crowd in the Eighteenth Century." *Past and Present* 50: 76–136.

Thrift, N. 1985. "Flies and Germs: A Geography of Knowledge" in *Social Relations and Spatial Structures*, edited by D. Gregory and J. Urry, pp. 366–403. (New York: St. Martin's Press).

U.S. Census Office, *Population of the United States, The 5th (1830), 6th (1840), 7th (1850) and 8th (1860) Censuses*. (Washington: Government Printing Office).

U.S. Census Bureau, 1975. *Historical Statistics of the United States: Colonial Times to 1970*. (Washington, DC: Government Printing Office).

U.S. Department of Commerce, 1930. *Statistical Abstract of the United States*. (Washington, DC: Government Printing Office).

Wade, R. C. 1959. *The Urban Frontier: Pioneer Life in Early Pittsburgh, Cincinnati, Lexington, Louisville, and St. Louis*. (Chicago: University of Chicago Press).

Chapter Six

Earle's Dialectical Policy Regimes and the Erie Canal

Anne E. Mosher

"Low Bridge"

I've got an old mule and her name is Sal
Fifteen miles on the Erie Canal
She's a good old worker and a good old pal
Fifteen miles on the Erie Canal
We've hauled some barges in our day
Filled with lumber, coal, and hay
And every inch of the way we know
From Albany to Buffalo
Chorus:
Low bridge, everybody down
Low bridge for we're coming to a town
And you'll always know your neighbor
And you'll always know your pal
If you've ever navigated on the Erie Canal

—Thomas S. Allen, 1905

Many American children learn Thomas Allen's "Low Bridge" as part of their elementary school history curriculum, committing to memory lyrics about a past that stands in marked contrast to today's world: mules, canal boats, lumber, coal, and hay, versus automobiles, interstate highways, plastic, computer chips, and unleaded gasoline. But "Low Bridge" (also known by the title "Erie Canal") does not simply make distinctions between past and present; its lyrics have been used to define, brand and sell to tourists and tour operators a region that heretofore has been known largely for blizzards, Golden Snowball Awards, and a lengthy cold and flu season. In print and web advertising, many businesses, not-for-profit organizations and governments at all jurisdictional levels along the Erie Canal (minor civil divisions, counties, the State of New York, and the U.S. federal government) are incorporating "Low Bridge" into a regional economic development strategy, invoking it—and the Erie Canal itself—to promote "Upstate" New York as an accessible recreational and cultural heritage playground (e.g., the Erie Canalway National Heritage Arena). The Erie Canal is being portrayed as a weekend getaway for New York City residents who seek "Life in the Past Lane" (Lockport Locks and Erie Canal Cruises 2007). Further, it is marketed as an easy diversion off the New York State Thruway for Niagara Falls-bound out-of-state and international visitors, a place where people can experience the "Other New York State of Mind" (Mower 2003). The hope is, of course, that New York City's escapees and the rest of the world's tourists will come to upstate, spend, and hasten a long-hoped-for economic shift away from the declining primary (mining, fishing, forestry, and agriculture) and secondary (fabricated or manufactured products) sector activities traditionally found along the Erie Canal corridor, toward a more-promising "new economy" of tertiary (services), quaternary (information processing, business administration, finance and insurance) and quinary (health, education, research, and recreation) sector activities.

Regional economic development strategies intended to hasten sectoral shifts are nothing new to the Upstate economy. In fact, their *national* history really begins there . . . with the creation of the Erie Canal (American Planning Association 2007). In the decade of the 1800s, landowners, investors and other members of the state's elite (many of whom resided in New York City and the lower Hudson Valley) came up with a grand plan: to build a 300-mile-long "artificial river" linking the Hudson River to Lake Erie (Sheriff 1996). This canal would allow for the establishment of primary and tertiary activities on land that previously had trouble participating in a market-based economy (Schein 1989; Miller 1979). At the time, however, many others considered the idea ill-timed and bordering on lunacy. Engineers noted the many large physical obstacles and technological problems that would have to be overcome to make the scheme a reality (Whitford et al. 1906). Potential investors estimated the expense and wondered if the canal would ever have enough traffic to make a profit, especially since it ran through a perceived wilderness that was devoid of traffic-generating population.

In the face of such opposition, canal supporters concluded that if a venture like this were to be pursued at all, it could not be by done by private investors alone (Bernstein 2005). Government would have to be involved in some way. Such support, however, would not come from the federal level. After canal supporters unsuccessfully petitioned President James Madison for assistance, the State of New York became the government entity that ultimately secured and guaranteed the financing, oversaw the massive construction project (including coordination of hundreds of contractors and thousands of workers), and amended the state constitution so as to have control in perpetuity over management and maintenance of the Erie Canal.

Thus the State of New York created a regional infrastructure that, after completion in 1825, precipitated a reduction in transportation costs between Upstate and Downstate by a factor of ten. Upstate farmers cleared more of their land and intensified production so as to participate in the market economy. Population flocked to once-sleepy villages like Buffalo, Rochester, Syracuse, Rome, Utica and Schenectady, remaking them into bustling manufacturing and mercantile emporia (Shaw 2004). The sectoral shift continued through the 1840s with the arrival of several short-haul railroads that trailed the canal's path and attracted various forms of manufacturing (Vance 1995). Downstate benefited given that: 1) much of the investment capital that built Upstate's canals came from the lower Hudson Valley and hence returned there as profit; and 2) Downstate's metropolis—New York City—became the transshipment hinge that connected the newly forged Great Lakes–Erie Canal–Hudson River transportation system to the rest of the Atlantic Basin (Meinig 1992).

State boundaries could not isolate the canal's transformative impacts. Almost immediately the Erie Canal began altering the State of New York's relationship with surrounding neighbors. As the canal brought more Euro-American settlers into the region, it hastened the full implementation of the land treaties that New York State had entered into (probably illegally) with the six-nation People of the Long House, the Haudenosaunee (Iroquois Confederacy) (Porter and Garrow 2005). The Canal also worried the British in Upper Canada as well as Pennsylvanians, Marylanders, and Ohioans into regional economic development/canal-building schemes of their own (Aitken 1952; Wallner 1973; Whebell 1969). Although New York politician DeWitt Clinton and other canal supporters had justified construction by arguing that it would bring to life the Federalist vision of a unified democratic republic of interconnected states, the Erie Canal actually amplified urban and interstate rivalries, and heightened already-emerging sectional differences between the U.S. North and South that would one day test the very concept of nationhood.

Thanks to professional historians, K–12 educators, and a History Channel documentary, the Erie Canal's function as an early regional development strategy is well known to the general public (Nash 2000). Most historical narratives that assess the impact of the Erie Canal, however, conclude in the 1860s, tacitly suggesting that the canal is no longer important (many Americans who live outside of the northeast are surprised when they learn that it still actually exists!) But the Erie Canal has survived, despite competition from the railroads, the internal combustion engine, and the creation of the St. Lawrence Seaway. Moreover, from the late-nineteenth century to the present day, it has continually contributed to, and has been shaped by, national controversies and international affairs. And yet, this last aspect of Erie Canal history is not well known—not even within New York State (Klein and New York State Historical Association 2001).

Only twice has the canal's story been brought into the "postbellum" era in a substantive way (Larkin et al. 2001). First is the work of New York State Engineer Nobel Whitford (Whitford et al. 1906; 1922), an appointed government official who knew in intimate detail the technical inner-workings of the canal and understood how they connected to the New York State institutional apparatus and political machine. His histories of the Erie Canal and its successor, the New York State Barge Canal, are remarkable reports. Whitford, however, in his treatment of the canal's postbellum history skirts around politically sensitive issues that formed the focus of so much of the historiography covering the earlier era, no doubt because he was hamstrung by his appointed position as a state officer and felt obliged to uphold professional allegiances within the engineering community. In the end, he presents an overwhelmingly celebratory and politically benign account of the Erie Canal.

Much of the same criticism can be leveled at the second attempt to bring the canal's story up to the present: Michelle McFee's (1998) historical overview of the canal's twentieth-century history. Like Whitford, McFee explains canal technology in copious detail but does not spill much ink regarding the intergovernmental politics that have kept the canal in operation to this day. The strength of her work lies elsewhere—first, in her presentation of some of the best photos from the New York State Archives' canal collection; and second, in her inclusion of reminiscences by the "canallers"—the people who actually lived and worked on the Erie Canal. Her book is an accessible and interesting account that puts some real names and faces to the fictional characters in Thomas Allen's "Low Bridge." And yet, despite Whitford and McFee's work, the question remains: what issues could the historiography of the postbellum canal address?

This chapter proposes an answer to this question through the application of a heuristic framework to Erie Canal history (and geography). Carville Earle's "Model of the Geographical Dialectics of American Policy Regimes" identifies and begins to explain several previously overlooked points of discussion regarding the political context in which the canal was created and exists (Earle 2003). Additionally, application to the Erie Canal affords the opportunity to critique Earle's theoretical framework and to discuss some of the issues that it raises about New York's role in American history more generally. Earle's model, as logically compelling as it is, thus cries out for further application at the international and regional scales. In this chapter, I focus primarily on the second of these scales (although I do mention briefly the international given the important role that the Erie Canal has played in the twentieth century in U.S.-Canada *and* U.S. allies relations). I ask: How well does Earle's model work in addressing the political geographical history of a region (upstate New York) and the infrastructural system that fostered its early development (the Erie Canal)? What will we learn from it regarding the late-nineteenth and twentieth-century roles that this regional infrastructure played in national and international affairs? Furthermore, because Earle's model addresses present-day conditions, what light might it shed on the regional economic policy regime in which "Low Bridge" and canal tourism have become a part? To answer these questions, it was first necessary to discuss in more detail Earle's model and its intellectual underpinnings (see chapter 2).

The question, however, is the extent to which they are related to the policies that New York State enacted to build the Erie Canal in the 1810s and 20s, widen its "prism" between the 1840s and 1860s, abandon it in favor of construction of the New York State Barge Canal in the 1900s and 1910s, redirect national focus away from it and toward the creation of the St. Lawrence Seaway in the 1950s, and spark its conceptual reinvention as a catalyst for tourism and real-estate development in the 1990s and 2000s.

INFRASTRUCTURES OF THE REPUBLIC AND THE DEMOCRACY

Having considered the basic political philosophies and attendant geosophies for either side of Earle's dialectical regime model, the question becomes one of how best to apply this model for the Erie Canal (chapter 2). The Erie Canal is not an explicit part of the empirical foundation from which Earle inductively created the broader theoretical framework. Earle did, however, have a good deal to say about the development of the nation's *infrastructure*—of which the Erie Canal is an implicit part. Earle's engagement with the Erie Canal is thus indirect, which makes the exercise of linking his model to the canal all the more challenging.

Infrastructure consists of the service-provision networks that allow people to live at high densities in towns and cities (Konvitz 1985). It also connects these people and cities into broader economic, social, and political networks. It includes things in the built environment like schools, police and fire departments, and libraries (the so-called "soft" infrastructures) and sewers, water mains, streetlights, electrical grids, airports, highways, railroads, ports, and canals (the so-called "hard" infrastructures). At several points in the argument, Earle discusses these infrastructures—either collectively or by referring to specific infrastructural systems, like the railroads or the internet backbone. The most extended empirical discussion comes in *The American Way*'s final chapter during the application of a hybridized Borchert/dialectical policy regime model to the evolution of the American city.[1] The best theoretical discussion, however, appears much earlier—in chapter 4—when Earle discusses the two policy regimes and how they fulfill certain spatial strategies through modification of the built environment.

On the one hand, Earle argues, Protectionist Elitist Republicanism, consisting of territorial and system expansion, demographic concentration, and areal functional specialization, *creates* infrastructural networks that extend the spatial scale over which urban jurisdictions and the federal state operate. More specifically, infrastructures of the republic are intended to: first, enhance property values as a means of capital accumulation for property owners; second, extend the sphere of the nation's economic influence toward the location of new resources; and third, reflect the goal of efficiency, meaning that people should cluster near the infrastructure as it will not be found everywhere. Additionally, under this rubric, new infrastructure is better than old as it reflects the most recent technology and engineering practices and is usually faster and more reliable.

On the other hand, liberal egalitarian democracies promote territorial and system infill, demographic dispersion, and intra-regional diversification which require the *reengineering* and *creative destruction* of the republic's networks in order to provide greater capacity and access. More specifically, infrastructures of the democracy are intended to: first, get goods and services to a mass of consumers in a more equitable fashion, meaning that people no longer have to cluster around the network but can instead spread out; and second, promote intra-regional development by creating more linkages between existing nodes within the network. Later, at the end of each Democracy, the economic and social burden of such an expanded system becomes so great and the system becomes so bogged down with traffic that the successive Republican regime comes to power promising system cutbacks and gridlock alleviating extensions into new territory. And so it goes over more than two centuries, periods of infrastructure creation followed by reengineering, creative destruction, and eventual replacement of that infrastructure with something "better."

Does this process of alternating policy regimes and their accompanying geosophies fit what is already known about Erie Canal history? More specifically, do the national mood-swings between Protective Elitist Republicanism and Liberal Egalitarian Democracy that Earle theorizes have any connection to the policy that was created toward, as well as the purpose of, the Erie Canal? Do the spatial strategies of Republican-style infrastructure creation and system extension and Democratic-style creative destruction/system saturation reflect what went on in Upstate New York, particularly during the twentieth-century period that historians have been slow to study? In what new directions does Earle's dialectical policy regime model direct possible research on the canal? To answer these questions, we need to: shift the discussion to a different geographical scale, re-orienting ourselves to look at New York State—the entity that built, owns and operates the Erie Canal; establish whether or not a pattern of alternating policy regimes like Earle's exists at the state level; and identify possible linkages between state-level policy regimes and the history of the Erie Canal's development.

The following section reports on my attempt to work through these questions. In it, I present several speculations about Earle's model, the geography of New York State politics, as well as the Erie Canal itself that have yet to be completely corroborated through a systematic analysis of primary evidence and the secondary literature. Although I have been researching and teaching about the Erie Canal for several years, the exercise of applying Earle's model to it has encouraged me to think in an entirely different way about this piece of infrastructure and the political context in which it sits. The dialectical policy regime model indicates some new directions in which research on the twentieth- and twenty-first-century Erie Canal could head and into which the existing historiography could be expanded.

DIALECTICAL POLICY REGIMES AND THE ERAS OF NEW YORK STATE POLITICAL PARTY DOMINANCE

Earle's decision to label the two policy regimes of American history as either republican or democratic might suggest that Earle saw the past as a contest between two rival political parties that since the mid-nineteenth century have dominated U.S. electoral politics. Throughout *The American Way,* however, Earle makes careful distinctions between parties and policies. Even though the nomenclature used in the dialectical policy regime model of republican and democratic is similar to political party nomenclature, Earle argues that politicians of a particular party affiliation can indeed participate in the erection of a policy regime that appears antithetical to the commonly recognized platforms on which their party stands. In other words, Earle believed that American history is sprinkled with Democrats (and before them, Democratic-Republicans) who have helped erect Republican policy regimes and Republicans (and before them, Federalists and Whigs) who have helped erect Democratic policy regimes. Rather, for Earle what made an era a Republic or a Democracy is the tenor of the entire body of national-level policy that was enacted over longish periods of time and the extent to which its content displays either a tendency toward protectionist elitism or free-trade egalitarianism. It's not solely about whether or not the majority of politicians holding elected office at a particular time have Ds or Rs behind their names. That point must be kept in mind when applying the dialectic regime model to any jurisdictional unit besides the federal government, and that includes New York State.

Nevertheless, a cursory comparison between the elitist/egalitarian tendencies of state-level policy and the platforms of New York State's political parties shows some correlation over more than two centuries (Klein and New York State Historical Association 2001). (In looking at policy regimes at the state level, it is probably less useful to consider protectionism and free-trade tendencies as these internationally oriented policies generally have been articulated at the federal level and not by the state.) Federalists, Whigs, and Republicans tended to support and enact policy that could be characterized as elitist while Democratic-Republicans and Democrats erected policy that tended more toward egalitarianism (at least until the late 1950s). In this context, therefore, I use the party affiliation of elected officials (when viewed in the context of New York State political history) as a surrogate for an in-depth policy content analysis similar to the one that Earle did for *The American Way.* This is justifiable, I believe, because my task here is not to construct a full-blown geo-political history of New York State, but instead to use Earle's model as a means to identify and reconsider key moments in Erie Canal history.

To ascertain whether or not New York state politics has displayed a rhythm similar to the one suggested by Earle's dialectical policy regime model, I have created the "elected seat integration index" (ESII). This index is deduced by recording on an annual basis (from 1789 to 2006) the political party affiliation of the New York State Governor, the two U.S. Senators from New York State, and the party of the majority of U.S. House of Representatives from New York State. (A possible refinement to the index includes annual evaluation of the New York State Senate and Assembly, but that is a major undertaking that I am leaving for a future project.) The index also considers how well the above political slate meshes with the party affiliation of the U.S. President as well as the majority parties in the entire U.S. Senate and the entire House of Representative. The annual results suggest the party leanings of the New York state electorate. Given fluctuations in the index (noise in the data), I have identified and graphed general trends by calculating the index average by decade for each party (figure 6.1).

Low values for the ESII indicate a lack of party dominance within the state and little correlation between the party of state officials and the party of the U.S. President and congressional majorities. High values indicate party

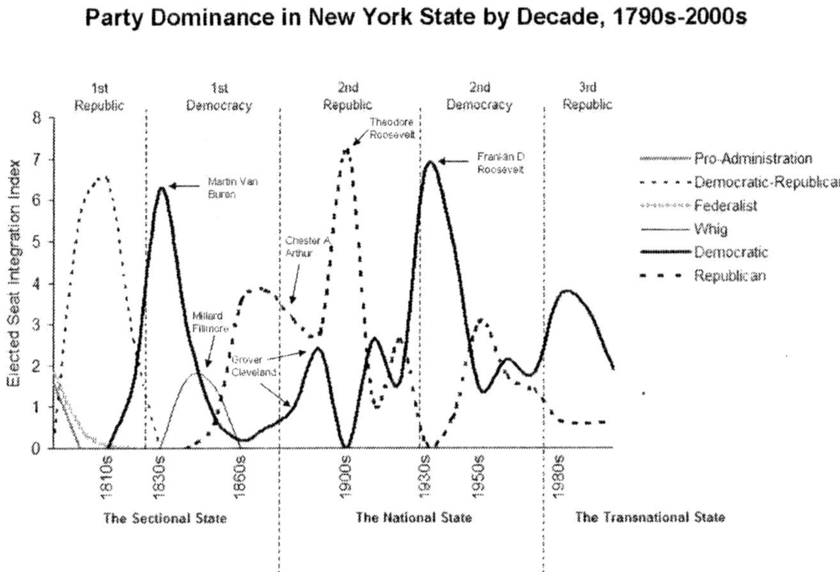

Figure 6.1. Party Dominance in New York State by Decade, 1790s–2000s

dominance within the state and a strong correlation between the party of state officials and the party of the U.S. President and congressional majorities. Medium values indicate either: (1) party dominance within the state but little correlation between the parties of state officials and the U.S. President and congressional majorities; or (2) strong correlation between the parties of state officials and the U.S. President and congressional majorities, but lack of party dominance within New York State. Also indicated in figure 6.1 are the six "New York Presidencies": Martin Van Buren (1837–1841), Millard Fillmore (1850–1853), Grover Cleveland (1885–1889, 1893–1897), Chester A. Arthur (1881–1885), Theodore Roosevelt (1901–1909), and Franklin Delano Roosevelt (1933–1945). These presidencies help to explain some aspects of the ESII and further link the party curves to well known historical moments in American history.

Considered simultaneously, the ESII curves for each political party suggest a cyclical rhythm to New York state politics that at times corresponds to the one suggested by Earle's dialectical policy regime model. Three points must be made, the first concerning the peaks in party influence in New York State and their relationship to the New York Presidencies. The three highest peaks reflect electoral "coat-tail" effects during decades when U.S. Presidents hailed from New York State (Martin Van Buren, Theodore Roosevelt, and Franklin Delano Roosevelt). At these points, the native son's popularity helped carry other party members into federal and New York state office (Morris 1979; Rayback 1983; Watkins 1999).

The peaks, however, are smaller for Millard Fillmore, Grover Cleveland and Chester Arthur. Fillmore, vice-president and a member of the Whig Party, was never popularly elected as president; he assumed the office after President Zachary Taylor's death. Nor was his party in existence very long, the Whig Party having grown out of opposition to the Jacksonians in the 1830s and 1840s. It essentially fizzled out nationally during the 1850s over disagreements about the issue of slavery (Holt 1999).

Cleveland, a Democrat, has the distinction of being the only president to serve two non-consecutive terms of office—one during the 1880s and the other during the 1890s. The middling position of the Democratic Party's ESII at this point reflects a temporal dilution of Cleveland's influence spread over two decades (whereas most of the other presidencies occurred over a single decade); of course, the middling position of the index may also reflect Cleveland's classically liberal stance (international free-trade, domestic elitism) that made him operate similarly to some of the Republicans who held office during the Second Republic. New York voters could vote for him as a Democrat and stay true to their Republican consciences (Faulkner 1959).

Similar to Fillmore, Arthur (a Republican vice-president who was widely distrusted when he came into office owing to a number of questionable episodes in his early political career) only assumed the presidency after James Garfield's assassination; the middling position of the Republican Party's ESII at this point reflects not only ambivalence within New York state over party preference but also the diluting impact of sharing the decade of his presidency with New York Democrat Grover Cleveland (Reeves 1975).

More important are the three New York-based presidents who helped to generate high peaks in their parties' strength (Van Buren, Theodore Roosevelt, and Franklin D. Roosevelt). Significantly, each one played a role in the life of the Erie Canal during the time in their careers when they were earning their political stripes at the New York state level.

As might be expected from a good egalitarian, as a New York State senator, Van Buren initially opposed the Erie Canal because he believed that it was too risky and would, if successful, only benefit Upstaters. He ultimately convinced the state legislature that the canal should be built in segments; tolls generated by the already-completed portions would help defray the cost of additional segments (Bernstein 2005). (Van Buren's lifelong engagement with infrastructure definitely merits additional research; apparently his attitude on "internal improvements" flip-flopped several times during the course of his political career in the U.S. Senate and as president.)

Moving forward in time to the 1890s, elitist (albeit a rather weak one) Governor Teddy Roosevelt commissioned a major study of the entire New York state canal system in response to growing concerns that the state was feeding a white elephant that could not possibly continue to compete with the railroads (Whitford, Williams, and New York (State). State Engineer and Surveyor. 1922). The study also came on the heels of a major embezzlement scandal associated with an aborted piecemeal widening of the canal's main trunk line during the early 1890s. The report concluded that a New York canal could still serve an important role—particularly because it offered competition to the railroad and its presence served as an indirect form of state price intervention. However, the system itself was completely outdated. New port facilities (including modern grain elevators) needed to be constructed, the canal prism needed to be widened and deepened, and—most of important of all, the stone masonry lining needed to be scrapped in favor of canalized rivers and cement-lined locks and trenches that could withstand the wakes created by engine-driven boats (Larkin et al. 2001). (Up to this point, traffic on the Erie Canal was still pulled by mule.) TR threw his support behind the report and did not waiver in his enthusiasm even after he had left office to become William McKinley's vice president. The New York State Barge Canal thus owes its existence partly to his efforts; further, what Roosevelt learned about canals from this exercise seems also to have played a role in his political position on the construction of the Panama Canal (Grasso and Vaala 2003).

TR's cousin, Franklin Delano Roosevelt, viewed and used the canal somewhat differently. On the one hand, the canal system served a very personal purpose. He used it—a state facility—instead of the privately owned railroads to conduct state-wide tours as both candidate and governor, thus allowing him to be a stronger critic of the railroads and avoiding accusations of preference toward any particular company. On the other hand (and as we will see below), FDR used the canal as a means to non-transportation-related ends. As governor, for example, FDR authorized a program that put the unemployed back to work filling in large segments of the old Erie Canal. He also joined ranks with other Great Lakes states politicians (including his Democratic gubernatorial predecessor Al Smith) and entrepreneurs who argued that the New York State Barge Canal needed to be "federalized," widened and deepened yet again in order to create an "All-American" shipping lane that would run from Oswego on Lake Ontario to Albany on the Hudson River (Mosher In preparation-b). Handing the canal over to the federal government would help stem the drain on the state's coffers and the expected federal improvements would be a boon to central and eastern Upstate New York. The New York State legislature even went as far as to pass legislation in April 1930 that would allow for the intergovernmental transfer of responsibility to occur.

As president, however, FDR changed course on the canal—arguing that it should not be federalized. Government funds would be better spent, in his opinion, on a joint international venture (with Canada) that would create the St. Lawrence Seaway. The Seaway itself wasn't the prize in all of this, even though Great Lakes grain dealers really wanted it so they could more easily participate in the liberal free-market international economy that FDR was helping to erect. Rather, what FDR wanted out of the St. Lawrence Seaway project was the right for the United States to generate hydroelectric power along the St. Lawrence River. This cheap power would benefit the entire industrial northeast (and hence, the entire nation). Thus Roosevelt, like Martin Van Buren before him, reversed position on the canal—in this case putting national concerns above more sectional ones once the spatial scope of his responsibilities widened from New York State to the entire nation.

A second point to be made from the ESII for New York State concerns two apparent inversions in policy regime sequencing—once under the Sectional State and then again under the Transnational State. In both cases, New Yorkers elected several decades-worth of politicians to state and federal office who were slightly-to-completely (depending upon the individual in question) out of step with the overarching federal-level policy regime. In the case of the Sectional State, this may reflect New York State's relative disinterest in the concept of national federation when compared to ten of the original U.S. states (Shechter 1985). It may also reflect the presence of a large population of renters and small landowners who wished to dismantle the feudal-like social system that had been in place in the Hudson Valley since the beginning of Dutch colonization (Meinig 1966).

In the case of the Transnational State, the inversion reflects the election of mainly Democrats during: (1) three Republican presidencies (five terms in all); (2) more than a decade of Republican domination over the U.S. Congress; and (3) three terms of a Republican governor. However, this is not a strong inversion with Democrats autocratically ruling the local day. A closer look at the policy enacted at the state level during this period indicates a preference for fiscal conservativism, brought on by concerns over how to fund in perpetuity the behemoth public infrastructural system that the Second Democracy created. This shift toward fiscal conservativism makes New York like much of the rest of the nation (Schneier and Murtaugh 2001).

What sets New York apart from many other states, however, is continued popular support for a number of socially progressive issues—including the existence of spatially diffuse educational and health care systems that serve people close to where they live, as well as belief in things like women's reproductive rights, gun control, and anti-smoking legislation. New Yorkers share these concerns with the majority of the electorate in some other northeastern states, thus creating a swath of "Blue (Democratic) States" across the traditional American industrial core as depicted in the famous 2000, 2004, and 2008 presidential election outcome maps. The popular interpretation of these maps is that the country is on the verge of being torn apart again by deep ideological and regional divisions (Farhi 2004; Frank 2004; Klinkner 2004).

Although interesting, the Blue State/Red State map is a cartographic contrivance. If election results are considered at the county or precinct level, a different pattern emerges. This also happens if the binary blue-red classification scheme is expanded to include shades of purple that indicate varying degrees of strength for the two candidates (Democratic candidate = blue and blueish purples; Republican candidate = red and reddish purples.) What emerges from these maps is a picture of the Downstate/Upstate divide that Erie Canal tourist operators are latching onto with their "other New York state of mind" tagline. New York City tends more toward Democratic blue with surrounding suburbs a mixture of magenta and burgundy. Upstate tends ever-so-slightly toward the Republican red, with notable sprinklings of dark magenta and burgundy around blue centers in Albany, Syracuse, Rochester, Ithaca, and Buffalo (Vanderbei n.d.).

Aesthetically pleasing as the "Purple Map" is, there is a working reality to the Blue/Red divide when it comes to New York's engagement in federal politics. By electing Democrats to a Congress where the balance of power was held by Republicans during much of the 1990s and 2000s, New Yorkers saw some erosion in their ability to bring home federal "bacon." Upstate Republican Representatives, however, parlayed their party affiliation and their House seniority into key committee appointments that allowed them to direct federal money to their home districts. They (Representatives James Walsh and Sherwood Boehlert, in particular) were the ones who pushed for the creation of the Erie Canalway National Heritage Corridor (Schumer, Clinton, and Walsh 2003).

If Democrats have been pushing canal-related issues in Washington, they are certainly doing it with a lower profile than the Republicans. Exceptions include now-deceased Senator Daniel Patrick Moynihan and current New York State Attorney General Andrew Cuomo. In the late 1970s and early 1980s, the mounting push toward fiscal conservativism within the state had convinced many Upstaters that when forced to make hard choices, New York State would amend its constitution and abandon the canal completely given how little traffic it carried and because it was now one of a number of responsibilities shouldered by the New York State Department of Public Works (predecessor of the New York State Department of Transportation). Moreover, the Army Corps of Engineers had resurrected the call for federalization. Similar to FDR before him, during a state-wide canal boat tour,

Senator Moynihan lamented that the canal had deteriorated but felt quite strongly that this—the last working canal in the United States not owned and operated by the federal government—should stay in state hands (Perlez 1982). At various times during his nearly twenty-three years in the U.S. Senate, he used his influence to acquire federal funds that would help the state with repairs and upgrades (Mosher in preparation-a).

These infusions of congressional capital were sporadic, however. To solve the problem, in 1992 at the behest of Governor Mario Cuomo, the State transferred responsibility for the barge canal not to the federal government as some had feared, but to the New York State Thruway Authority, where it would supposedly be "protected" from the funding vacillations linked to electoral politics, where thruway tolls could be used to fund consistently the canal's operation and maintenance, and where the Thruway Authority could bundle the I-90 New York State Thruway and the Erie Canal into a regional economic development plan for Upstate. What the transfer has meant, however, is that the canal has become part of the strange, almost-untouchable and quite legendary world of the New York State public authorities (Caro 1975; Heiman 1988).

Remember the comedic movie gesture in the 1997 Barry Sonnenfeld film *Men in Black* that put MIB's New York City headquarters inside the exhaust fan station of the Triborough Bridge and Tunnel Authority's Brooklyn-Battery Tunnel? As Zed, the MIB director explains during James Edwards's initiation into MIB (in that very building), "You are no longer part of 'the system.' We're above the system. Over it. Beyond it." This dialogue plays upon the popular understanding that New Yorkers have regarding public authorities (like Triborough) within their state. The public authorities are somehow beyond control, even by the state government. Their perceptions were only confirmed in 2003 when it came to light that the Canal Corporation, a subsidiary of the Thruway Authority, had entered into an illegal contract with Buffalo businessman Richard Hutchens that had awarded Hutchens exclusive residential development rights on state land along the *entire* barge canal route—from Buffalo to Albany *and* along remaining feeders (Mosher in preparation-c). Evidence had been brought to the State Comptrollers office indicating that Hutchens had lobbied the Canal Corporation in the mid-1990s for this right and that the Corporation's ensuing public solicitation was based largely on one of his proposals. Of the thirty-three parties who responded to the Corporation's solicitation, only three received any follow-up contact from the Canal Corporation about the matter, whereas the Canal Corporation insisted to state auditors that it had contacted them all. Luckily, the comptroller's office had the authority to rescind the contract. When this happened, Comptroller Alan Hevesi (Democrat) said,

> Development along the Erie Canal will be an important part of upstate economic development efforts in the coming years. But there is no excuse for not giving every potential developer an equal opportunity to compete for the right to build. When the State offers a valuable opportunity, it must use a fair and open competitive process to award it. That is not only in the interest of fairness for the vendors, but also to ensure that the taxpayers receive the best possible deal. (Office of the New York State Comptroller 2003)

Clearly, in less than two decades a perceptual shift regarding the canal had taken place. Going from being forgotten and taken for granted, it now was being viewed as a potential social and economic asset.

In the mid-1990s, around the time that Hutchens approached the Canal Corporation, Clinton Administration Housing and Urban Development Secretary Andrew Cuomo's was devising his own Erie Canal strategy that would help develop its potential as a social and economic asset. In October 1997 he announced the Erie Canal Initiative—a program that made over $130 million in federal grant money available to 57 communities along the Erie Canal for the development of heritage tourism and recreation resources. Although I have yet to learn about the actual implementation of this program and its effectiveness, many New York Republicans at the time speculated that Cuomo was interested in the canal only as a means to foster political support around Upstate for a future gubernatorial bid—which did indeed happen, unsuccessfully, in 2002 (Cuomo—who was elected to the office of New York State Attorney in 2006—is the eldest son of Mario Cuomo, who served as New York State Governor between 1983 and 1995). There is some evidence, however, that the money his program provided helped build a cooperative network of Erie Canal communities who, with the support of Republican U.S. House Representatives, successfully lobbied Congress for the establishment of the Erie Canalway National Heritage Corridor in 2000.

The third and final point related to political party dominance in New York State concerns the early onset of the Second Republic and Democracy under the National State. Both anticipate the national shift by a decade or more. In the case of the Second Republic, the shift may have occurred early because of the prolonged democratic phase during the Sectional State era, time enough for New York state politicians to enact a policy regime that had raised social expectations, changed cultural values about the meaning of citizenship, substantially reworked the existing infrastructural system so as to make it more egalitarian, but that also led not only New York State but the entire nation into major crisis (Klein and New York State Historical Association 2001). By the 1840s, Martin Van Buren's "Albany Regency" within the New York Democratic Party could not sustain control over the legislative process—due largely to mounting concerns over the State's fiscal solvency. The State had deepened, widened and realigned the Erie Canal along much of its course and was building numerous feeder lines that would penetrate every corner of the state. Tolls, however, were not increasingly relative to this construction due to the competition posed by improved roads and the nascent railroad system. If this wasn't enough, by the 1850s, the Democratic Party's problems took on an ideological dimension. The national organization contended that the issue of slavery should be left to the western territories to decide when they achieved statehood. Downstate Tammany Hall Democrats tended to align with this position, due to New York City's heavy involvement in the southern cotton industry and ancillary trades. Upstate Democrats, however, tended to gravitate more toward the newly emerged Republican Party stance (that federal—not state—decree should abolish the practice of slavery at once and for all). In 1860, a bipartisan coalition of Upstate voters and Downstate Republicans narrowly decided (by a margin of 8 percent) the issue—not only for New York state but for the entire nation as well when they gave New York's 35 Electoral College votes to Lincoln. (Without these votes, the Illinoisan would not have been able to attain the 150 electoral seats needed to win. New Yorkers supplied a 28-vote surplus.) Shortly thereafter, southern states began seceding from the nation. In response, New Yorkers—particularly those Upstate—applied to the war effort the industrial and commercial assets that had originally developed because of the existence of the Erie Canal. They supplied armaments, uniforms, logistical and hierarchical leadership, financial capital, and thousands of soldiers. Republican New York State thus played a leading role in enforcing the concept of a federal union and, in the process, helped erect and dominate the economy and society that characterized Earle's National State after 1877.

New York also led the way out of the Second Republic and into the Second Democracy during the crisis of consumption that Earle identifies as the Great Depression of the 1930s. Although the early part of the crisis stemmed from wild fluctuations in New York City's financial market, Downstate's diversified economy was able to absorb the initial blows and the City did not feel the full effects until the winter of 1931–1932. By that time, however, Upstate localities had already suffered from factory layoffs and closures, bank foreclosures, out-migration and a drastically eroded tax base (Watkins 1999). New York State Governor Franklin D. Roosevelt initially responded by pushing legislation that would stabilize industry. But as the crisis wore on, mayors and county executives pressed for a state bailout that would help financially strapped municipalities that (along with private charitable concerns) could no longer meet their traditionally accepted responsibility for the "worthy poor." The number of unemployed and vagrant persons had simply grown too large.

As a consequence, in October 1931 the state legislature and FDR created the New York State Temporary Emergency Relief Administration, an agency that indirectly re-distributed state aid to the poor without creating a New York version of the British dole (New York State Temporary Emergency Relief Administration 1934a, 1934b, 1937; Mosher 2006). The philosophy behind their actions was the largely bi-partisan belief that most New Yorkers would rather go hungry than accept charity; what the unemployed really wanted was to work. Thus TERA provided funds to municipalities for state-approved but local proposed "make work" projects.

Even though municipalities struggled with a process that became a direct forerunner of the modern grant-in-aid leveraging process, TERA provided nearly five billion dollars in funds that went toward completion of a series of long-delayed municipal housekeeping tasks across New York State. As part of this, in several Upstate communities, TERA workers filled in the old Erie Canal that had been made obsolete by the construction of the New York State Barge Canal in the 1910s.

This process operated so efficiently in Rome, New York, that in 1933 then-Governor Herbert Lehman (D) and the TERA state-level director, Harry Hopkins, held Rome up as model for how a new "cooperative" form of intergovernmental relations could work. Notably, TERA's architects and administrators (including Hopkins) were the very same people whom FDR later tapped to create the alphabet soup of programs that became part of the New Deal after Roosevelt's election to the U.S. presidency in 1932 (Bremer 1975). Although these programs created all sorts of new infrastructure that would put New Yorkers back to work and provide services to the people of the state of New York for many years to come, it must be noted that with all of this construction had come destruction as well—a point that Earle explicitly embeds within the dialectical policy regime model.

In summation, the ESII suggests that three general eras exist within New York State political history: a Democratic-Republican/Democratic phase that extends from the late seventeenth century to the 1830s, a Whig/Republican phase from the 1840s through the 1910s, and a Democratic phase from the 1910s to the present day. Contained within these eras, of course, are fluctuations within party dominance as well as shifts in party platforms and operating practices. There are big differences, for instance, between the Second New York State Democratic Era as it existed under FDR's presidential administration when compared to how it existed during the presidency of George W. Bush. In the 1930s and 40s, the electorate, the Democratic Party, as well as the state itself, set the pace for the rest of the country politically, socially, economically and culturally. In the 2000s, however, New York seemingly has less influence (a trend that really began in the 1950s) (Martis and Elmes 1993). Of course, the second Bush's administration's handling of the wars in Afghanistan and Iraq and the national electorate's growing unhappiness with the direction that the country seems to be headed may signal a national shift back toward New York's democratic tendencies (although a single election year [2008] does not a trend make). Much depended on the outcome of the 2008 Presidential elections in which two New Yorkers battled it out for the top spot. Neither candidate, however, represented anything close to the extreme within their respective political parties. Rather, they each reflected the rather ambivalent tone of current New York State politics—fiscally conservative and socially moderate Rudolph Giuliani (R) versus fiscally moderate and socially progressive Hillary Rodham Clinton (D). If anything, both typify two different but quite similar slants on an American version of neoliberalism (Harvey 2005).

ASSESSING THE DIALECTICAL POLICY REGIME MODEL

Clearly, Earle's dialectical policy regime model functions as any good heuristic model should: it encourages one to rethink and refine analytical categories and forces comparison between logically deduced predictive outcomes and what seems to have occurred in real life. This particular model, however, presents some real challenges for application at a scale other than the national one that Earle so skillfully worked through for us in *The American Way.*

First, the model really necessitates a thorough understanding of not only the geographical development of a region, state or city over a very long historical timeframe, but also an equally good understanding of two centuries-worth of public policy. Having attempted to apply the model to the relatively "simple" case of the Erie Canal, my feeling is that I have only just scratched the surface and that further application of the model would best be done as a collaborative interdisciplinary team involving geographers, political historians, and political scientists. This realization makes me all the more appreciative of Earle's incredible effort to tackle the national-scale project single-handedly.

Second, the cyclical conceptualization of time that Earle embeds within the model makes it difficult to use the diachronic (chronologic) *and* synchronic (one time period) forms or argumentation that typify historical geography. Neither of those modes function very well and if used tend to obscure Earle's larger "we have all been here before" point. In fact, figuring out the organizational structure for this chapter has been one of the most challenging intellectual exercises I've ever under taken! It took several false starts to come to this realization: staying true to Earle's concern for dialectic tension between policy regimes means that application of this model to a region is not the same thing as working through a stage model, like Meinig's "American West Model," or Whebell's "Corridor Theory of Urban Systems," in the context of a region like the Upper Mississippi Valley (Meinig 1972; Whebell 1969; Sheridan 1983). What this model encourages is historical comparison: what do moments in American history, separated by fifty to sixty years from each other, have in common? How do the spatial patterns in existence at these moments compare? Are they similar? If not, why are they different? While historians are quite adept at this sort of argumentation, for historical geographers this seems to be outside the normal mode of operation. And perhaps this underscores another possible difference between historical geography and geographical history.

Third, the fact that the policy regime timing and sequencing that Earle proposes doesn't work perfectly at the New York state level really begs the question that Earle alludes to but never really answers in *The American Way*: what impact does the structure of federalism have on the implementation of policy regimes? That is, to what extent do intergovernmental relations between different jurisdictional levels matter to the process of crisis and recovery that Earle describes? As political scientist Daniel Elazar argued, the nature of intergovernmental relations within U.S. federalism has changed form several times (Elazar 1981). These changes have profound implications for how federal policy gets articulated where people actually live. Further, each U.S. state has a different (and ever changing) philosophy regarding how and under what circumstances it will engage the federal system. Within individual states, certain state agencies have reputations of playing better with minor civil divisions and with the fed than others. Is it any wonder then that Earle chose to bypass the quandary of the Fifty States to look instead at the articulation of federal policy at the scale of the city? Given the relative disengagement of the individual U.S. states from the affairs of the cities found within them (reflecting something similar to the "Stadtluft macht frei" [city air makes a person free] mentality of the Medieval period within western Europe), the federal government has long played an important role in urban affairs—especially in the Second Democracy and Third Republic (Vance 1990). The city scale thus makes a better proving ground for understanding how policy regimes translate into spatial patterns and built environment. States, however, constitute a different sort of challenge.

Still, there is concordance between Earle's dialectical policy regime model and the geographical historical development of the Erie Canal

<table>
<tr><th></th><th>Earle's State Definitions</th><th>National Policy Regime Phases</th><th>Earle's Predicted Geosophies toward Infrastructure</th><th>Eras of New York State Political Party Dominance</th><th colspan="6">Erie Canal Eras</th></tr>
<tr><td rowspan="6">← Synchronic Dimension →</td><td rowspan="2">Sectional State</td><td>First Republic
1790s-1820s/30s</td><td>Creation and extension</td><td rowspan="2">Democratic-Republican/Democratic Era
1790s-1840s</td><td colspan="6">Planning and Constructing Clinton's Ditch
1699-1825</td></tr>
<tr><td>First Democracy
1820s/30s-1878</td><td>Re-engineering, creative destruction, system redundancy</td><td colspan="6">System-wide Capacity Enlargement, Realignment, and Construction of Feeder Canals
1835-1862</td></tr>
<tr><td rowspan="3">National State</td><td rowspan="2">Second Republic
1880s-1930s</td><td rowspan="2">Creation and extension</td><td rowspan="2">Whig/Republican Era
1850s-1910s</td><td colspan="6">Piecemeal Capacity Enlargement
1895-1898</td></tr>
<tr><td colspan="6">Planning and Constructing the New York State Barge Canal
1899-1918</td></tr>
<tr><td>Second Democracy
1930s-1980</td><td>Re-engineering, creative destruction, system redundancy</td><td rowspan="2">Democratic Era
1910s-2000s</td><td colspan="2">All American Canal v. St. Lawrence Seeway
1930s-1950s</td><td colspan="2">Rationalist Administrative Reorganization
1920s-1960s</td><td colspan="2">Abandonment of Enlarged Clinton's Ditch
1920s-1930s</td></tr>
<tr><td>Transnational State</td><td>Third Republic
1980 to present</td><td>Creation and extension</td><td colspan="3">Re-imaging the Canal for Recreation and Heritage Tourism
1970s to present</td><td colspan="3">Federal Intervention, Public Authorities & Keno Capitalist Development
1980s to present</td></tr>
<tr><td></td><td colspan="10">← Diachronic Dimension →</td></tr>
</table>

Figure 6.2. Comparison of Earle's Dialectical Policy Regime Model and the Historical Development of the Erie Canal

(figure 6.2). Moreover, the federal policy context may not always have mattered in the daily operation of the canal, but the ability of the people of the State of New York to use the canal as a way to compete with other U.S. states for population and business has always been of utmost concern.

For me, the real value of Earle's dialectical policy regime model has been that it has guided me in new directions in my quest to research and write a geographical history of the twentieth- and twenty-first-century Erie Canal. The dialectical policy regime model pushes me to go far beyond the "social production of the built environment" perspective that I had previously been using. As I mentioned at the outset, little academic work has been done on the canal during this period and what has been done sidesteps political questions almost entirely—and I was about to do the same thing. Further, within that historiography, the twentieth century becomes a time simply of decline and then eventual rebirth due to heritage tourism, when in fact application of Earle's model has led me to believe that there was a lot more going on than that. I had acknowledged as interesting the issues related to ongoing administrative restructuring due to state devolution, the push for real-estate development, and the canal's role in international relations as but had not really considered that they might be part of the landscape-driven story that I was going to tell. Now, I think that they are *the* story of the social production of landscape along the New York State's twentieth and twenty-first century canals.

Further to this, Earle has led me to believe that current Upstate marketing and regional branding efforts (largely being conducted under the auspices of federal and private initiatives) are not simply part of an economic development strategy but are also a form of a Protectionist Elitist Republicanism that is intended to create areal functional specialization and make Upstate a beneficiary of regional functional interdependency. The periphery is trying to take advantage of the core. Although things may be different Downstate in the Democratic-leaning Big Apple, for the "Apple Knockers" who live in the Erie Canal communities of "Low Bridge" fame, the Third Republic has definitely arrived.

NOTE

1. I find it interesting and curious that Earle did not include in his discussion the Adams model of American city structure, especially given how closely linked the Adams and Borchert models have become in the standard urban geography curriculum. Adams (1970), like Earle, links his empirical analysis to economic cycles and presents a graphic rendition of the model that is remarkably similar to Earle's. Adams

theorizations about policy, however, link mainly to federal building finance programs and not to broader concerns of political philosophy.

BIBLIOGRAPHY

Adams, J. S. 1970. "Residential Structure of Midwestern Cities," *Annals of the Association of American Geographers* 60, no. 1:37–62.

Aitken, H. G. J. 1952. "Financing the Welland Canal: An Episode in the History of the St. Lawrence Waterway," *Bulletin of the Business Historical Society* 26 no 3.

American Planning Association. 2007. *Pathways in American Planning History: A Thematic Chronology*. <http://www.planning.org/pathways/regional.htm>.

Bernstein, P. L. 2005. *Wedding of the waters: the Erie Canal and the making of a great nation*. 1st ed. (New York: W.W. Norton).

Borchert, J. R. 1967. "American Metropolitan Evolution," *Geographical Review* 57, no 3:301–332.

Bremer, W. W. 1975. "Along the 'American Way': The New Deal's Work Relief Programs for the Unemployed," *Journal of American History* 62 no 3:636–652.

Caro, R. A. 1975. *The Power Broker: Robert Moses and the Fall of New York*. (New York: Random House).

Earle, C. 1992. *Geographical Inquiry and American Historical Problems* (Stanford U. Pr).

———. 2003. *The American Way: A Geographical History of Crisis and Recovery*: (Lanham, MD: Rowman & Littlefield).

Elazar, D. J. 1981. "The Evolving Federal System," *Proceedings of the Academy of Political Science* 34, no 2:5–19.

Farhi, P. 2004. "Elephants Are Red, Donkeys Are Blue, Color Is Sweet, So Their States We Hue," *Washington Post*, November 2, C01.

Faulkner, H. U. 1959. *Politics, Reform and Expansion, 1890–1900*. (New York: Harper & Row).

Frank, T. 2004. *What's the Matter with Kansas? How Conservatives Won the Heart of America* (New York: Metropolitan Books).

Grasso, T. X., and L. Vaala. 2003. "Who is the "Father of Today's Erie Canal?" *Canal Town Clarion* 1 no 2:1–3.

Harvey, D. 2005. *A Brief History of Neoliberalism*. (New York: Oxford University Press).

Heiman, M. K. 1988. *The quiet evolution: power, planning, and profits in New York (*New York: Praeger).

Holt, M. F. 1999. *The Rise and Fall of the American Whig Party: Jacksonian Politics and the Onset of the Civil War*. (New York: Oxford University Press).

Klein, M. M., and New York State Historical Association. 2001. *The Empire State: a history of New York*. (Ithaca; Cooperstown: Cornell University Press; New York State Historical Association).

Klinkner, P. A. 2004. "Red and Blue Scare: The Continuing Diversity of the American Electoral Landscape," *The Forum* 2, no 2.

Kondratieff, N. 1935. "The Long Wave in Economic Life," *Review of Economic Statistics* 17:105–115.

Konvitz, J. W. 1985. *The urban millennium: the city-building process from the early Middle Ages to the present.* (Carbondale: Southern Illinois University Press).

Larkin, F. D., J. Daniels, J. West, and New York State Archives Partnership Trust. 2001. *Erie Canal: New York's gift to the nation: a document-based teacher resource.* 1st ed. (Peterborough, NH; Albany, NY: Cobblestone Pub. Co.: New York State Archives Partnership Trust).

"Lockport Locks and Erie Canal Cruises." *Banquets and Parties* 2007, <http://www.llecc.com/banquets.html> (December 2007).

Martis, K. C., and G. A. Elmes. 1993. *The Historical Atlas of State Power in Congress, 1790–1990.* (Washington, D.C.: Congressional Quarterly, Inc).

McFee, M. A. 1998. *A long haul: the story of the New York State Barge Canal.* (Fleischmanns, N.Y.: Purple Mountain Press).

Meinig, D. W. 1966. "The Colonial Period, 1609–1775". *Geography of New York State*, edited by. J. H. Thompson. (Syracuse: Syracuse University Press).

———. 1972. "American Wests: Preface to a Geographical Interpretation," *Annals of the Association of American Geographers* 62, no 2:159–184.

———. 1986. *Atlantic America, 1492–1800.* Vol. 1, *The shaping of America: a geographical perspective on 500 years of history.* (New Haven: Yale University Press).

———. 1992. *Continental America, 1800–1867.* Vol. 2, *The shaping of America: a geographical perspective on 500 years of history.* (New Haven: Yale University Press).

———. 1998. *Transcontinental America, 1850–1915.* Vol. 3, *The Shaping of America.* (New Haven: Yale University Press).

———. 2004. *Global America, 1915–2000.* Edited by T. s. o. A. a. g. p. o. y. o. history. (New Haven: Yale University Press).

Miller, R. B. 1979. *City and hinterland: a case study of urban growth and regional development.* (Westport, CT: Greenwood Press).

Morris, E. 1979. *The Rise of Theodore Roosevelt.* (New York: Ballentine).

Mosher, A. E. 2004. *Capital's utopia: Vandergrift, Pennsylvania, 1855–1916, Creating the North American landscape.* (Baltimore: Johns Hopkins University Press).

———. 2006. "Low Bridge!/No Bridge!: The Temporary Emergency Relief Administration and the Erie Canal at Rome, 1931–1934". (presented in *Conference on New York State History.* New York City).

———. In Preparation-a. New Regionalism and the Shifting Geography of Federalism: The Case of the Erie Canalway National Heritage Corridor.

———. In preparation-b. The Shifting Inter-Scalar Politics of Federalism: The Debate over the All-American Canal and St. Lawrence Seaway

———. In Preparation-c. State Devolution and the Emerging Geography of Regional Keno Capitalism: The Case of the Erie Canal

Mower, E. 2003. Welcoming Address. In *Erie Canal Convocation.* (Utica, New York).

Nash, B. 2000. The Erie Canal In *Modern Marvels*: History Channel.

New York State Temporary Emergency Relief Administration. 1934a. Emergency Relief in the State of New York: Statutes, Regulations, and Opinions and Interpretations of Counsel: New York State.

———. 1934b. Relief Activities of City and County Welfare Districts in Cooperation with the State Temporary Emergency Relief Administration, November 1, 1931–December 31, 1933: New York State.

———. 1937. *Five million people, one billion dollars. Final report of the Temporary emergency relief administration, November 1, 1931–June 30, 1937 . . . June 30, 1937.* (Albany, NY).

Office of the New York State Comptroller. 2003. Hevesi Rescinds Approval Of Canal Corp. Contract With Hutchens Because Agency Provided False & Misleading Information October 20th).

Perlez, J. 1982. Moynihan Mixes Politics And History on Boat Trip. *New York Times*, September 6, 21.

Porter, R. O., and C. E. Garrow. 2005. *Legal and Policy Analysis Associated with Migrating Indigenous Peoples: Assessing the Impact on the Haudenosaunee Within New York State--Discussion Draft. In Working Paper Series* (Syracuse: The Center for Indigenous Law, Governance & Citizenship at Syracuse University College of Law).

Rayback, J. C. 1983. Martin Van Buren: His Place in the History of New York and the United States. *New York History* 64:121–135.

Reeves, T. C. 1975. *Gentleman Boss: The Life of Chester Alan Arthur.* (New York: Knopf).

Schein, R. H. 1989. A Historical Geography of Central New York: Patterns and Processes of Colonization on the New Military Tract, 1782–1820. Thesis (Ph.d.), (Syracuse University).

Schneier, E., and J. B. Murtaugh. 2001. *New York Politics: A Tale of Two States.* (Armonk, NY: M.E. Sharpe).

Schumer, C., H. R. Clinton, and J. Walsh. 2003. Congress Approves $600,000 for Erie Canal *Heritage Corridor Commission.*

Shaw, D. 2004. *City building on the eastern frontier: sorting the new nineteenth-century city, Creating the North American landscape.* (Baltimore: Johns Hopkins University Press).

Shechter, S. L., ed. 1985. *The Reluctant Pillar: New York State and the Federal Constitution.* (Troy: Council for Citizenship Education, Russell Sage College).

Sheridan, A. M. 1983. The Development of Nucleated Settlement Systems: The Case of the Upper Mississippi Valley, 1800–1860, *Geography,* (Pennsylvania State University, University Park, PA).

Sheriff, C. 1996. *The artificial river: the Erie Canal and the paradox of progress, 1817–1862.* 1st ed. (New York: Hill and Wang).

Vance, J. E. 1995. *The North American Railroad: its origin, evolution, and geography.* (Baltimore: Johns Hopkins University Press).

Vance, J. E., Jr. 1990. *The Continuing City: Urban Morphology in Western Civilization.* (Baltimore: Johns Hopkins University Press).

Vanderbei, R. J. 2007. *Election 2004 Results* n.d., May 10, 2007. <http://www.princeton.edu/~rvdb/JAVA/election2004/>.

Wallner, P. A. 1973. *Politics and Public Works: a Study of the Pennsylvania Canal System, 1825–1857 History*, (Pennsylvania State University, University Park, PA).

Watkins, T. H. 1999. *The hungry years: a narrative history of the Great Depression in America*. 1st ed. (New York: Henry Holt & Co).

Whebell, C. F. J. 1969. "Corridors: A Theory of Urban Systems," *Annals of the Association of American Geographers* 59 (1):1–26.

Whitford, N. E., New York (State). State Engineer and Surveyor., M. M. Beal, and United States. Dept. of the Treasury. Bureau of Statistics. 1906. *History of the canal system of the state of New York, together with brief histories of the canals of the United States and Canada*. (Albany, NY: Brandow printing company).

Whitford, N. E., F. M. Williams, and New York (State). State Engineer and Surveyor. 1922. *History of the barge canal of New York State*. (Albany, NY: J. B. Lyon, printers).

Wright, J. K. 1947. Terrae Incognitae: The Place of Imagination in Geography. *Annals of the Association of American Geographers* 37, no. 1:1–15.

Chapter Seven

The Interplay of Manufacturing Employment and Population Concentrations in the United States, 1840–1990

Samuel M. Otterstrom

The development of the population landscape in the United States has been marvelously complex. The tremendous variety of historical geographies at work can belie some basic forces that have influenced population growth in all parts of the country. The effect of manufacturing location on population and settlement patterns is one factor that deserves attention. People settle in environments that will provide them a living, and employment opportunities arise where there are people. The introduction of manufacturing can radically expand the carrying capacity of an area once reliant on agriculture and local services. Together, these factors can bring about the multiplication of residents in urban areas where there was once a lower population threshold; however, it is less clear how relative concentrations of manufacturing jobs relate temporally to shifting population concentration patterns.

To help answer the question of relative timing, this research provides a comprehensive baseline analysis of national and regional population and manufacturing concentration patterns and relationships from 1840 to 1990 using data derived from a historical United States GIS. I reason that manufacturing employment concentration in the United States was an important precursor to greater population concentration, and that over time, manufacturing and population concentration levels have converged because of both urbanization and manufacturing dispersion.

Carville Earle (2003) argued for the connection of his political regimes to the spatial attributes of the economic and urban society in the United States. In considering Moran's *I* statistic (Moran 1948) as a measurement of spatial concentration in population he stated:

> In the first American state (1780–1880), concentration reaches its highest levels at the end of the First Republic (to 1830) and then, after a half century of

> demographic dispersion during the First Democracy, falls to its lowest level in 1880. The cycle is repeated in the second American state (1880–1980); spatial concentration rises sharply in the 1880s with the installation of the Second Republic and the rise of mass production (Earle 2003: 356).

In terms of manufacturing concentration Earle reasoned that concentrations in manufacturing were cyclical like population, but that they lagged the concentration trends of the populace by at least a decade (2003: 356). Earle uses the research of Kim (1998) to support this view. Kim measured the dispersion and concentration of different manufacturing industries among regions. In contrast to Earle, I argue that manufacturing concentrations did not follow population concentration, but were in actuality the harbingers of future population changes.

Besides the main issue of concentration timing, I will also address three other related questions: How concentrated was manufacturing employment between 1840 and 1990, and where was it the most concentrated? What were the trajectories of manufacturing concentration trends in relation to population concentration shifts? What is the significance of the changing differential between manufacturing and population concentration over time?

To address these questions, I outline the trends of concentration in manufacturing employment for U.S. counties at the national (contiguous United States), regional (census divisions), and city-system (major cities and their related hinterlands) levels from 1840–1990 (see Pred 1980 for a discussion of the nature of city-systems). I then compare these with population trends to determine how manufacturing employment concentration has related to population concentration. The process is straightforward and yields valuable results.

INFLUENCE OF MANUFACTURING ON POPULATION

Our understanding of the geographic relationship between population growth and manufacturing development is continually being clarified. In the economic history of the United States manufacturing has been a pivotal activity. Its apex has come and gone, but its role in moving the nation from an extractive and agrarian-based society to a nation dominated by services cannot be dismissed. The timing of manufacturing's ascent as a core economic activity in the United States underscores the part that industry played in bringing greater concentration or urbanization in landscapes of formerly scattered farmsteads and small cities. This effect appears evident even though manufacturing has never employed more than 50 percent of workers in this country. Because of its enduring impact, manufacturing continues to receive a tremendous amount of attention by researchers seeking to understand regional economic growth (Walker and Lewis 2001).

Manufacturing has been a catalyst to urbanization and to population concentration (Bogart 1998); not only did it provide large numbers of jobs focused in advantageous sites, but the new technologies and products made by this industry created new economic opportunities and industries. The agglomeration economies that developed in large cities accelerated this growth; cities that garnered early industrial firms had an advantage over other cities that did not adjust to the new economic realities (Pred 1966).

Many explanations have been proffered over the years as to the timing, impact, and spatial relationships of the manufacturing industry with ensuing settlement patterns. Through this process, scholars have developed a number of models that integrate various growth factors into their structure. The temporal appearance of manufacturing in these models ranges from late in the development process (Hoover and Fisher 1949), to a more intermediate position (North 1955; Muller 1976), to a very early and central role in population growth (Page and Walker 1991; Isard 1990; Leven 1993). Whenever manufacturing did enter into the growth equation, it is apparent that some cities and regions grew at the expense of others because of their geographic advantages and earlier entrances into the industrial scene (Pred 1965; Meyer 1983).

Other important factors have complemented the effect of manufacturing and have either constrained or enhanced population growth in regions. These include the dimensions of service economies, agricultural change, resource locations, transportation routes, trade patterns, attractiveness, and hinterland size. Many studies have considered these factors at a large scale (North 1961; Dunn 1980; Perloff et al. 1960; Duncan et al. 1960; Berry and Horton 1970). Other scholars have looked at specific regions (e.g., Muller 1977; Cronon 1991; Higgs 1969; Schnell and McLear 1972; Stobart 2000). Still others have emphasized one or a small number of important factors such as transportation (e.g., Vance 1970; Conzen 1975), attractiveness (Fotheringham et al. 2000), hinterland characteristics (Page 1998), and the connections of the frontier and city regions with various parts of the country (Pred 1976; Meyer 1980).

In all of the research that has been conducted on the factors behind settlement growth, one area of study that has received less attention is the significance of the spatio-temporal shifts in the relative distribution of people compared with these factors. We know that economic forces and geographic situations influence population patterns, but it is less clear how quickly population distributions change as a result of relevant influences. At this point, manufacturing employment data are the most complete of any of the possible explanatory variables for the time period in question; therefore, manufacturing is the focus of this study. Most of the arguments above concerning manufacturing's impact on population patterns show that when concentration in industry (industrialization) occurs, concentration of people (urbanization) follows (Walker and Lewis 2001). However, these analyses have not determined how long an imbalance in relative concentration lasts or how long it takes for similar levels of concentration in industry and population density to develop.

Thus, the theoretical construct of this chapter is comprised of three main threads of thought that I will illustrate in the succeeding sections. First, manufacturing in its initial manifestation is necessarily a more concentrated phenomenon than general population settlement. Second, people have become more concentrated partly by following manufacturing opportunities through migration away from the farm to urban industrial zones. Third, as the settlement landscape has matured from early to post-industrial patterns, manufacturing has tended to suburbanize, agglomerate, and disperse at the same time that population was first concentrating, and then, more recently, deconcentrating away from urban cores. This approach blends the Page and Walker (1991) argument that manufacturing and population grew together, with a disparity in the relative distribution of population and manufacturing across the nation from 1840 to 1990 that I reveal in this chapter. I illustrate how the incongruities of this spatial relationship diminished over time as the two population components converged in a time-lagged fashion that partly followed the cyclical patterns envisaged by Earle (2003), but which differed from his view in some important ways.

RATIONALE, DATA, AND METHODS

To show this theoretical relationship I need to accurately portray and analyze both large- and small-scale geographic trends over a long period of time. In this way, a clearer picture of the relative connections of population and manufacturing concentration can be explicated. Because of the complexity of this issue, one method and one scale are not sufficient to give a complete picture of manufacturing employment concentration and its relationship to population concentration. Therefore, I take a varied approach that explores this issue from a number of vantage points.

All data are at the county level and built into a historical GIS from a combination of historical US Censuses and a historical set of digital county maps known as *HUSCO 1790–1999* (Earle et al. 1999). Population data are from the decennial censuses from 1840 through 1990. Manufacturing employment data are from various censuses of manufactures administered nearest the decennial years. County areas are included in the *HUSCO* digital county boundary files for each decade with those from the nineteenth century being estimates calculated from the county boundary files themselves, while the county areas of the twentieth century were taken from the census tabulations. Alaska and Hawaii are not included in the analysis because of their late date of entry into the United States and their separation from the contiguous states of the country.

The total number of employees in manufacturing includes salaried workers and wage earners through 1900. After 1900, the total contains only wage earners and not salaried officials and clerks. The dates of the manufacturing censuses coincide with the years of the population censuses through 1890. The 1900, 1910, 1920, and 1930 manufacturing data are from the Census of Manufactures collected the year before (1899, 1909, 1919, and 1929). Data for 1940 through 1980 come from the digital version of the *County and City Data Book* (U.S. Census 1980) for the census years. The 1990 data are from the 1992 Census of Manufactures (see also appendix C).

In this chapter I follow three steps to assess the relationship between manufacturing and population concentration. The first step is to figure the Hoover concentration index of population and manufacturing employment for each census from 1840 onward using county data to illustrate city-system, regional, and national combinations (Hoover 1941), as well spatial autocorrelation concentration measures for all counties of the nation. The second step is to calculate differentials (the differences between Hoover indices of manufacturing employment concentration and population concentration) for each of these three spatial scales. These differentials provide relative values that can be easily compared with like figures from other regions across the country. Finally, I develop a general model of concentration relationship between manufacturing and population.

The first step includes using the Hoover index of concentration for manufacturing employment as well as for population. The Hoover index is valuable because it gives an easily understood picture of the relative distribution of a particular phenomenon across a landscape. I calculate the manufacturing employment and population Hoover index for the nation, all regions, and all city-systems, using county level data for each decade.[1] The historical GIS is integral here as it includes all counties from 1840 to 1990 with their attendant areas and populations. In every decade the GIS was used to determine what city-system or region each county fell within historically. This is important because boundaries were rapidly changing up until the early part of the twentieth century. Below is a short description of the Hoover index. It is calculated in the following manner:

> Let P_{it} be the fraction of a nation's [or other area's] population in sub-area I in year t and let a_i be this area's fraction of the nation's [or other area's] land area, and let there be k sub-areas. Then, the Hoover index, H_t is given by
>
> $$H_t = 2(\sum_{I=1}^{k} |P_{it} - a_i|) \times 100$$
>
> (Vining and Strauss 1976: 2)

The index has potential values from 0 to 100. High values mean a higher concentration of manufacturing employment (or people), or a very uneven distribution of such employees. Low values mean a low concentration of employees, or in other words, a landscape of more equally dispersed industry. In essence, the index indicates the percentage of manufacturing employees in the study area that would have to be moved across county lines to make an even distribution of employees. An increase in the Hoover index between decades likely means that manufacturing growth or relocation among counties was very uneven. On the other hand, a decreasing Hoover index value points to manufacturing jobs spreading to areas that were previously less densely filled with manufacturing. This occurrence could indicate either suburban growth in counties bordering metropolitan areas or expressly rural expansion in areas more distant from the regional cores.

How does the Hoover index of manufacturing employment relate to a Hoover index calculated for the total population? I address this question in the second step by calculating differentials. These differentials measure the spread between manufacturing employment concentration and population concentration for the same aggregation of counties. I compute these differentials for the nation, regions, and city-systems after calculating both the manufacturing employment and the population concentration indices.

The other concentration measure is spatial autocorrelation which is a helpful additional analytical resource. One weakness of the Hoover Index is that it cannot show the degree of clustering in population or manufacturing densities. For example, the Hoover index of two regions could be exactly the same, but the pattern of clustering could be quite different between the two. Thus, spatial autocorrelation can give us a valuable complementary view to the Hoover index. At the "global" level, the spatial autocorrelation measure (Moran's *I*) (Moran 1948) reports the degree of concentration or dispersion within the nation as a whole using county level population and manufacturing densities and spatial relationships. A positive Moran's *I* value (up to +1) points to "spatial" concentration, or a clustering of like densities in population or manufacturing employment, while a negative result (to –1) indicates dispersion or clustering of dissimilar values. A value near 0 indicates little or no spatial autocorrelation. A z-value test of the Moran's *I* statistic indicates statistical significance. I calculate global Moran's *I* statistics using the historical United States GIS of counties (and their changing boundaries) for each census year for both population density and manufacturing employment density to allow for an analysis of spatial autocorrelation differentials as well.

In my analysis I compare Earle's assessment of the timing of manufacturing concentration vis-à-vis his periodic model with my results that consider concentration and dispersion overall and not among different industries as Kim (1998) did. This will allow me to determine if national level manufacturing concentration trends have actually followed the regime cycle rubric that Earle proposed. In his model there should have been demographic dispersion during the First Democracy (between 1828 and 1877) and during the Second Democrary (1932–1970s). On the other hand there should have been concentration during the Second and Third Republics (1880s–1932 and 1980s onward, respectively) (Earle 2003: 350–351). Did manufacturing employment follow this pattern, or did population follow the lead of manufacturing in its spatial configuring?

Finally, after considering manufacturing concentrations and manufacturing versus population differences at national, regional, and city-system levels, I synthesize a model of the differentials' telling trends through time. Differentials are powerful measures that show how similar or dissimilar the concentration levels of manufacturing employment and population are. In other words, they illustrate the degree to which manufacturing employment concentration leads or lags behind population concentration. Differentials can also be compared across time and region because differentials control for geographical variations in county area or region makeup. When calculated, underlying variable spatial characteristics are canceled out when each population concentration index is subtracted from its related manufacturing employment index. Thus, differentials provide a clearer view of the temporal and spatial interactions and patterns of manufacturing employment concentration versus population concentration.

NATIONAL MANUFACTURING CONCENTRATION

At the national level, the major focus is to determine and analyze overall trends of manufacturing employment concentrations. The statistics from this level of geography are beneficial because they provide a baseline that averages out local population extremes. This baseline serves as a starting point for a comparison of national values with regional and city-system numbers. The baseline also shows the limits, intensity, and shifts of manufacturing concentration that signal significant transitions in the manufacturing sector and the settlement distribution of the population of the United States.

National Measures

Manufacturing employment has been quite concentrated among all counties in the nation since the first census of manufactures was taken (see table 7.1) (1820 statistics are included even though there is a gap in 1830 and 1840 marks the start of a more consistent tabulation of manufacturing by the census). In fact, manufacturing employment has been more concentrated than population concentration since 1840. This point is notable since population concentration levels have always been fairly high at the national scale. Even so, manufacturing employment's high concentration is reasonable in light of the more important role that urbanized areas have usually played in manufacturing growth (e.g., economies of scale and externalities) (Pred 1965).

The pattern of manufacturing concentration for the nation using county-level data has been one of high levels of employment concentration that have gradually shifted to lower levels. In 1840, the Hoover index of manufactur-

Table 7.1. National Hoover Index of Manufacturing Employment Concentration and Differentials with Population Concentrations (Man. – Pop)

Year	*Concentration*	*Differential*
1820	66.79 (86.32)	13.47
1830		
1840	64.35 (81.93)	19.07
1850	81.73 (83.81)	16.08
1860	79.48 (81.86)	19.94
1870	79.24 (79.82)	16.24
1880	81.46 (81.79)	22.61
1890	80.06	23.99
1900	78.55	23.90
1910	77.49	24.97
1920	77.99	24.11
1930	77.89	21.98
1940	76.56	20.23
1950	74.83	15.95
1960	72.54	10.94
1970	70.34	7.15
1980	67.49	5.54
1990	68.76	5.71

(Numbers in parentheses were figured using a contemporary (1970) total area)

(From 1890 on the total area of the country was essentially constant)

ing employment stood at 64.29. Ten years later, it had jumped to 81.73. This means that in 1850, nearly 82 percent of manufacturing jobs would have had to be relocated across the nation to make them evenly distributed. This high value was mostly due to the effect of the great increase of land enumerated by the census in the far West, which had little manufacturing activity at the time.[2] From this peak, the Hoover index has fallen during every decade except the 1870s, 1910s, and 1980s. In 1990 the index stood at 68.89, which remained above the national population Hoover index value (62.61). The trend line emphasizes that manufacturing continues to be a highly concentrated economic activity, but not to the degree that it was 150 years ago.

An analysis of the trends in spatial autocorrelation of all counties for each decade portrays a different, yet useful view of population settlement patterns compared with the Hoover results. Spatial concentration using Moran's *I* was quite low throughout the latter part of the nineteenth century (table 7.2). This low level continued until 1930. After 1930 there was a historic break from previous patterns marked by a very significant increase in autocorrelation, which paralleled the rise of manufacturing and decline of agriculture as important employment sectors across the nation. The decrease in autocorrelation between 1980 and 1990 may be attributed to both the overall loss of manufacturing employment during the 1980s and the movement of a large number of the remaining jobs to areas outside of traditional manufacturing regions.

Table 7.2. National Moran's *I* Spatial Concentration in Manufacturing Employment and Population with Differentials (1820–1990)

Year	*I-Man*	*Z-Man*	*Prob Man*	*I-Pop*	*Z-Pop*	*Prob-Pop*	*I-Diff*	*Z-Diff*
1820	0.0478	3.44	0.0006	0.0557	3.95	0.0001	–0.0079	–0.51
1830				0.0332	3.21	0.0013		
1840	0.0094	1.76	0.0784	0.0190	2.48	0.0133	–0.0096	–0.72
1850	0.0132	2.10	0.0361	0.0100	0.82	0.4094	0.0032	1.27
1860	0.0131	1.96	0.0499	0.0140	1.87	0.0618	–0.0009	0.09
1870	0.0126	1.76	0.0780	0.0170	2.05	0.0401	–0.0044	–0.29
1880	0.0087	1.38	0.1681	0.0162	1.96	0.0506	–0.0075	–0.58
1890	0.0082	1.26	0.2066	0.0174	2.12	0.0338	–0.0092	–0.86
1900	0.0190	2.26	0.0238	0.0337	3.63	0.0003	–0.0147	–1.37
1910	0.0367	4.34	0.0000	0.0480	5.34	0.0000	–0.0114	–0.99
1920	0.0148	3.44	0.0006	0.0247	4.11	0.0000	–0.0099	–0.67
1930	0.0153	3.45	0.0006	0.0710	8.97	0.0000	–0.0558	–5.52
1940	0.1217	13.39	0.0000	0.0831	10.33	0.0000	0.0386	3.06
1950	0.1104	13.00	0.0000	0.0887	11.04	0.0000	0.0217	1.96
1960	0.1738	19.10	0.0000	0.1570	17.58	0.0000	0.0169	1.52
1970	0.2212	23.86	0.0000	0.1907	20.95	0.0000	0.0305	2.91
1980	0.1962	23.12	0.0000	0.1928	21.94	0.0000	0.0034	1.18
1990	0.0324	7.36	0.0000	0.1922	22.05	0.0000	–0.1598	–14.69

(*I* scores, Z scores, Probabilities [Prob], and differentials [Diff] between Population [Pop] and Manufacturing [Man])

The differences between the Hoover index of concentration and the spatial autocorrelation measures are due, in part, to the way that concentration is measured by the indices. The Hoover index tends to rise when density increases disproportionately in one or more counties compared with other counties in the region (even if the counties are not contiguous); while at the same time, spatial autocorrelation tends to decrease because these same counties have become less like their neighbors. This contrast between the two methods helps explain the decline in spatial autocorrelation from 1970 to 1990 and the rise in the Hoover index from 1980 to 1990 (i.e., this difference shows evidence of manufacturing employment change in non-contiguous counties during the 1980s). Thus, using both methods to analyze manufacturing concentration over time gives a more complete picture of its changing geographical nature.

National Differentials

Plotting the differentials (differences) between the concentration measures of population and manufacturing employment reveals the important shift from a large gap in concentration to a very similar level of concentration of these two variables (table 7.1 and figure 7.1). The Hoover index differentials are high and variable until 1880; the differential peaks in 1910 when manufactur-

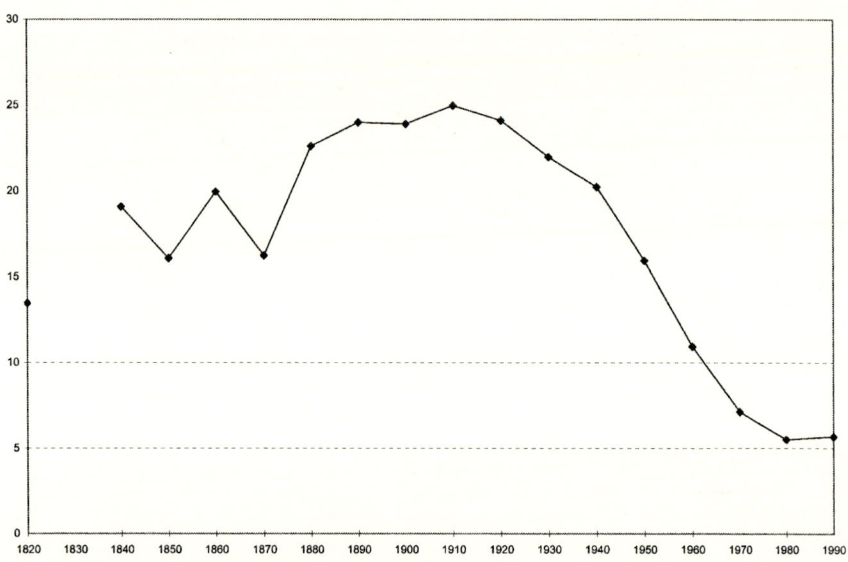

Figure 7.1. Differentials between National Manufacturing Employment and Population Concentration Hoover Index Values 1820–1990

ing employment was some 25 points more concentrated than population. The year 1910 marked the end of the frontier period of population deconcentration (Otterstrom 2003). After 1910, population began to concentrate while manufacturing employment began to spread more evenly. These two factors led to a large decrease in the differential until it reached its lowest point of 5.54 in 1980. The fact that manufacturing concentration and population concentration had become very much alike by 1990 is an indication of greater spatial equality in manufacturing employment distribution than ever before.

The trends in the differentials of the spatial autocorrelation Moran's *I* illustrate the similarities between population and manufacturing employment spatial concentration until the important shift that occurred from 1930 to 1940 (table 7.2). The slight edge that population held over manufacturing employment through most of the period before 1920, points to the more intense concentration of manufacturing in city centers (i.e., more dissimilarity between the urban centers and surrounding counties). Except for 1850, population exhibited slightly more spatial autocorrelation than manufacturing employment from 1840 through 1930. Between 1920 and 1930 manufacturing employment suffered losses in many areas, which allowed spatial concentration of manufacturing employment to remain low, while at the same time population spatial concentration increased because of the spread of urban areas.[3] This combination prompted a large decline in the differential.

From 1930 to 1940, the negative differential shifted abruptly to positive territory in which manufacturing concentration led population concentration. The substantial changes exhibited during this ten-year period may be related to the important role that government intervention played in stimulating economic growth in specific locations. The positive differential that developed in the 1930s continued through 1980, but was most significant through 1970. This positive trend reflects the large increases in manufacturing employment in suburban areas, thus increasing spatial clustering of counties with similar manufacturing employment densities.

During the 1980s spatial concentration of manufacturing employment dropped precipitously, resulting in the lowest differential for the whole study period, because of the opposite effects of rising population concentration combined with declining manufacturing employment spatial concentration. The large drop of manufacturing concentration mirrors the sizable losses in manufacturing employment in this decade.[4] So, in essence, the decline in manufacturing in the 1980s did not occur in a spatially uniform manner; Hoover-like concentration increased while spatial concentration decreased.

In summary, since 1840, manufacturing employment has generally tended to be much more concentrated than population according to the Hoover index. It was not until the twentieth century that population began to approach the concentration levels of manufacturing employment. The large but declining differentials during most of the study period show how population concentration *did* lag behind manufacturing concentration at first, and that high manufacturing employment concentration has been a general precursor to rising population concentration. On the other hand, spatial concentration measured using Moran's *I* tells a different story that emphasizes the greater relative clustering of population for most decades until 1940 when growth of manufacturing spilled over into the suburbs and neighboring counties from inner cities. In 1990, the contraction of manufacturing during the 1980s manifested itself in the great decline in manufacturing spatial concentration and hence in the population/manufacturing differential.

Regional Patterns

National-scale patterns of manufacturing concentration are naturally related to the regional levels because the regions are components of the nation (see figure 7.2 for regional boundaries); however, there are significant degrees of variability among U.S. regions across space and time that make this more refined scale deserving of particular attention. Using the historical GIS to determine regional population and area statistics I calculated regional Hoover indices for manufacturing employment and population among the counties of each region. The general trends in concentration were: first, volatile swings in the nineteenth century; second, relative stability and regional similarity from around 1900 to the 1930s; and third, divergence and regional spread from the 1930s to 1990 (table 7.3). The year 1980 marked the greatest spread between the most concentrated region (Mountain), and the least concentrated (East South Central). The difference was over 36 Hoover index points. By 1990, the Mountain and Pacific regions were the most concentrated in manufacturing employment while the East South Central and South Atlantic were the least concentrated. The Pacific, West South Central, and Mountain regions are the only ones that did not follow a slight downward slide in concentration after 1930. While the concentration levels for the Pacific and West South Central regions were fairly steady during this later period, levels in the Mountain region generally increased. All regions except the Pacific concentrated between 1980 and 1990, which was a break from previous trends for the six regions just noted. This turnaround appears to be a function of uneven spatial losses of 3.8 million manufacturing jobs during the decade.

Comparison of the national and regional Hoover index values for manufacturing is of special interest. During all years studied, manufacturing employment at the national level has been more concentrated than the average of all the regional values. This is an indication of the high density of manufacturing

Figure 7.2. Regional Boundaries of the United States

jobs in the Northeast and Midwest compared with other parts of the country (making a high concentration value). In contrast, within the regions in this part of the country (East North Central, Middle Atlantic, and New England), manufacturing employment has been fairly evenly distributed; therefore, the regional indices are generally lower than the national index.

The five-decade period from 1930 to 1980 was the longest time period in which deconcentration was most evident across regions (table 7.3). Between 1910 and 1930, concentration was slightly more common, while during the two previous decades the trend was toward deconcentration. Indeed, this four-decade pattern of concentration for twenty years and deconcentration for twenty years appears to have extended back to 1850. Therefore, notwithstanding overall regional variability, alternating rhythms of concentration and deconcentration have existed since 1840; these rhythms were tempered only by an unusually long deconcentration phase during the mid-nineteenth century.

The great shift toward increasing concentration of manufacturing jobs in the 1980s was extraordinary; indeed, such a trend had not occurred since the 1920s. This movement followed in opposition to a general dispersion of population that occurred during the 1970s (Vining and Strauss 1976). The shift back to manufacturing employment concentration in the 1980s occurred as manufacturing employment itself was entering a significant dive. Also

Table 7.3. Regional Manufacturing Employment Concentration Using the Hoover Index

Year	Pacific	Mountain	W. N. Central	W. S. Central	E. S. Central	South Atlantic	New England	Mid. Atlantic	E. N. Central	Nation
1820			57.84	80.19	55.08	51.73	51.28	47.83	78.55	66.79
1830										
1840			58.46	74.40	52.14	56.15	51.47	43.60	58.29	64.35
1850	85.50	68.65	81.81	79.55	55.04	62.45	61.96	57.93	59.40	81.73
1860	79.23	74.64	69.74	66.67	49.72	60.75	62.79	61.77	52.87	79.48
1870	75.71	64.49	75.55	71.01	52.75	61.52	62.35	56.89	49.47	79.24
1880	80.16	73.04	71.22	66.44	57.59	65.99	64.87	65.82	58.45	81.46
1890	74.71	74.22	74.22	70.28	60.69	66.06	64.65	66.65	60.31	80.06
1900	71.84	72.38	74.19	61.88	56.68	57.75	63.88	64.30	63.67	78.55
1910	70.77	66.43	74.76	59.87	53.73	55.02	64.80	63.60	65.66	77.49
1920	69.85	64.34	75.78	61.83	55.38	57.00	66.79	63.29	68.71	77.99
1930	68.59	65.57	76.61	62.75	56.75	56.96	66.90	63.90	69.98	77.89
1940	70.49	63.10	73.75	60.44	53.91	55.55	65.51	64.07	67.56	76.56
1950	69.21	65.56	72.30	60.89	49.92	52.02	65.51	62.77	65.25	74.83
1960	72.39	70.19	69.10	61.69	44.63	50.36	64.96	60.94	61.61	72.54
1970	73.08	71.19	66.51	61.13	39.74	47.27	63.72	58.55	59.18	70.34
1980	72.23	73.36	63.70	60.08	37.01	45.14	62.66	55.80	55.84	67.49
1990	71.80	75.70	67.83	65.52	42.15	50.04	63.17	58.05	57.96	68.76

during this decade, population returned to a concentrating trend. Therefore, during the 1980s manufacturing employment became more concentrated by virtue of job losses and spatial contraction of the remaining industries, even as overall population concentrated on account of real growth and a renewed push toward urbanization.

Regional Differentials

To see the particular relationship of manufacturing employment to population concentration in regions we look again at the differentials (table 7.4). The year 1890 marked the greatest difference between manufacturing concentration and population concentration. Before 1890, manufacturing employment was generally more concentrated than population, which indicated rising differentials throughout most of the period. During the Civil War (1860s) the North and parts of the West exhibited a slowdown in manufacturing employment concentration and a severe drop in the growth of settled land; the effect was to increase population concentration in those areas. On the other hand, the South (South Atlantic, East South Central, and West South Central) continued to exhibit higher differentials.

Since 1890, the general move in regional differentials was negative during every decade except the 1980s. Although both population and manufacturing employment became more concentrated in the 1980s, manufacturing's concentrating shift exceeded that of population in all but the Pacific and Mountain regions. Therefore, most regional differentials increased during the decade, reversing the downward trend that had begun nearly 100 years earlier. This means that over the past century, population has consistently concentrated at a higher rate than manufacturing employment across regions. The differentials not only show the expected higher manufacturing concentration levels, but they also highlight the rapid convergence of values in all regions from about the 1930s to 1990. Of particular note, three regions—South Atlantic, East South Central (just 1980), and Middle Atlantic—had greater population concentration than manufacturing concentration in 1970 and 1980. These three regions were relatively dispersed in their population concentration and even more dispersed in terms of manufacturing employment. In contrast, in 1890 the South Atlantic and East South Central regions had the greatest disparity between manufacturing concentration and population of any region. These findings are an indication of the industrial development that focused on many rural locations in the South following World War II.

Because differentials cancel out the unique underlying geographies of population and manufacturing employment of each region, significant urbanization and manufacturing patterns can be revealed, which would otherwise

Table 7.4. Regional Differentials Between Manufacturing Employment and Population Concentration (Man. - Pop.)

Year	*Pacific*	*Mountain*	*W. N. Central*	*W. S. Central*	*E. S. Central*	*S. Atlantic*	*New England*	*Mid. Atlantic*	*E. N. Central*
1820			16.71	25.19	14.32	18.47	7.35	10.90	8.02
1830									
1840			19.50	29.27	21.39	17.78	14.27	12.93	6.98
1850	10.35	25.86	12.40	21.73	28.67	27.20	22.22	25.31	16.36
1860	10.29	32.63	17.49	24.72	26.79	27.90	20.22	25.79	18.86
1870	11.28	9.03	10.94	26.54	27.74	28.84	17.16	17.88	19.46
1880	22.07	20.19	22.51	19.60	35.22	34.95	16.74	24.19	30.02
1890	21.21	23.41	29.98	24.47	40.17	36.27	12.78	20.53	30.14
1900	19.07	24.57	31.72	19.77	37.24	29.01	9.84	14.11	31.14
1910	15.29	20.88	36.79	23.84	34.45	27.56	7.90	9.38	28.47
1920	11.61	19.62	37.85	24.11	33.88	25.38	7.57	6.63	25.03
1930	6.99	19.73	37.35	24.57	30.84	22.67	6.40	5.08	20.08
1940	9.34	16.86	32.78	21.00	27.41	19.34	4.84	5.27	17.76
1950	6.77	14.73	28.11	16.12	18.18	11.81	4.50	3.86	12.96
1960	7.86	13.93	20.78	10.48	7.85	5.97	3.42	1.59	6.96
1970	7.40	11.39	14.98	6.82	1.08	–0.12	1.74	–0.58	3.81
1980	8.55	12.46	12.02	4.69	–1.11	–1.67	2.04	–1.02	2.51
1990	8.40	12.03	12.41	6.48	2.62	1.49	2.88	0.97	4.16

be hidden under less straightforward numbers. For example, by 1910 the West North Central region had the highest differential and continued to hold that position until 1990 (except in 1980, when it was just below the Mountain region differential). The West North Central region comprises much of the prime farmland of the nation. The high differentials from this area point to a traditionally less industrial-based rural realm compared with other parts of the country.

In other parts of the country, the Pacific, Middle Atlantic and New England regions' differentials separated from the other regions from 1880 to 1910, and by 1930 they were nearly thirteen points below the next lowest region. This great drop in differentials was propelled by the tremendous urbanization that occurred in these Atlantic and Pacific core areas. After 1930, the differentials in the other regions began to drop, thus bringing all regions into closer proximity. The precipitous decline in the South Atlantic and West North Central was caused by both population concentration and manufacturing deconcentration that helped narrow the regional differentials. The maximum spread (from highest concentration region to lowest concentration region) was over 32 points in 1930, but was just 12.5 points in 1990. By 1990, the nation had become much more homogeneous in its internal manufacturing/population concentration patterns than ever before.

In summary, manufacturing employment concentration has led population concentration across the majority of regions since at least 1840. For nearly a century (1890 to 1980), population concentrated and manufacturing employment deconcentrated, which caused regional differentials to fall dramatically. From 1980 to 1990, more rapid concentration in manufacturing than in population resulted in an increase in differentials. This reverse constituted a clean break from the trends of the previous ninety years. But this "break" prodded the nation into the most regional similarity that it has ever seen in the relative distribution of manufacturing jobs and population.

CITY-SYSTEM PATTERNS

The city-system level allows us to look closely at specific cities and their hinterlands to see how their population distributions have related to manufacturing employment (see appendix A). Because of important geographic distinctions and differences in settlement timing, concentration levels of manufacturing employment in U.S. city-systems have varied widely over time. On average, concentration at this smaller geographic grouping of counties has been less than the regional or the national averages of Hoover values. This is largely because of the deconcentrating effect of smaller, more homogeneous groups of counties. Even with lower overall concentration and a high degree of variability, the most consistent attribute across city-systems has been manufacturing employment concentration exceeding and leading population concentration.

A useful way to get a rough but understandable picture of the major concentration trends is to sum decadal city-system changes in the Hoover index of manufacturing employment. This calculation treats all regions equally. A positive value for the decade means that the city-systems, in general, were moving towards concentration, while a negative number indicates the opposite. This method magnifies much of the movement in manufacturing concentration that was depicted at the national scale (figure 7.3).

The trend of city-system manufacturing employment concentration consists of five main periods: positive growth from 1840 to 1870, intense increase from 1870 to 1890, definite slowing from 1890 to 1920, a slow downward slide from 1920 to 1980, and finally, a burst of concentration in the 1980s. The net result was that levels of overall manufacturing concentration in 1990 were similar in many respects to that of 1890 even though manufacturing employment grew from less than five million in 1890 to nearly seventeen million in 1990. However, the general trend hides the existence of important clusters, since individual city-systems have developed spatial patterns of manufacturing distribution to match their unique regional geographies.

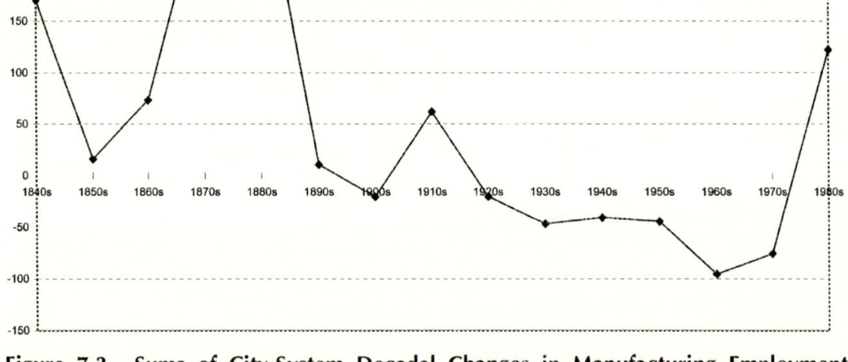

Figure 7.3. Sums of City-System Decadal Changes in Manufacturing Employment Concentration 1840–1990

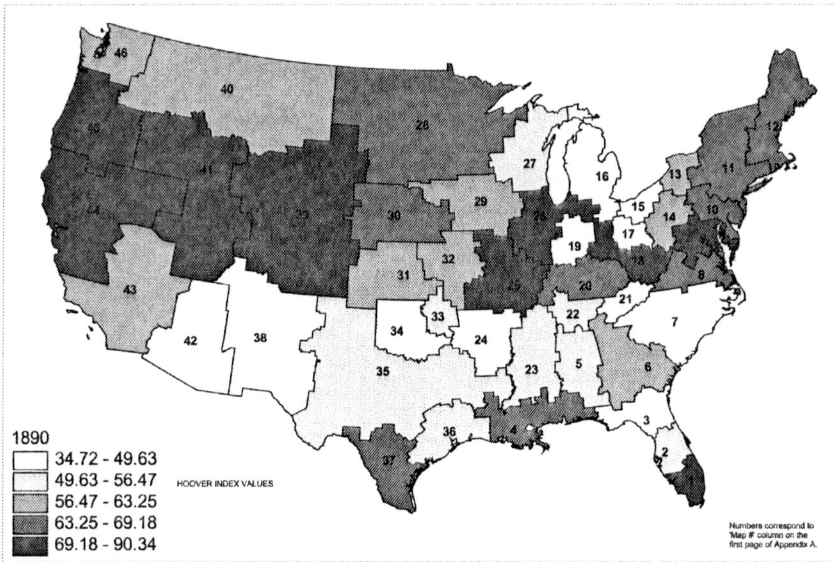

Figure 7.4. Hoover Index of Manufacturing Employment Concentration for City-Systems in 1890

In 1890, both high and low concentration levels were spread around the nation in a somewhat haphazard manner (figure 7.4). Miami had the highest concentration value at a tremendous 90.34, even though it was next to relatively dispersed Tampa and Jacksonville.[5] The other highly concentrated city-systems shared the middle latitudinal tier while the most deconcentrated areas were spread throughout the nation. By 1990, the most densely concentrated city-systems were clustered in the Southwest, while those in the Southeast were the most dispersed. This shift between 1890 and 1990 emphasizes the process of regional convergence over the intervening century (figure 7.5).

The period from 1890 to 1980 highlights how the nation transitioned from the peak of manufacturing growth into a long period of deconcentration. The 1890s saw a precipitous drop in total concentration change as most of the East and South declined. During the following decade there was an even greater slowdown; just three city-systems concentrated by more than five points, while six systems deconcentrated by more than five points. There was a slight resurgence in the 1910s, which was followed by an overall manufacturing concentration drop from 1920 through 1980. This sixty-year period was one of great growth in manufacturing employment. In many city-systems, especially in the East, the increases were spread over counties which previously had few manufacturing jobs.

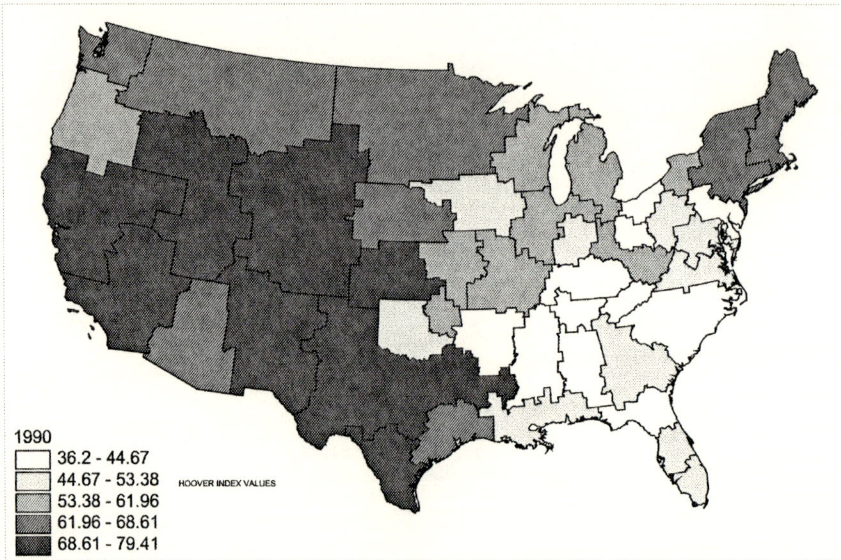

Figure 7.5. Hoover Index of Manufacturing Employment Concentration for City-Systems in 1990

In the 1980s, significant losses in manufacturing employment were coupled with increases in manufacturing concentration across much of the nation. Some sixteen city-systems concentrated by more than five points. In contrast, during the 1970s just one city-system registered such a large amount of concentration. To further emphasize the about-face in trends from the 1970s to the 1980s, only four city-systems declined in concentration during the 1980s as compared with thirty-four in the 1970s.

City-System Differentials

What then is the relationship between manufacturing employment concentration and population concentration at the city-system clustering of counties? Simply put, manufacturing employment concentration has usually exceeded population and has led the way to higher concentration in both distributions (appendix B). In all decades, a majority of the city-systems have been more concentrated in manufacturing employment than in population, even during the early period between 1850 to 1860 when many city-systems, which were just emerging in the frontier had higher levels of population concentration.[6] It was not until 1980 that more than a handful of city-systems (13) registered population concentration greater than manufacturing. Ironically, that year also marked the end of the great population deconcentration of the 1970s

(Long and Nucci 1997). This meant that manufacturing deconcentrated even faster than population during the decade.

Overall, differentials saw a tremendous increase from 1840 to 1890, followed by a parallel decline from 1910 to 1980 (figure 7.6). In a majority of city-systems, differentials between manufacturing employment and population concentration peaked between 1890 and 1910. Some twenty-five city-systems, clustered in the mid-section of the nation, had manufacturing employment concentration of at least 25 points above population concentration in 1910 (figure 7.7). This indicates that in these city-systems there was tremendous spatial disparity between the location of manufacturing jobs and the distribution of the overall population.

From 1910 through 1920, rising population concentration and falling manufacturing concentration slowly eroded the concentration advantage of manufacturing employment. After 1920, the general downward trend was even more pronounced. The number of city-systems with very high differentials (over 25 points) began to shrink towards the northern Great Plains until only Wichita remained in that category in 1960. In that same decade, four city-systems had negative differentials (population more concentrated than manufacturing employment). These were Portland (OR), Jacksonville (FL), Richmond (VA), and Washington, D.C. Clearly, population and manufacturing had experienced converging trends across the country since 1910.

Figure 7.6. Sum of Differentials in the Hoover Indices for City-System Manufacturing Employment and Population Concentration 1820, 1840–1990

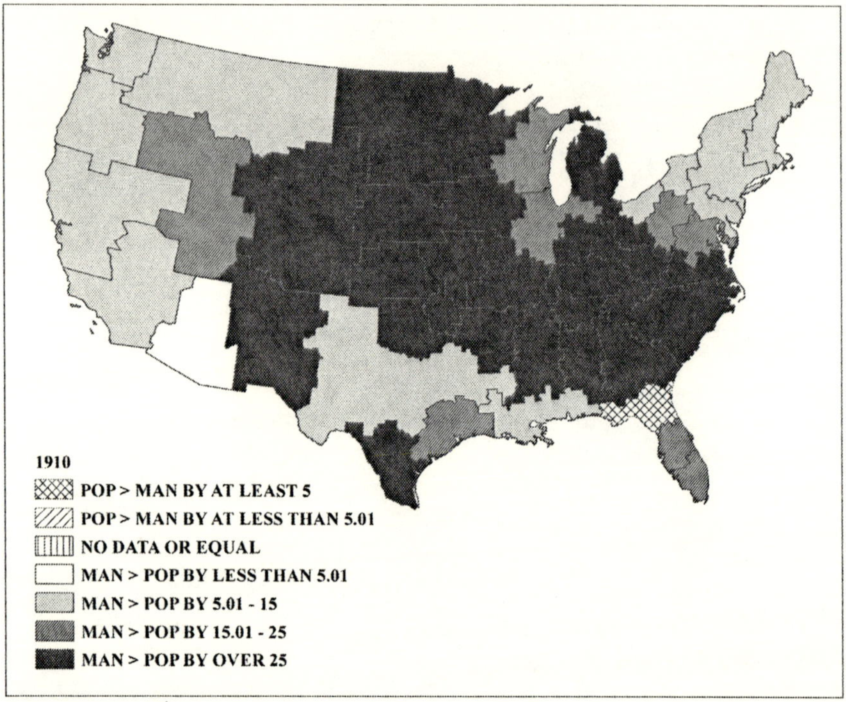

Figure 7.7. Differentials between Manufacturing Employment and Population Hoover Indices of Concentration for City-Systems in 1890

Just as at the national and regional scales, the 1980s proved to be a rebound year in city-systems for both population concentration and manufacturing employment concentration even though manufacturing across the nation experienced a net loss of jobs. A majority of the city-systems in 1990 had differentials between 5 and 15 points, while only the Washington D.C. city-system showed a negative differential less than –5. Washington's high number of white-collar government workers may be part of the reason for why it had a greater concentration of population (figure 7.8).

CONCLUSION

Over the past 150 years, manufacturing employment has tended to be more concentrated than the general population. This fact has been shown through the use of the differential of the Hoover indices of population and manufacturing. The significant point is that the relative concentration of industry to

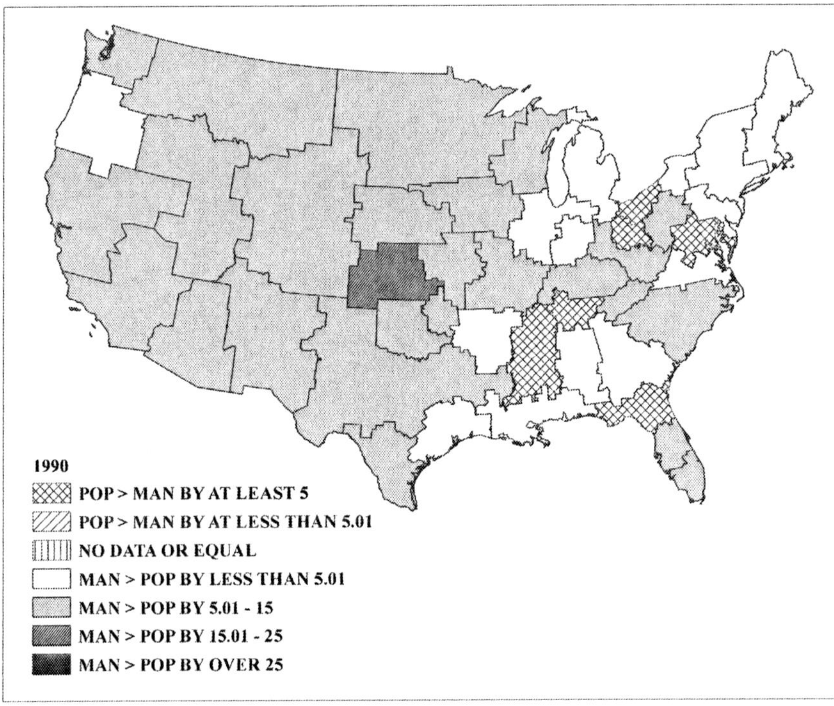

Figure 7.8. Differentials between Manufacturing Employment and Population Hoover Indices of Concentration for City-Systems in 1980

population has shifted according to a strongly regular pattern—one where population and manufacturing concentrations have converged over time.

At the national level, the Hoover index manufacturing concentration was very high through the late 1800s reaching a value above 81. The index gradually declined to its 1990 level of 68.76. Population, on the other hand, tended to disperse until it found a Hoover index low point of 52.94 in 1910. After that, urbanization finally began to outweigh rural settlement growth and the population concentrated for many decades, with only a short pullback during the 1970s. Combining the manufacturing and population trends results in three periods: divergence, convergence, and balance (figure 7.9).

During the divergence between 1840 and 1910, increasing differentials pointed to greater unevenness in the population/manufacturing landscape (see figure 7.1).[7] This was the lag period, when frontier settlement was still growing vigorously, but at the same time, many important eastern cities were expanding very rapidly. New and relocated manufacturing jobs continued to

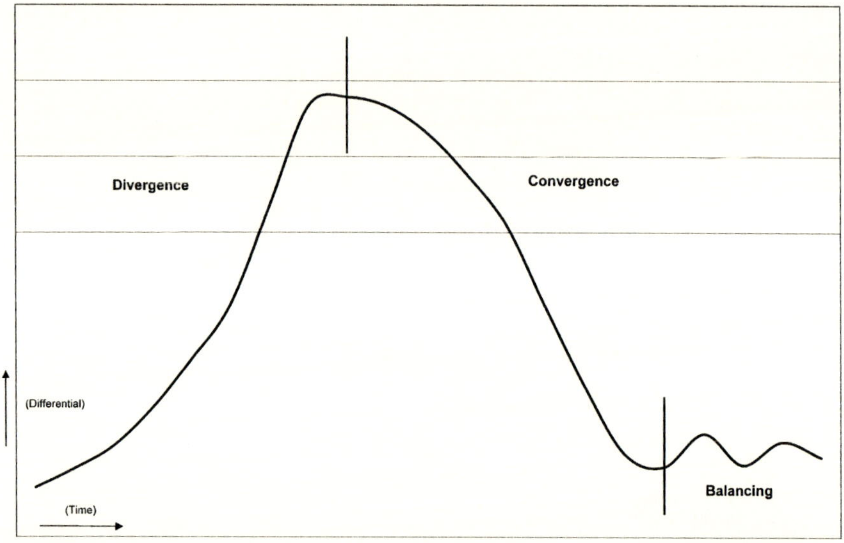

Figure 7.9. Generalized Model of Trends in Differentials between Manufacturing Employment and Population Hoover Indices of Concentration

be concentrated while only a portion of the overall population followed this urbanizing trend. This was due in part to the fact that dispersed agricultural and other resource extractive industries still employed a large portion of the population. For example, even though manufacturing jobs were dispersing at the national level from 1900 to 1910, the overall populace was spreading out even more quickly. Additionally, a look at the great increase in differentials from 1870 to 1880 shows the heightened divergence caused by the population dispersing while manufacturing was concentrating.

The convergence period started after 1910. The combined effect of large numbers of people moving from periphery areas to core urban realms and the continued dispersal of industry from the traditional manufacturing belt to other areas across the country moved the nation into greater relative spatial similarity in respect to manufacturing jobs and population. This process illustrates the geographically opportunistic way in which both the general populace and those locating manufacturing establishments acted in their reconfigurations. During this period, industry reached outward to areas where few manufacturing jobs had been, while the general population was attracted toward these and other related urban opportunities.

The final period of achieving balance, or dynamic equilibrium, is the one with the shortest history. After the intense convergence from 1910 to 1980, the relative importance of manufacturing took a sharp downward turn.

Jobs were lost in the 1980s, so firms retrenched into fewer locales, causing concentration. Population concentrated as well, placing the nation in near balance or in a dynamic equilibrium. This balance is not static, but appears to be working toward more subdued shifts. This relative concentration does not necessarily point to an exact correlation in 1990 in the relative densities of the two distributions; however, the degree to which the differential has converged is evidence of important spatial processes prodding the nation toward greater relative geographic continuity in manufacturing and population distribution.[8]

A different picture of the relationship between manufacturing and population comes from the Moran's *I*. Relative differentials were quite small between 1840 and 1920, slightly favoring population, showing how similar the clustering of similar densities of population and manufacturing employment were. Then, the spatial concentration of industry experienced a marked increase after 1930, powerfully illustrating the great outward spread of manufacturing jobs during the Great Depression and World War II. Additionally, differentials showed an about-face that occurred during the 1930s, so that by 1940 manufacturing employment actually showed more significant clusters of similar density than population. This elevated pattern continued until 1980, and then the loss of manufacturing jobs in the 1980s precipitated a marked drop in manufacturing spatial concentration. Thus for the first century (1840 to 1940) population led manufacturing in terms of spatial clustering, but the great rise in spatial autocorrelation of manufacturing from 1940 to 1980 illustrates how manufacturing employment had its own period of greater levels of autocorrelation, but which evaporated by 1990.

Earle's (2003 chapter 12) argument for the periodic dispersion and concentration effects of different policy regimes finds some credence here when the differentials of the population and manufacturing employment Hoover indices are considered (see figures 7.1 and 7.6). Through the First Democracy, population dispersion around the country combined with already high manufacturing concentration translated into larger and larger differences in their respective relative geographies (between 1840 and 1880). Between the 1880s and the 1930s manufacturing retained its high concentration level, while population switched from dispersion to concentration after 1910 so that this Second Republic period was characterized by continuing high total differentials. The Second Democracy (New Deal) followed with dispersion in manufacturing employment, but *not* in population, which continued to concentrate. This meant that differentials rapidly disappeared during the period. The Third Republic since the 1970s has been hit with a leveling out of the differentials as population concentration has slowed to a near standstill and manufacturing has shrunk in importance as its deconcentration trend has ceased.

Thus, the coordinated movements in concentration of these two variables show periodic switches, but perhaps the most important trend change has to do with the larger-scale shift from the Sectional State of the 1780s to 1870s to the National State of the 1880s to 1980 (Earle 2003). In this more expansive view the first century was characterized by divergence between the relative locations of the general people and manufacturing employment, while the coordinated character of the ensuing National State century led to the convergence of manufacturing and population geographies. Even though Earle argued for the decline of national-level spatial concentration effects from the different policy regimes, this research has shown that they were still evident after the 1880s (Earle 2003: 358–9).

A process of divergence, convergence, and balance is not limited to the national scale. Many of the regions and city-systems have experienced the same process, although the timing and intensity of the differential swings vary according to where the city-systems are located. For instance, the Mountain West region was moving through convergence in 1990 while New England, with its much longer settlement history, had already reached a balanced position. City-systems such as New York and Philadelphia have converged, while others such as Richmond and Nashville saw population concentration move past manufacturing concentration and continue in that condition for two to three decades prior to 1990.

Moving from the general to the particular brings out noticeable differential patterns, which may or may not follow the national trend. However, it is apparent that even in these distinctive places, divergence and convergence is often the rule (usually with more of the convergence coming from population concentration and less from manufacturing dispersion). Specific city-system trends support the larger picture and give researchers the consistent framework to guide their search for the geographic and historic causes behind the spatial restructuring of population and manufacturing in this nation. Examples of recent specific regional studies that could use this type of data include Walker's (2001) work on San Francisco, Hise's (2001) essay on Southern California, and Muller's (2001) treatment of Pittsburgh and its environs.

High levels of manufacturing concentration were a vital indicator of the point that population concentration would likely reach as urbanization entered a strong phase in the twentieth century. Initial manufacturing concentrations foreshadowed both population concentration and manufacturing dispersion. In essence, population and manufacturing have met in the middle and now overall population and manufacturing employment are both concentrated at similarly high levels, with manufacturing concentration usually being just above population concentration. This convergence trend is key to understanding the complex relationship between overall settlement patterns and manufacturing locations.

The economy of the United States is rapidly changing and unpredictable. The impact of the evolving manufacturing sector on settlement patterns is particularly difficult to adequately assess; however, manufacturing's relevance in influencing population shifts cannot be ignored. The fact that population concentration has so clearly diverged then converged in relation to manufacturing employment concentration, even at various scales, shows how helpful industry can be in explaining the current and historical population distributions of the United States.

NOTES

1. Kim (1995) calculated regional Hoover indices for manufacturing specialization at the regional level, but did not look at how spatially concentrated overall manufacturing employment.
2. If the current area of the contiguous United States is used to calculate the index for 1840, the value is actually 81.93 (see the values in parentheses in table 7.1).
3. Total employment in manufacturing in 1920 was 9,096,000 and 8,836,000 in 1930.
4. Total employment in manufacturing in 1980 was 21,871,000 and 18,008,000 in 1990.
5. Miami's high manufacturing concentration lasted for only a few decades.
6. This was due in part to the fact that these fledgling city regions had very few manufacturing jobs at the time.
7. The two downward spikes of the 1840s and 1860s were caused by the inclusion of the lands west of Missouri in 1850 (for the 1840s) in the calculations and by the tremendous disruption of the Civil War which effectively slowed frontier settlement (for the 1860s).
8. At the aggregated regional level divergence lasted until 1890, convergence from 1890 to 1970, and balancing from 1970 to 1990. At the aggregated city-system level divergence lasted until 1900, convergence from 1900 to 1970, and balancing from 1970 to 1990.

BIBLIOGRAPHY

Bogart, W. 1998. *The Economics of Cities and Suburbs.* (Upper Saddle River, NJ: Prentice-Hall Inc).

Berry, B., and F. Horton, eds. 1970. *Geographic Perspectives on Urban System.* (Englewood Cliffs, NJ: Prentice-Hall Inc).

Conzen, M. 1975. "A Transport Interpretation of the Growth of Urban Regions: An American Example." *Journal of Historical Geography* 1:361–382.

Cronon, W. 1991. *Nature's Metropolis: Chicago and the Great West.* (New York, NY: W.W. Norton and Company)

Duncan, O., W. Scott, S. Lieberson, B. Davis, and H.Winsborough. 1960. *Metropolis and Region.* (Baltimore, MD: The John Hopkins Press).

Dunn, E. 1980. *The Development of the U.S. Urban System.* (Washington DC: Resources for the Future).

Earle, C. 2003. *The American Way: A Geographical History of Crisis and Recovery.* (Lanham, MD: Rowman & Littlefield).

Earle, C., S. Otterstrom, and J. Heppen. 1999. *HUSCO—1790–1999* [Historical United States County Boundary Files on CD-ROM]. (Baton Rouge, LA: Geoscience Publications).

Fotheringham, A., T. Champion, C. Wymer, and M. Coombes. 2000. "Measuring Destination Attractivity: a Migration Example." *International Journal of Population Geography* 6: 391–421.

Higgs, R. 1969. "The Growth of Cities in a Midwestern Region, 1870–1900." *Journal of Regional Science* 9: 369–375.

Hise, G. 2001. "Nature's Workshop Industry and Urban Expansion in Southern California, 1900–1950." *Journal of Historical Geography* 27: 74–92.

Hoover, E. 1941. "Interstate Redistribution of Population, 1850–1940." *Journal of Economic History* 1: 199–205.

Hoover, E., and J. Fisher. 1949. "Chapter V." *Problems in the Study of Economic Growt.* (New York: Universities-National Bureau Committee for Economic Research).

Isard, W. 1990. *Location Analysis and General Theory: Economic, Political, Regional and Dynamic, v 1.* (New York, NY: New York University Press).

Kim, S. 1995. "Expansion of Markets and the Geographic Distribution of Economic Activities: The Trends in U.S. Regional Manufacturing Structure, 1860–1987." *Quarterly Journal of Economics* 110: 881–908.

———. 1998. "Economic Integration and Convergence: U.S. Regions, 1840–1987." *Journal of Economic History* 58: 659–683.

Leven, C. 1993. *Regional Changes in Urban and Metropolitan Population in the United States.* (Washington DC: Urban Institute Press).

Long, L., and A. Nucci. 1997. "The Hoover Index of Population Concentration: A Correction and Update." *The Professional Geographer* 49: 431–440.

Meyer, D. 1980. "A Dynamic Model of the Integration of Frontier Urban Places into the United States System of Cities." *Economic Geography* 56: 120–140.

———. 1983. "Emergence of the American Manufacturing Belt: An Interpretation." *Journal of Historical Geography* 9: 145–174.

Moran, P. 1948. The Interpretation of Statistical Maps. *Journal of the Royal Statistical Society* B: 243–251.

Muller, E. 1976. "Selective Urban Growth in the Middle Ohio Valley, 1800–1860." *Geographical Review* 66: 178–199.

———. 1977. "Regional Urbanization and the Selective Growth of Towns in North American Regions." *Journal of Historical Geography* 3: 21–39.

———. 2001. "Industrial Suburbs and the Growth of Metropolitan Pittsburgh, 1870–1920." *Journal of Historical Geography* 27: 58–73.

North, D. 1955. "Location Theory and Regional Economic Growth." *Journal of Political Economy* 63: 243–258.

———. 1961. *The Economic Growth of the United States 1790–1860.* (New York, NY: W.W. Norton and Company).

Otterstrom, S. 2003. "Population Concentration in United States City-Systems from 1790 to 2000: Historical Trends and Current Phases." *Tijdschrift voor Economische en Sociale Geographie* 94: 477–495.

Page, B. 1998. "Charting the Middle Ground: History, Geography and City-Hinterland Relations in the Great West." *Ecumene* 5: 81–104.

Page, B., and R. Walker. 1991. "From Settlement to Fordism: the Agro-Industrial Revolution in the American Midwest." *Economic Geography* 67: 281–315.

Perloff, H., E. Dunn Jr., E. Lampard, and R. Muth. 1960. *Regions Resources and Economic Growth.* (Baltimore, MD: The Johns Hopkins Press).

Pred, A. 1965. "Industrialization, Initial Advantage, and American Metropolitan Growth." *Geographical Review* 55: 158–185.

———.1966. *The Spatial Dynamics of U.S. Urban-Industrial Growth, 1800–1914.* (Cambridge, MA: The MIT Press).

———. 1976. "The Interurban Transmission of Growth in Advanced Economies: Empirical Findings versus Regional-Planning Assumptions." *Regional Studies* 10: 151–171.

———. 1980. *Urban Growth and City-Systems in the United States, 1840–1860.* (Cambridge, MA: Harvard University Press).

Rand McNally & Co. 1990. *Rand McNally Commercial Atlas and Marketing guide.* (Chicago: Rand McNally & Co).

Schnell, J., and P. McLear. 1972. "Why the Cities Grew: a Historiographical Essay on Western Urban Growth 1850–1880." *Bulletin, Missouri Historical Society* 28: 162–177.

Stobart, J. 2000. "In Search of Causality: A Regional Approach to Urban Growth in eighteenth-century England." *Geografiska Annaler* 82: 149–163.

U.S. Census. 1980. *County and City Data Book.* (Washington, D.C.: U.S. Department of Commerce, Bureau of the Census, 1940–1980 for each census year, available electronically from the Inter-university Consortium for Political and Social Research).

Vance, J. Jr. 1970. *The Merchant's World: The Geography of Wholesaling.* (Englewood Cliffs, NJ: Prentice-Hall Inc).

Vining, D., and A. Strauss. 1976. *A Demonstration that Current Deconcentration Trends are a Clean Break with Past Trends.* (Philadelphia, PA: Regional Science Research Institute).

Walker, R. 2001. "Industry Builds the City: The Suburbanization of Manufacturing in the San Francisco Bay Area, 1850–1940." *Journal of Historical Geography* 27: 36–57.

Walker, R., and R. Lewis. 2001. "Beyond the Crabgrass Frontier: Industry and the Spread of North American Cities, 1850–1950." *Journal of Historical Geography* 27: 3–19.

APPENDIX A: HOOVER INDEX OF MANUFACTURING EMPLOYMENT CONCENTRATION FOR CITY-SYSTEMS

	Map #	*1820*	*1840*	*1850*	*1860*	*1870*	*1880*
Atlanta	6	40.65	37.64	45.04	42.84	45.29	56.40
Birmingham	5	48.70	38.46	33.89	36.13	35.13	44.76
Boston	12	56.18	55.05	64.70	65.44	65.47	67.57
Buffalo	13	47.85	32.77	40.53	45.57	42.86	49.00
Charlotte	7	35.86	33.04	34.61	30.15	34.80	39.89
Chicago	26		33.60	43.35	44.55	49.82	63.08
Cincinnati	18	51.16	49.97	58.01	64.25	63.38	68.58
Cleveland	15	26.36	18.01	24.79	34.13	30.77	44.51
Columbus	17	40.23	32.56	39.07	35.75	32.14	40.09
Dallas	35	18.70	27.66	71.52	33.44	44.47	43.75
Denver	39					52.85	64.47
Des Moines	29		31.40	37.98	41.98	44.49	50.53
Detroit	16	43.92	60.99	45.20	41.33	42.17	45.03
El Paso-Albuquerque	38			51.43	50.26	46.33	46.94
Houston	36			36.80	37.01	39.44	48.45
Indianapolis	19	78.42	30.05	41.80	36.76	34.45	44.19
Jacksonville	3	23.52	38.20	47.08	37.47	46.44	41.18
Kansas City	32		43.56	51.01	40.49	43.62	52.16
Knoxville	21	41.96	32.09	29.95	31.74	39.12	47.07
Little Rock	24		51.28	36.85	26.21	36.66	41.97
Los Angeles	43			46.77	52.00	52.66	58.42
Louisville	20	46.71	43.71	57.87	52.66	57.08	63.24
Memphis	23	49.32	39.59	33.37	34.97	43.87	45.36
Miami	1		34.37	28.15	22.80	26.42	28.08
Milwaukee	27		65.55	51.66	47.56	49.95	60.33
Minneapolis	28			46.44	52.84	74.05	57.31
Nashville	22	37.16	33.71	37.45	34.73	34.78	45.21
New Orleans	4	65.96	55.62	53.08	53.11	58.78	69.38
New York	11	42.46	42.70	57.66	59.24	56.08	64.66
Oklahoma City	34						
Omaha	30			26.24	40.74	42.47	45.02
Philadelphia	10	42.87	43.21	58.89	64.98	61.13	67.18
Phoenix	42					31.59	35.91
Pittsburgh	14	43.02	38.05	48.63	55.01	56.64	61.55
Portland	45			61.72	70.23	68.62	62.02
Richmond	8	41.59	42.67	51.26	55.75	56.59	64.25
Salt Lake City	41			35.46	46.71	57.72	61.49

	Map #	*1820*	*1840*	*1850*	*1860*	*1870*	*1880*
San Antonio	37			46.43	43.59	40.89	56.66
San Francisco	44			32.61	52.09	70.89	80.61
Seattle	46				58.00	42.49	66.62
Spokane	40				59.69	50.91	56.08
St. Louis	25	51.25	52.62	63.19	65.70	67.89	74.35
Tampa	2			33.13	39.49	34.60	44.46
Tulsa	33					8.02	14.15
Washington D.C.	9	36.88	41.76	65.48	64.42	65.02	76.27
Wichita	31				42.51	33.26	35.32

APPENDIX A. (*Continued*)

	1890	*1900*	*1910*	*1920*	*1930*	*1940*
Atlanta	56.97	49.72	54.25	59.65	54.94	55.29
Birmingham	54.02	50.00	48.10	51.06	52.19	48.99
Boston	67.63	66.88	67.54	68.98	69.10	66.91
Buffalo	58.55	51.96	55.13	57.56	60.24	59.16
Charlotte	47.26	46.67	44.99	44.66	47.97	46.59
Chicago	69.89	71.63	72.42	72.91	72.76	71.36
Cincinnati	74.62	72.03	66.34	68.70	71.12	67.36
Cleveland	50.24	49.85	51.25	55.43	54.28	51.38
Columbus	41.55	47.88	49.24	51.96	53.34	49.66
Dallas	52.68	56.73	59.37	60.49	59.53	61.91
Denver	71.85	73.96	73.58	66.51	64.73	69.79
Des Moines	60.33	58.30	62.13	64.83	67.26	66.06
Detroit	49.45	54.51	60.74	68.67	70.18	68.01
El Paso-Albuquerque	44.04	60.78	61.18	66.57	69.39	54.73
Houston	50.51	48.42	46.21	53.28	60.74	63.88
Indianapolis	48.85	54.56	55.00	56.94	56.53	52.35
Jacksonville	34.87	21.95	22.91	33.60	26.59	37.01
Kansas City	62.01	69.54	71.45	74.58	72.50	71.51
Knoxville	49.63	53.24	45.27	45.58	56.28	47.88
Little Rock	45.45	41.71	43.49	46.72	44.37	37.41
Los Angeles	60.48	71.38	73.41	76.77	84.04	86.67
Louisville	67.34	68.84	68.50	68.74	71.82	66.10
Memphis	54.73	46.67	43.09	44.89	42.18	45.20
Miami	90.34	84.44	59.56	57.46	34.61	48.30
Milwaukee	52.65	58.40	60.29	62.05	65.14	62.15

	1890	*1900*	*1910*	*1920*	*1930*	*1940*
Minneapolis	65.09	67.40	69.24	69.74	71.18	67.93
Nashville	53.90	54.92	55.07	56.18	60.11	47.27
New Orleans	69.18	51.53	46.32	44.72	44.42	50.87
New York	66.11	66.03	66.43	67.45	68.48	69.70
Oklahoma City	34.72	42.26	57.73	62.40	57.00	57.68
Omaha	67.80	70.40	73.20	75.43	70.14	71.05
Philadelphia	64.29	61.30	60.13	59.20	56.30	53.71
Phoenix	35.98	37.53	32.10	33.80	31.51	38.65
Pittsburgh	63.25	60.25	58.48	57.21	59.78	59.60
Portland	70.53	71.23	70.49	68.69	58.67	57.13
Richmond	67.08	65.80	45.38	61.01	60.88	51.55
Salt Lake City	71.46	78.79	71.95	68.97	67.83	69.64
San Antonio	63.66	70.46	68.99	64.12	65.87	69.35
San Francisco	76.82	77.62	73.97	72.12	70.47	73.98
Seattle	63.90	56.34	56.93	59.19	54.23	55.78
Spokane	62.39	68.25	60.88	57.42	62.76	61.68
St. Louis	79.59	78.66	77.29	77.10	75.23	69.78
Tampa	51.78	52.58	48.09	51.61	49.46	47.98
Tulsa	56.47	47.61	62.98	62.34	62.89	58.95
Washington D.C.	80.58	75.58	54.62	72.51	73.05	66.82
Wichita	58.04	61.20	63.18	67.66	65.32	65.82

APPENDIX A. (*Continued*)

	1950	*1960*	*1970*	*1980*	*1990*
Atlanta	50.02	49.74	46.97	44.17	51.67
Birmingham	43.74	39.71	34.16	31.60	38.83
Boston	67.18	66.24	64.87	63.92	64.11
Buffalo	58.92	58.11	56.57	52.97	56.65
Charlotte	44.10	41.63	36.89	34.21	39.86
Chicago	69.51	65.83	62.30	60.05	60.09
Cincinnati	64.24	61.01	59.78	55.70	62.22
Cleveland	48.93	48.22	44.73	40.81	41.23
Columbus	47.39	45.19	43.92	39.69	41.84
Dallas	63.48	63.52	65.60	65.84	69.95
Denver	72.42	75.68	77.07	78.25	78.56
Des Moines	62.47	55.93	50.90	46.26	47.62
Detroit	64.83	60.70	57.94	53.92	56.79
El Paso-Albuquerque	55.68	63.43	67.40	72.63	73.07

	1950	*1960*	*1970*	*1980*	*1990*
Houston	65.09	67.88	66.33	64.19	64.83
Indianapolis	49.20	39.07	41.51	38.54	45.72
Jacksonville	39.58	41.65	39.08	37.79	42.62
Kansas City	68.87	63.85	60.41	56.88	60.73
Knoxville	46.37	44.74	38.42	36.55	42.00
Little Rock	35.86	35.14	34.37	33.00	40.12
Los Angeles	85.52	84.15	82.27	80.06	79.41
Louisville	60.70	53.30	48.21	42.25	45.40
Memphis	43.35	37.87	33.13	31.53	35.79
Miami	53.54	58.66	55.99	53.75	53.28
Milwaukee	62.18	61.58	60.19	58.46	57.52
Minneapolis	69.69	67.90	66.91	67.04	66.67
Nashville	43.05	35.26	29.91	28.12	35.04
New Orleans	47.16	47.58	44.13	43.79	45.53
New York	68.77	67.32	65.24	62.31	63.98
Oklahoma City	56.74	57.76	54.07	52.66	53.41
Omaha	71.26	67.02	63.79	62.39	67.48
Philadelphia	51.38	48.82	44.84	42.26	42.72
Phoenix	45.88	66.34	67.55	68.89	69.07
Pittsburgh	56.96	53.99	50.21	48.39	48.51
Portland	54.14	55.03	58.63	59.79	60.90
Richmond	44.62	45.61	42.51	41.74	51.51
Salt Lake City	73.17	70.87	71.37	74.59	75.60
San Antonio	70.51	70.87	68.68	69.52	69.78
San Francisco	72.24	72.58	75.48	74.80	73.75
Seattle	56.93	61.06	62.67	63.82	66.40
Spokane	62.94	60.08	57.95	62.03	63.99
St. Louis	67.61	64.91	60.74	54.73	57.47
Tampa	49.56	50.26	49.92	46.73	47.19
Tulsa	60.75	58.83	53.15	49.30	57.03
Washington D.C.	62.02	59.55	55.29	50.39	48.66
Wichita	71.26	70.91	67.92	68.17	72.36

APPENDIX B: HOOVER INDEX DIFFERENTIALS FOR CITY-SYSTEMS (MANUFACTURING–POPULATION)

	1820	*1840*	*1850*	*1860*	*1870*	*1880*
Atlanta	–5.55	8.08	18.86	20.40	22.37	34.29
Birmingham	10.67	13.37	11.69	17.11	13.97	26.23
Boston	5.75	12.63	19.88	18.35	15.83	15.23

	1820	*1840*	*1850*	*1860*	*1870*	*1880*
Buffalo	6.51	5.07	10.54	17.16	12.34	20.02
Charlotte	15.57	13.03	17.27	14.85	17.97	24.09
Chicago	0.00	7.60	18.69	25.73	30.82	39.45
Cincinnati	5.80	7.51	15.71	23.39	23.28	32.44
Cleveland	11.39	7.82	15.52	23.72	14.79	25.07
Columbus	12.39	14.27	23.34	21.89	19.61	27.84
Dallas	4.30	8.92	0.66	–7.86	–9.47	–14.00
Denver					0.15	5.97
Des Moines		0.40	–1.78	2.66	13.31	30.02
Detroit	–13.81	–2.15	–9.57	–3.88	1.70	11.86
El Paso-Albuquerque			23.70	12.40	6.78	5.64
Houston			8.82	13.41	9.89	16.93
Indianapolis	12.01	8.09	26.68	24.23	20.98	29.97
Jacksonville	4.25	–1.83	12.31	4.84	9.69	7.19
Kansas City	0.00	7.30	20.35	7.48	18.98	34.21
Knoxville	10.38	6.65	8.57	11.81	18.74	28.01
Little Rock	–18.48	26.86	14.47	9.77	17.06	24.86
Los Angeles			–19.41	19.52	3.79	5.35
Louisville	11.48	18.02	34.95	31.89	37.17	44.40
Memphis	–9.86	6.13	7.53	15.92	20.90	26.45
Miami		27.33	–12.39	–20.04	–23.87	–25.78
Milwaukee	–39.08	–0.43	–12.73	–4.97	3.12	20.37
Minneapolis			–12.19	–17.81	–8.10	–4.74
Nashville	10.35	12.12	17.38	15.51	13.20	24.85
New Orleans	23.29	12.89	10.65	11.27	17.70	31.69
New York	9.45	13.45	25.84	22.44	15.03	19.72
Oklahoma City						
Omaha			–7.59	–23.49	–19.97	1.39
Philadelphia	11.55	10.44	23.79	28.08	24.02	27.77
Phoenix					–9.00	8.96
Pittsburgh	5.56	7.24	20.59	30.03	29.40	34.21
Portland			–4.89	1.25	11.96	12.33
Richmond	18.31	26.63	36.03	39.74	38.85	46.47
Salt Lake City			–27.00	–6.53	0.79	6.41
San Antonio			23.87	0.36	–0.42	22.58
San Francisco			–34.33	–14.20	4.88	18.83
Seattle				14.73	–4.01	25.62
Spokane				14.47	0.87	1.83
St. Louis	13.07	17.35	29.44	35.19	34.81	44.26
Tampa		–74.87	–5.55	–9.52	–2.98	17.60

	1820	1840	1850	1860	1870	1880
Tulsa					7.95	6.29
Washington D.C.	14.92	18.01	37.85	33.69	28.80	38.88
Wichita				–9.76	–11.67	–5.15
Average	4.82	7.93	9.94	11.08	10.93	19.46

APPENDIX B. (*Continued*)

	1890	1900	1910	1920	1930	1940
Atlanta	35.09	29.14	31.89	35.18	25.32	23.35
Birmingham	37.73	33.91	31.51	30.59	27.15	23.13
Boston	11.91	9.23	7.28	6.96	6.17	3.95
Buffalo	25.47	14.70	13.33	10.62	9.80	8.28
Charlotte	31.17	29.64	26.94	25.22	25.45	22.70
Chicago	35.30	30.36	25.43	20.53	14.85	13.74
Cincinnati	40.38	38.61	33.93	32.09	30.83	27.57
Cleveland	23.78	18.83	14.58	10.52	6.82	5.02
Columbus	27.87	30.78	27.51	25.85	22.49	17.84
Dallas	–1.59	4.37	12.70	12.08	15.67	17.34
Denver	19.75	24.30	26.61	20.12	18.16	21.43
Des Moines	44.24	42.83	42.99	43.01	43.46	40.51
Detroit	18.81	23.55	26.78	23.84	17.05	15.15
El Paso-Albuquerque	9.70	28.52	32.01	26.42	29.55	15.42
Houston	19.88	21.31	23.16	27.78	26.08	24.36
Indianapolis	32.34	33.92	31.62	28.58	24.83	19.38
Jacksonville	5.86	–7.00	–6.35	3.76	–5.24	3.75
Kansas City	41.51	44.27	41.57	40.96	35.04	32.41
Knoxville	30.34	37.52	29.49	27.63	32.67	23.58
Little Rock	28.13	25.99	26.13	28.98	23.07	16.27
Los Angeles	1.82	9.91	7.76	6.94	8.88	11.42
Louisville	47.81	49.68	48.22	46.79	44.94	39.52
Memphis	38.13	30.42	27.57	26.53	20.90	23.34
Miami	8.82	26.31	22.96	23.00	–7.12	2.19
Milwaukee	17.62	24.31	24.82	24.89	23.70	19.94
Minneapolis	16.99	22.29	33.24	34.27	34.50	28.91
Nashville	34.25	35.67	35.91	37.15	36.93	22.97
New Orleans	33.40	18.29	15.05	11.27	9.29	14.77
New York	15.65	10.36	5.57	3.56	2.21	3.25

	1890	*1900*	*1910*	*1920*	*1930*	*1940*
Oklahoma City	8.69	10.60	41.81	41.74	31.00	30.07
Omaha	25.01	29.31	36.01	38.47	32.20	31.34
Philadelphia	22.33	16.55	13.38	10.07	7.36	5.61
Phoenix	7.23	11.81	1.00	–0.94	–4.48	2.67
Pittsburgh	30.83	24.13	19.50	16.35	16.54	16.55
Portland	16.74	18.67	14.94	10.48	2.59	1.44
Richmond	45.65	42.52	34.89	28.77	27.50	16.55
Salt Lake City	18.61	28.45	22.51	16.00	12.64	13.62
San Antonio	29.80	32.42	31.03	18.07	16.73	19.75
San Francisco	15.53	16.45	11.71	7.04	4.77	9.72
Seattle	10.88	8.22	9.75	10.90	5.89	8.13
Spokane	8.82	20.00	15.49	20.09	23.65	21.40
St. Louis	51.08	48.06	42.10	37.74	31.43	26.09
Tampa	16.79	20.40	17.01	19.01	12.18	8.26
Tulsa	38.80	25.79	41.41	33.69	29.51	26.45
Washington D.C.	39.35	31.52	24.31	21.55	19.67	10.75
Wichita	18.89	20.55	33.30	36.90	34.28	31.64
Average	24.72	24.95	24.57	23.07	19.72	17.86

APPENDIX B. (*Continued*)

	1950	*1960*	*1970*	*1980*	*1990*
Atlanta	11.69	5.35	–1.07	–3.84	1.60
Birmingham	12.36	3.07	–4.11	–5.43	0.91
Boston	4.09	3.03	0.91	1.34	1.84
Buffalo	6.69	3.58	1.67	0.01	4.26
Charlotte	17.89	11.80	4.13	1.46	6.04
Chicago	10.90	6.22	2.55	1.59	1.14
Cincinnati	22.44	15.77	11.17	10.60	15.63
Cleveland	3.21	2.07	–0.90	–1.44	–0.20
Columbus	11.39	4.71	0.02	–2.98	–1.87
Dallas	16.63	11.57	9.42	8.06	8.37
Denver	19.66	16.63	13.87	15.16	12.78
Des Moines	33.09	22.98	14.97	9.72	9.74
Detroit	9.74	4.32	1.75	0.84	4.73
El Paso-Albuquerque	7.99	10.37	11.99	15.99	15.18

	1950	*1960*	*1970*	*1980*	*1990*
Houston	14.62	10.68	6.54	4.85	4.24
Indianapolis	12.84	0.36	1.00	–1.14	4.79
Jacksonville	0.96	–3.88	–8.49	–9.12	–5.62
Kansas City	24.42	13.88	7.82	4.98	6.73
Knoxville	19.02	15.41	7.43	6.29	10.87
Little Rock	9.56	3.59	1.07	–1.00	3.89
Los Angeles	10.75	9.81	9.41	9.73	12.93
Louisville	29.29	16.53	8.96	4.72	7.41
Memphis	16.70	6.26	–0.80	–3.35	–0.96
Miami	4.97	8.18	6.43	7.77	10.35
Milwaukee	16.60	11.62	8.29	8.14	6.58
Minneapolis	27.65	22.16	17.01	16.06	12.56
Nashville	13.76	0.09	–6.49	–7.58	–2.81
New Orleans	5.93	4.19	0.83	0.17	2.16
New York	2.57	1.10	–0.32	–1.03	1.28
Oklahoma City	22.11	15.20	8.15	6.49	5.16
Omaha	28.52	20.06	13.33	10.63	12.82
Philadelphia	2.99	1.50	–1.36	–0.90	0.72
Phoenix	0.27	13.55	11.19	11.29	10.19
Pittsburgh	12.73	8.08	4.41	5.30	5.82
Portland	–2.08	–1.40	0.09	2.20	2.73
Richmond	3.31	–1.38	–6.49	–7.00	0.53
Salt Lake City	12.11	5.76	4.18	6.99	7.00
San Antonio	13.94	10.85	7.08	7.80	7.12
San Francisco	6.03	5.21	7.29	8.83	8.74
Seattle	5.02	5.86	3.93	5.77	6.74
Spokane	17.26	12.48	7.83	9.53	9.93
St. Louis	20.04	13.47	7.06	3.96	6.44
Tampa	7.44	7.58	6.50	6.65	9.00
Tulsa	21.18	12.60	6.65	5.51	11.96
Washington D.C.	2.74	–2.08	–7.18	–8.58	–9.20
Wichita	33.60	25.91	20.97	19.88	21.14
Average	13.14	8.58	4.75	4.02	5.90

APPENDIX C: DATA AND METHODS INFORMATION

I used the "major trading areas" boundaries from the Rand McNally Commercial Atlas and Marketing Guide (Rand McNally & Co. 1990) to define my city-systems. The trade areas are groups of individual counties, with a central city or cities surrounded by the counties that are most economically tied to that metropolitan area. Using counties as the basic building blocks of city-systems is advantageous, because of the availability of manufacturing and population data for each census. The advantage that city-systems have over states for this type of analysis is that they form better economic regions by taking into account such factors as transportation, employment, and newspaper circulation. Alaska and Hawaii were not included because of their remoteness from the rest of the United States and their late admittance into the union.

Digital historical county boundaries from 1820 to 1990 were used to calculate population density, and assign counties to city-systems. To insure consistency and comparability of the statistics over time, I used the 1990 major trading area boundaries for each census year. As county boundaries changed between decades, especially before 1910, I assigned counties that fell into more than one city-system to the city-system that contained the center of the county in question. It is true that the actual city-systems of the United States have experienced changes over time, not only because of county boundary shifts, but also because of the evolution of city-systems' spheres of influence. Nevertheless, population concentration figures for trade areas that change every decade would be very difficult if not impossible to interpret.

I calculated the Hoover index of manufacturing employment concentration for each city-system using a total area figure which matched the area in the city-system at the date of census enumeration (see Appendix A for the complete table of manufacturing concentration). This varying area helps account for the large swings in manufacturing concentration in city-systems such as Dallas (1840–1860) and Tulsa (1880–1900). The effects of varying city-system sizes were helpfully canceled out when I calculated the differentials between manufacturing employment and population concentration (appendix B).

Manufacturing data for counties for the 1909 Census of Manufactures were never published. All that is available are state totals and figures for cities with over 10,000 inhabitants. I estimated county employment for 1909 using a database program. This was accomplished by entering the city (those with more than 10,000 inhabitants) and state totals for 1909 into data tables. I then calculated each county's proportion of the state total of manufacturing employees for 1899 (1900) and 1919 (1920), and averaged the two. This new figure was then multiplied for each county by the respective state totals in 1909. A second program insured that counties containing cities with over 10,000 people had an estimated number of manufacturing employees at least equal to the number reported for the particular city. When upward adjustments were made (to less than 20 counties), a proportional decline in employees occurred for other counties in order to keep the state total consistent. This left just a few counties with cities over 10,000 people whose estimated number of manufacturing employees was less than that reported for the city.

In 1992, the Census Bureau suppressed exact manufacturing data for over 600 counties so as to avoid disclosing information on individual companies. These I estimated. The Census did disclose the number of companies in each total employee class range for these counties. I used the midpoint of the indicated class to estimate each company's total employees; I then added these figures to obtain a total estimate for the county. The largest class was open-ended (250 and over). However, I used 793.42 as the average employee size for this class, as it most closely matched the total number of employees nationwide. This open-ended class is the most problematic because it covers such a large range so averaging employee figures for all such counties probably does not reflect the true situation. However, I still used these estimates because I did not discover a better alternative.

Chapter Eight

Regional Income Convergence and a Decennial Core-Periphery Regionalization of the United States 1929–2000

John Heppen

Scholars have devoted a lot of attention to differences in regional incomes in the United States and variations in regional economic development. From historians like Douglas North (1966) to geographers John Agnew (1987) and Carville Earle (2001; 2003) different theories have been proposed in explaining the significance and causes of different income levels in the United States from 1790 to the present. Regardless of theory the geography and most importantly the changing geography of regional incomes remain an important topic and hypothesis for investing problems in the historical geography of the United States. There are three purposes of this essay. The first is to provide a regional division of the United States using a core and periphery method for analyzing the regional geography of the United States. The second is to examine changes in the core and periphery structure of the Untied States and to determine if regional incomes have become more or less spatially concentrated through from 1929 to 2000. The third is to test Earle's (2003) theory of regional volatility in incomes from the 1930 to 1980 period and for regional stability in incomes afterward using a core and periphery model. Regional volatility and stability was measured by comparing regional convergence or divergence of incomes. This study is different in that it identified core and peripheral regions free of any predetermined regional geographic boundaries and then studied regional stability or volatility.

Regions are vital in studying the geography of the United States and key to analyzing the political economy of the country through time. A regional approach to researching and teaching the geography of the United States is vital since it allows one to study or illustrate a topic in more manageable pieces. Comparative and historical studies employing a regional approach have revealed problems in defining regions. Wishart (2004) called upon geographers to reexamine their regional approach in order to present other narratives and interpretations. Authors of textbooks on the regional geography of North America recognize a South, Northeast, New England, Midwest, West, and Great Plains among other regions (Birdsall, Florin, and Price 1999; Getis, Getis, and Quastler 2001; McKnight 2004; Patterson 1994). Other studies base regions on cultural, social, and historical patterns (Gastil 1975; Garreau 1981; Zelinsky 1994; 1980; 1973). Systematic studies placed states into core and peripheral regions based on their position in the world-economy (Agnew 1987; Bensel 1984). Bensel (1984) noted that comparative analysis with arbitrary regions of the United States based on history, culture, or ethnicity is difficult. Therefore, there is a need for a regional geography of the United States, which uses a core-periphery approach in order to make regional comparative and historical studies easier as well as demonstrate how changing regional geographies are tied to wider cyclical trends in the world-economy and the regional and national growth of the U.S. political economy.

One school of thought believes that regional trade between the East, South, and West was responsible for the economic growth of the United States during the nineteenth century (North 1966). Another school of thought sees the development of three regional agricultural belts beyond the Appalachians as spurring economic growth before the Civil War (Earle 2001). Regardless of the view, the United States has been at the forefront of the world-economy since World War II as the hegemonic core power (Wallerstein 1991; Agnew 1987).

The world-economy is the current capitalist economy with an extensive and complete single division of labor possessing an integrated set of production processes that interact with each other through an instituted or created market (Wallerstein 1991:13). Within this world-economy, there are core states (countries) with higher incomes, more advanced technologies and production systems and peripheral regions with lower incomes and less-advanced industries, which primarily serve as providers of resources, agricultural products, low-cost labor, and markets for value-added manufactured goods and services from the core (Wallerstein 1991). There are also semi-peripheral states with characteristics of both the core and periphery. The core and periphery construct can be applied to regions within larger countries like the United States.

Within the United States, core and peripheral regions have been identified using two main methods. Agnew (1987) and Earle (2003) used the multi-state, census divisions as their unit of analysis. The core was identified as the Northeastern United States from Southern New England to the Mid-Atlantic west to the Lower Great Lakes, while the periphery was composed of the South and the West. Bensel (1984) divided the country into trade areas based on a dominant urban center and surrounding rural hinterland. Bensel (1984) examined sectional stress between the traditional Northeastern core area and the peripheral Southern and Western regions of the Untied States. What is missing in this core and peripheral regionalization of the United States is a critical approach to this regional scheme, which tests the assumptions of core in the Northeast and a periphery in the South and West. This test is important since a shift of many core processes to the periphery is a major theme of the contemporary political economy of the United States.

There was a gradual shift beginning after World War II in many core production processes to the periphery caused by higher production and labor costs due to older capital; higher social welfare benefits; higher taxes; environmental amenities; and a perceived better business climate in the South and West (Bensel 1984; Cobb 1984; Agnew 1987). The economic slowdown of the 1970s and restructuring of the 1980s accelerated this movement as firms shifted capital and production to peripheral regions of the United States attempting to regain profits and higher returns on their investments (Agnew 1987). This regional shift occurred within a broader framework of cycles of growth and stagnation in the world-economy and alternating policy regimes in the United States, which at various times favor policies that encourage regional volatility or regional stability (Earle 2003). One type of policy regime identified by Earle (2003), Free Trade Masses (FTM), from 1930 to 1980 favored a mass distribution of resources that encouraged regional volatility. The other type, Protectionist Elite (PE) from 1980 to the present, promoted a more elite distribution of resources encouraging regional stability. The impacts of these policy regimes on the regional geography of the United States played an important role in the purpose of this research. A greater explanation of the regimes will follow in this essay.

This essay begins with a brief examination of previous core and peripheral approaches; then it will explain its methodology of regionalizing the United States at the state-level approximately every ten years; and it will follow with an explanation on how the two alternating policy regimes affected regional volatility and stability. Subsequently, an examination of regional convergence or divergence of income and the regional core and peripheral configurations will be presented and analyzed in accordance with the purposes of this research.

REGIONS, INCOMES, INCOME CONVERGENCE, AND POLICY REGIMES

Previous research with an emphasis on regional incomes and regional income convergence has employed fixed regional categories of New England, Middle

Atlantic, East North Central, West North Central, South Atlantic, East South Central, West South Central, Mountain, and Pacific following conventional United States Census Bureau categories (see Agnew 1987; Barro and Sala-i-Martin 1992; Barro and Sala-i-Martin 1991; Bernard et al. 1985; Earle 2003; Easterlin 1961; Kim 1995; Kim 1998). This chapter is different in that it regionalizes the country into five regions based on a core-periphery approach at the state-level approximately every ten years from 1929 to 2000. The terminology is borrowed from Wallerstein's World-Systems Theory (1979; 1991). The United States is a core country of the world-economy having advanced production systems, higher incomes, and other capital-intensive activities associated with a core country. However, core countries do have regions with peripheral characteristics. The United States has a core region in the Northeast and two peripheral regions based primarily in the South and West (Bensel 1984; Agnew 1987; Earle 2003). Political and geographic conflict flared between the core based in the industrial Northeast and Great Lakes and a peripheral South and West that desired different government policies favoring their regions especially during the twentieth century (Bensel 1984; Agnew 1987; Earle 2003). This conflict coincided with a larger temporal rubric of alternating policy regimes.

Two policy regimes have alternated in approximately fifty-year intervals since the 1780s. Republics (1780s–1828, 1880s–1930, 1980–present) combine liberal preferences for elitist domestic policies, producer revolutions, regional specialization and stability with republican preferences for nationalistic foreign policies and expansion, and demographic concentration—establishing dense settlements in frontier areas (Earle 2003:15). Democracies (1828–1877, 1930s–1980) combine Republican ideas of egalitarian domestic policies, diversified and volatile regions and consumer revolutions with internationalist views of free trade, geographical consolidation and demographic dispersion—filling up the spaces between previously established frontier settlements (Earle 2003:15).

The alternating periods are triggered by the cyclical crisis in capitalism corresponding with the 45 to 60 year periods of Krondratieff (1934, 1985) long waves. The first part of the wave, the A phase, is associated with rising prices and economic growth and the B phase, the second part of the wave, is associated with declining prices and economic stagnation. The good times coincide with the A phase of the Kondratieff cycle as the diffusion of new techniques and technologies brings about rising incomes and bad times are associated with the B phase (Earle 2003). The result of the B phase during the Great Depression forced the creation of the New Deal and free trade policies (Earle 2003). In response to these crises in the B phase, society turned to innovations to bring back profits. Innovations diffuse geographically from source areas as result of the economic crisis and the desire to bring back prosperity or good times (Earle 2003:18–22).

During American Republics or Protectionists Elite (PE) regimes, regional incomes remain stable since the regime pursues policies that do not favor redistribution of resources or preferences to disadvantaged regions. Regions that provide lower labor costs should remain regions of low-cost labor for producers. Democracies or Free Trade Masses (FTM) regimes on the other hand exhibit regional volatility. They wish to see regions with lower shares of national income catch-up and promote policies that encourage regional economic development and a lessening of regional inequalities. It is during this phase that manufacturing processes diffuse from core regions to peripheral regions to save labor costs. The onset of the Great Depression coincided with a regime change in the United States as Roosevelt's New Deal signified a major policy change in the US. Federal spending and the acknowledgment of the South as the nation's number one economic problem meant that federal resources were redirected to this poorest and most peripheral region of the United States. After WWII, many producers in the industrialized Northeast relocated labor-intensive activities to the South for cheaper wages and tax breaks (Cobb 1984; Agnew 1987; Bensel 1984). In addition, Southerners and Southern governments during the time actively promoted themselves to Northern industries as a low-cost region with obedient and non-union workers in the midst of a growing Sunbelt market (Cobb 1984: 51–67). The Northeast during this time was burdened with aging capital and higher production costs associated with higher energy costs, social services, and labor unions beginning in the 1970s (Bensel 1984; Agnew 1987). Furthermore, the South and West became home to a higher concentration of defense contractors and federal defense contract dollars compared to the Midwest (Markusen et al. 1991).

With the relocation of capital to the South and the change to a Republican regime favoring protectionist and elite policies, regional incomes should remain stable. Further equalization of regional incomes is not promoted since producers would be prevented from capitalizing on cheaper labor in other regions. Therefore, regional incomes should be volatile as measured by regional income convergence from 1930 to 1980 and stable as measured by regional incomes remaining more stable or slightly diverging from 1980 to 2000. Previous research has found income convergence across U.S. states and regions from the nineteenth century through the twentieth century with an emphasis on the rapid income convergence of Sunbelt regions (Barro and Sala-i-Martin 1992; Barro and Sala-i-Martin 1991; Bernard et al. 1985; Easterlin 1961; Kim 1995; Kim 1998).

DATA AND METHODS

In order to regionalize the United States, personal per capita income at the state-level in current dollars was collected from the U.S. Census Bureau decennially from 1929 to 2000 for the forty-eight contiguous states (U.S. Census Bureau 2003). Per capita income was standardized as a percentage of the national per capita income. For example if per capita income in the United States for 1940 was $595, California with a per capita income of $844 registered 142 percent of the country's per capita income. These data were subjected to a k-means cluster analysis to regionalize the country. The purpose of cluster analysis is to minimize the within-group variation while maximizing the between-group variation or in this case clustering states with similar income levels (Rogerson 2001). A k-means cluster analysis must begin with a predetermined number of groups with a minimum of one member for each group since this method clusters observations by giving each group a centroid, or center position of data (Rogerson 2001). Cluster analysis provided final cluster centers for each group. Five clusters were pre-selected in order to identify a core, near-core, middle, semi-periphery, and periphery regions of the United States decennially from 1929 to 2000. The final cluster center for per capita income as a percentage of national per capita income was used to determine whether each group belonged to the core, near-core, middle, semi-periphery, or periphery. The core regions in this study were the states with the highest income. Core regions had the highest final cluster center. The near-core region in this study represented states with slightly lower incomes than the core states or the second highest final cluster center. In the broader sense, the core and near-core in this study represented an upper-income region. The periphery represented the region with the lowest income, least economic development with more labor-intensive economic activities providing foodstuffs and raw materials to the core. The periphery had the lowest final cluster center. The semi-periphery represented a region with slightly higher incomes than the periphery or the second to the lowest final cluster center. The states grouped in the middle are states final cluster centers third for each decade.

The period of this study (1929–2000) coincided with the last two policy regimes in the United States identified by Earle (2003). The year 1929 marked the first year per capita income data became more easily available from the US Census Bureau. In addition the time period chosen closely matched with the fourth cycle of the Kondratieff wave from the Great Depression to 2000 as well as the the alternating free trade masses redistributed regimes (FTM) and protectionist elite regimes (PE) of 1930–1980 and 1980–present respectively.

Moran's *I* test for spatial autocorrelation measured levels of spatial autocorrelation of income from 1929 to 2000. Moran's *I*, a global measure of spatial autocorrelation, determined the degree of spatial dependence, or the degree to which the income was clustered by state. Interpretation of Moran's *I* was simple. As Moran's *I* approaches 1, the degree of spatial autocorrelation increases, while a Moran's *I* of 0 indicates a random pattern. In testing for Earle's hypothesis, Moran's *I* should steadily weaken and decline from 1929 to 1980 and then become stable or increase from 1980 to 2000. A first-order binary contiguity spatial weights matrix recorded the spatial arrangement of the 48 states created from an Arcview Shapefile of the 48 contiguous United States. A regular matrix of spatial weights (W) captured the spatial relationship of the states. In a binary contiguity matrix element, w_{ij} is assigned a value of 1 if the states (i and j) shared a common boundary (i and j were "neighbors"), and a value of 0 if they were not neighbors (Heppen 2003). The queen measure of contiguity was used which recorded states as neighbors sharing common corners.

SPATIAL ANALYSIS OF INCOME 1929 TO 2000

Income in the United States followed a pattern predicted by Earle (2003). Moran's *I* test for spatial autocorrelation for per capita income as percentage of national income showed a decline during a FTM period and an increase beginning in a PE regime. From 1929 to 1980 Moran's *I* declined every decade. The sharpest decline occurred from 1970 to 1980 during a period of economic stagnation, rising oil prices, and slow growth. During this decade, the Sunbelt boom magnified as many producers within the United States shifted production facilities out of the traditional manufacturing core of the Northeast and Great Lakes to facilities in the South and West (Agnew 1987; Bensel 1984). This was consistent with the redistributive policies of the FTM regime and the relocation of capital and production to lower cost labor regions in the South and West. Spatial autocorrelation of income increased sharply from 1980 to 1990 consistent with the PE regime theorized to take place beginning in 1980. PE regimes favor an elite distribution of resources and income. Even though spatial autocorrelation of income mildly declined in 2000, Moran's *I* for 2000 was higher than the measure for 1980—suggesting income stability.

Another method to measure income stability, convergence, and divergence is to examine state membership in each category from decade to decade. Theoretically, under the FTM regime there should be a leveling of state membership with decreases in the number of states in the core and periphery and increases in the middle groups. The number of states in

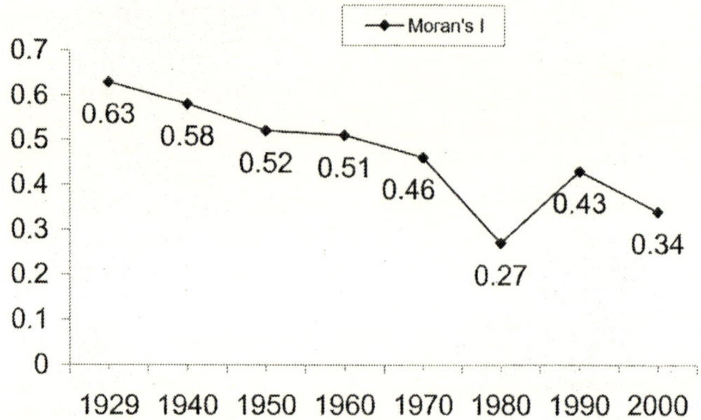

Figure 8.1. Spatial Autocorrelation of Per Capital Income as Percentage of National per Capita Income 1929–2000 State Level

the middle category reached its highest memberships from 1950 to 1980. During the 1940 to 1980 period, the number of states in the periphery dramatically decreased. In 1940, fourteen states were peripheral and in 1980, only four states were peripheral. From 1950 to 1980, the average number of states in the core remained at five. A different pattern emerged in 1990 as the number of states in the core decreased to one, the number of states in the middle declined, and the number of states in the periphery ballooned to 16 in 1990. During the PE regime, the number of states in the two bottom groups increased and then remained stable from 1990 to 2000. States in the middle declined from 1980 to 2000 and remained stable from 1990 to 2000. In summary, there is strong evidence that the FTM period smoothed over regional differences in state income as the number of states joining the middle group and leaving the periphery increased, suggesting the distribution of resources and regional income volatility.

Table 8.1. State Membership in Each Type of Region 1929–2000

Region	*1929*	*1940*	*1950*	*1960*	*1970*	*1980*	*1990*	*2000*
Core	5	1	6	7	5	5	1	1
Near-Core	9	8	9	13	4	7	6	4
Middle	15	9	17	17	22	19	11	11
Semi-Periphery	10	16	11	8	14	13	16	18
Periphery	9	14	5	3	3	4	14	13

Source: Author

CONVERGENCE AND DIVERGENCE OF REGIONAL INCOMES

Examining regional incomes as a percentage of national income for the five regions found evidence of regional volatility and convergence from 1930 to 1980. Incomes among all five regions converged between 1940 and 1980. The most dramatic convergence occurred from 1940 to 1950 followed by a steady convergence from 1950 to 1980 with 1980 being the decade where incomes came closest to converging. It is theorized that politics played a role in that era of convergence since the power of Southern Congressman and the alliance between the New Deal Northerners and Southern Democrats brought programs like the Tennessee Valley Authority to the South and the need for year-round military training brought even more federal dollars to the periphery (Bensel 1984; Cobb 1984; Agnew 1987; Hooks 2001). However, Johnston (1980) found no link between congressional committees and the allocation of federal funds to home states during that time. A period of divergence from 1980 to 1990 occurred during the first decade of the current PE regime and was followed by a relatively steady period from 1990 to 2000. The last two decades indicates an elitist preference for core regions and regional income stability consistent with American Republics.

This study next will examine the composition and geography of the five regions through time. It begins with the two regions at opposite ends of the spectrum—the core and the periphery—since they represent the two regions where income convergence and divergence were most pronounced. This will be followed by the near-core and end with the middle and semi-periphery two regions containing the most members with the widest geographic range.

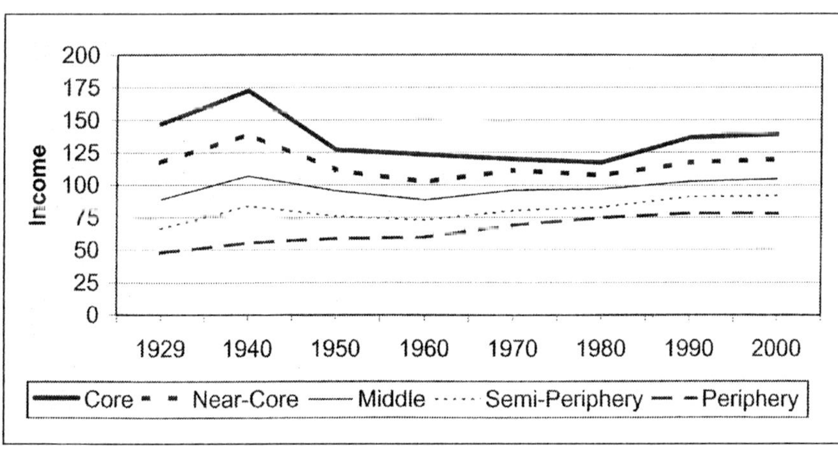

Figure 8.2. Regional Incomes U.S. 1929–2000 as a Percentage of National Income

THE CORE REGION 1929–2000

The core region of the United States followed a history of expansion and contraction during the seventy-year period. New York, Connecticut, Delaware, and Illinois were the core in 1929. The core then shrank from 1929 to 1940 during the Great Depression to just Delaware. It expanded from one member in 1940 (Delaware) to an average of five states from 1950 to 1980 offering evidence of income dispersion and regional volatility California and Nevada were added to the core for 1950. The movement westward of the core represented a shift to the Sunbelt and the growth of California after World War II (McWillilams 1949). California benefited from its Pacific position and the growth of aerospace and defense industries as it became part of a "Gunbelt" (Markusen et al. 1991; Crump 1989; Crump and Archer 1993). For 1960, the core reached seven states, but at the height of membership, it was still concentrated in the Northeast.

During the FTM regime, the core's income as measured as a percentage of national per capita income declined from 172.6 to 127.2 percent from 1940 to 1950 and continued a steady decline down to 117.4 percent in 1980. However, the figure increased sharply from 1980 to 1990 to 136.5 percent and remained relatively stable from 1990 to 2000—consistent with the PE regime that began in 1980. The transition to a PE regime was reflected in the contraction of the core down to Connecticut by 1990 and 2000. In summary, the main story of the core was one of limited expansion and an excursion to

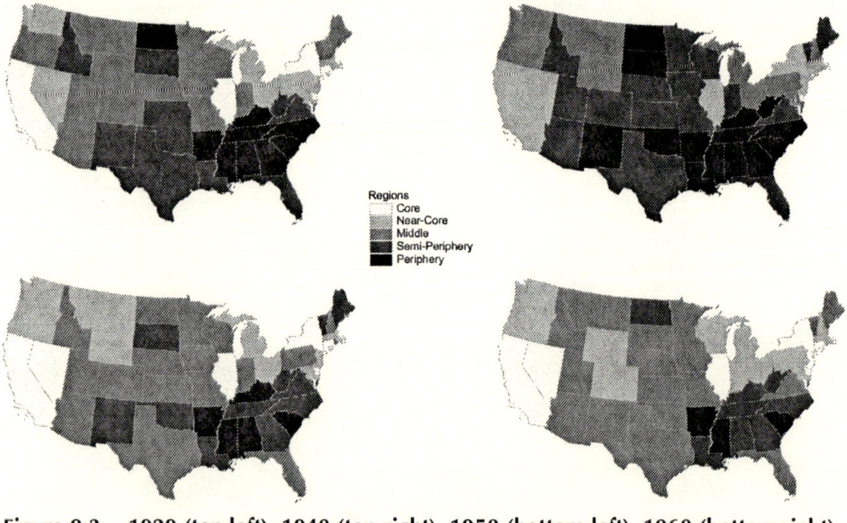

Figure 8.3. 1929 (top left), 1940 (top right), 1950 (bottom left), 1960 (bottom right)

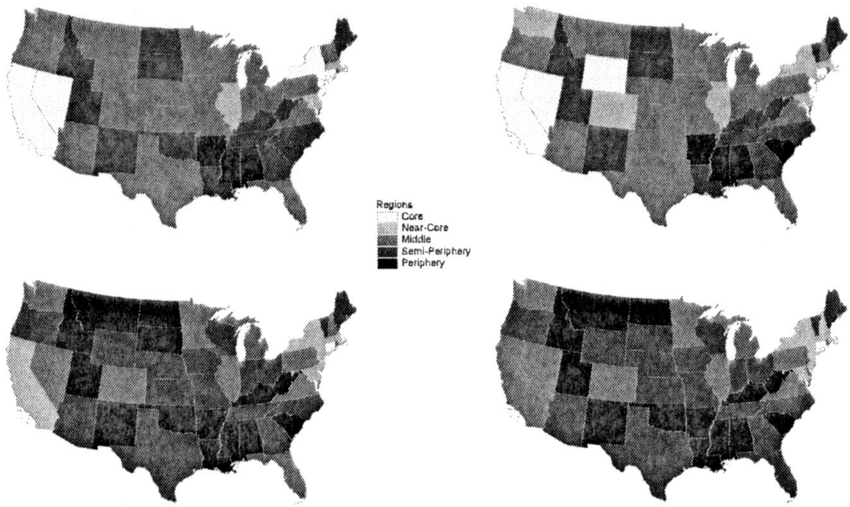

Figure 8.4. 1970 (top left), 1980 (top right), 1990 (bottom left), 2000 (bottom right)

the West Coast during the FTM regime and contraction from 1980 to 2000 in the new PE regime.

THE PERIPHERY 1929–2000

The periphery most closely followed Earles' theory of regional volatility and regional stability through regimes. The number of states in the periphery rose from 1929 to 1940, but then dramatically declined and stayed low from 1950 to 1980 following the redistributive policies of the FTM regime. In 1940, the periphery was Southern and Western. Then the periphery shrank down to just Southern States from 1950 to 1980, but the states, which have remained most consistently in the periphery—Alabama, Arkansas, Mississippi, and South Carolina—saw their per capita income increase while staying in the periphery. Income in the periphery improved dramatically through time, as it was less than half of the national figure in 1950 and near 80 percent of the national value in 2000. Thus the difference between the core and periphery steadily declined after 1940 and came closest to convergence in 1980 with 42.9 percentage points separating the core and periphery. However, the difference between the regions dramatically increased to 61 percentage points from 1960 to 2000. Temporally, the spatial inequality closed during the FTM regime, but it reemerged at the beginning of the PE regime. Even though the income inequality was not as large as it was in the beginning of the last FTM regime the convergence trend ended.

In summary, the change to a PE regime from 1980 to 1990 saw the number of states in the periphery balloon to fourteen from four while the number of states in the core fell to one. But from 1990 to 2000 the number of states in the periphery remained high but relatively stable. The redistributive policies of the New Deal, New Frontier, and Great Society were evident from 1929 to 1980 as those FTM policies were a catalyst for the Civil Rights Movement and Sunbelt boom. Increasing political, social, and economic opportunities for blacks and the greater economic integration of the South helped equalize regions—an important goal of FTM regimes.

THE NEAR-CORE, 1929–2000

The near-core remained relatively stable in income while experiencing great geographic volatility. Beginning with a base in the Northeast and Great Lakes, it expanded to include Western states, but with the start of a PE regime in 1980 it contracted. The expansion and contraction periods were consistent with policies of FTM and PE regimes respectively. Regional convergence peaked in 1960 with an income at 102 percent of the nation and a wide geographic distribution of membership from New England, the industrial states of Pennsylvania, Ohio, Michigan, Wisconsin, Indiana, and some Western states. From 1929 to 1950, the near-core averaged nine members with most states from the traditional manufacturing belt of the Northeast and Lower Great Lakes and Western states. Beginning in 1970, the near-core contracted with fewer members in the West and Industrial Midwest. By 2000, it clustered exclusively in the Northeast. The Northeast is the historic center of political and economic power in the country from colonial times and the current PE regime continues that trend. Together with the core, the near-core forms an upper-income region of the country concentrated in the Northeastern third of the country.

The story of the near-core was one of expansion and then contraction consistent with the changing policy regimes. The near-core which had an optimistic pattern of expansion to the West during the FTM regime with roots in the industrial core of the country has shrunk to a Northeastern corridor dominated by the Baltimore-Washington metro area and the Boston and New York City regions bordering the only core state of 2000—Connecticut. In some regards this can be interpreted as a troubling outcome of the PE policies of the Reagan Revolution.

THE MIDDLE AND SEMI-PERIPHERY 1929–2000

For much of its history, the middle was geographically in the middle as states of the Great Plains, Interior, and Midwest formed this group. Additionally, the middle for five of the eight decades of this study was the largest group. The middle and semi-periphery are linked from 1940 to 2000. As membership in the middle increased the membership of the semi-periphery decreased from 1940 to 1980. From 1940 to 1980, Sunbelt states such as Florida, Texas, and Virginia left the periphery and semi-periphery and joined the middle.

Many of these Sunbelt states were part of the Gunbelt, which received a disproportionate share of federal and defense department funds during the Reagan Administration (Markusen et al. 1991; Crump 1989; Crump and Archer 1993). Hooks (2001) found evidence that from 1950 to 1990 federal investment in military facilities resulted in greater gains in manufacturing in Southern counties versus Northern counties. Social attitudes embracing militarism and warfare also helped these Southern states (Lind 2002). Some states, which received a disproportionate share of defense spending from administrations since the 1980s, have left the periphery and semi-periphery. The last two decades period of income convergence—1970 and 1980—saw the largest number of states in the middle with 22 and 19 states respectively, and almost every region of the country represented in the middle. Florida, Texas, and Virginia became members of the middle group, while most of the South, Northern New England, and some Western States remained in the periphery and semi-periphery.

Unfortunately, the semi-periphery from 1990 and 2000 became the largest region replacing the middle. This trend followed the predictive pattern associated with a shift to a PE regime from the FTM regime. The semi-periphery expanded as Southern and Western states and industrial states of the Midwest joined former middle states Florida and Texas in the semi-periphery. The trend of the semi-periphery growing to include Sunbelt states, states of the traditional manufacturing belt, Washington State and the states of the Great Plains is a disappointing but predictable trend. The irony of this expansion of the semi-periphery and periphery is that many of those Gunbelt and Sunbelt states did not benefit in the long-term. Being part of the Gunbelt was no ticket to the core or near-core even though the income differences between the core and the periphery and semi-periphery were not as large as they were at the beginning of the last FTM regime.

CONCLUSION

There were three purposes in conducting and presenting this research. The first purpose was to provide a systematic regionalization of the geography of the United States using a core and periphery method. This research found continuity and change in the regional geography of the United States using a core and periphery method. Many states, which were core or near-core, became semi-peripheral and some peripheral and semi-peripheral states improved to near-core and core status. Cyclical economic patterns and the resulting policy responses have clearly changed the regional geography of the country. States and regions which were considered backward or behind suddenly saw new investment and migration giving the country a new region called the Sunbelt while regions of older capital and population decline and became called the Rustbelt. Referring to these regions as Sunbelt or Rustbelt did not tell the full story of regional change or fully integrate the global and national processes working to change the geography of the country. Applying a systematic method and referring to places as core or periphery makes comparative, historical, and contemporary research and teaching more systematic, replicable, and meaningful. Tying these approaches with cultural-historical approaches broadens our understanding of the regional geography of countries and places within the changing dynamics of the world-economy and allows predictions of future regional trends and regional geographies of the United States.

The second purpose of this research was to examine changes in the core and periphery structure of the Untied States and to determine if regional incomes have become more or less spatially concentrated through time. Regional incomes in the US became less spatially concentrated until 1980 and then it increased from 1980 to 1990. There was a decline in the spatial concentration of income from 1990 to 2000, but the level of spatial concentration was higher than 1980. The regional composition of the upper-income groups followed a similar pattern of spatial concentration. In 1929, the core included California, Illinois, New York, Connecticut, and Delaware. From 1940 to 1980, the core and near-core regions expanded to Western and Midwestern States as the middle group of states expanded with the addition of former periphery and semi-periphery states. In the last 20 years, the periphery and semi-periphery grew in membership as states tumbled down from the middle and near-core. The growing peripheral regions once again created a disadvantaged Southern and Western region of the country similar to last PE regime before the Great Depression as the core in 2000 contracted to only one state—Connecticut.

The third purpose of this research was to test for Earle's (2003) theory of regional volatility and stability as measured by convergence and divergence in incomes during policy regime shifts in the United States. Incomes between core and peripheral regions were more volatile during the FTM phase and more stable during the PE phase as hypothesized. What made these results important was that instead of traditional or fixed regions based on social or cultural constructs a core-periphery approach was used. The key moments which spurred regional volatility were the Great Depression, World War II, and the economic crisis of the 1970s. The Second World War and Great Depression forced a massive federal intervention into the economy and society of America as the country mobilized to fight the Depression and contribute to the war effort. The period from 1940 to 1950 saw the greatest rate of income convergence. Afterwards, 1950 to 1980 saw a slower rate of income convergence between regions as the FTM regime initiated by Roosevelt and the New Deal continued. This period was marked by American dominance in the world-economy, the cold war military-industrial complex, and the civil rights movement, and the beginning of the Sunbelt boom. In 1980, the gap between the core and periphery came closest to convergence. But, the economic crisis during the 1970s signaled the need for new innovations and the Reagan Revolution of the PE regime followed.

The economic crisis of the 1970s caused by rising energy costs; foreign competition in steel, automobiles, and appliances; aging capital; and higher costs for social services ushered in the PE regime. The reaction to the crisis by the new PE regime was to force firms and governments to be more competitive and seek out cheaper labor; more flexible production systems, and increased government incentives and tax breaks. The Reagan Revolution brought in an era of favoring elites and producers. From 1980 to 1990, the gap between core and periphery regions increased and the number of states in the last two categories increased in number and geographic scope into the West and Midwest. There are now more states in the periphery and semi-periphery than there were in 1980, while the number of states in the core and near-core has decreased.

Future research will need to first explain the wider political implications in elections and administrations caused by changing core and periphery regional geographies of the country. Second, it should examine the changing social geographies resulting from core and periphery regional change. In conclusion, a systematic approach to the regional geography of the US has merit. It provides an approach which lends itself to comparative analysis and allows scholars to make more sound conclusions. Together with cultural-historical approaches the approach gives a more complete picture of the changing regional geography of the United States.

BIBLIOGRAPHY

Agnew, John. 1987. *The United States in the World-Economy*. (Cambridge: Cambridge University Press).

Barro, Robert, J and Xavier Sala-i-Martin. 1991. "Convergence across States and Regions," *Brookings Papers on Economic Activity* 1, 107–182.

———. 1992. "Convergence," *The Journal of Political Economy* 100, no. 2, 223–251.

Bernard, L. Weinstein, Harold T. Gross, and John Rees. 1985. *Regional Growth and Decline in the United States Second Edition*. (New York: Praeger Publishers).

Bensel, Richard Franklin. 1984. *Sectionalism and American Political Development 1880–1980.* (Madison: The University of Wisconsin Press).

Birdsall, Stephen, S., John W. Florin, and Margo L. Price. 1999. *Regional Landscapes of the United States and Canada, 5th Edition.* (New York: John Wiley & Sons, Inc).

Cobb, James, C. 1984. *Industrialization and Southern Society 1877–1984.* (Lexington: The University Press of Kentucky).

Crump, Jeff. 1989. "The Spatial Distribution of Military Spending in the United States 1941–1985," *Growth and Change* 12:38–62.

Crump, Jeff and J. Clark Archer. 1993. "Spatial and Temporal Variability in the Geography of American Defense Outlays," *Political Geography* 12:38–63.

Earle, Carville. 2001. "Beyond the Appalachians 1815–1860," *North American The Historical Geography of a Changing Continent*, edited by Thomas F. McIlwraith and Edward K. Muller, 165–188. (Lanham, Maryland: Rowman & Littlefield Publishers, Inc).

———. 2003. *The American Way A Geographical History of Crisis and Recovery.* (Lanham: Rowman & Littlefield Publishers, Inc).

Easterlin, Richard, A. 1961. "Regional Income Trends, 1840–1950," *American Economic History*, edited by Seymour E. Harris, 525–547 (New York: McGraw-Hill Book Company Inc).

Gastil, Raymond. 1975. *Cultural Regions of the United States.* (Seattle: University of Washington Press).

Garreau, Joel. 1981. *The Nine Nations of North America.* (New York: Avon Books).

Getis, Arthur, Judith Getis, and I.E. Quastler. 2001. *The United States and Canada, The Land and People.* (Second Edition. New York: McGraw-Hill).

Hooks, Gregory. 2001. "Guns and Butter, North and South The Federal Contribution to Manufacturing Growth 1940–1990," *The Second Wave Southern Industrialization from the 1940s to the 1970s*, edited by Philip Scranton, 255–285, (Athens: The University of Georgia Press).

Johnston, Ronald J. 1980. *The Geography of Federal Spending in the United States of America.* (New York: John Wiley & Sons, Ltd).

Kim, Sukkoo. 1995. "Expansion of Markets and the Geographic Distribution of Economic Activities: The Trends in U.S. Regional Manufacturing Structure, 1860–1987," *The Quarterly Journal of Economics* 110, no. 4, 881–908.

———. 1998. "Economic Integration and Convergence: U.S. Regions, 1840–1987," *The Journal of Economic History* 58, no. 3, 659–683.

Knox, Paul, John Agnew, and Linda McCarthy. 2003. *The Geography of the World Economy Fourth Edition.* (London: Arnold).

Kondratieff, Nicolai. 1935. "The Long Wave in Economic Life," *Review of Economic Statistics* 17:105–115.

Kondratieff, Nicolai. 1984. *The long-wave cycle.* (New York: Richardson and Snyder).

Lind, Michael. 2002. *Made In Texas: George W. Bush and the Southern Takeover of American Politics.* (New York: Basic Books).

Markusen, Ann, R. P. Hall, S. Campbell, and S. Deitrick. 1991. *The Rise of the Gunbelt: The Military Remapping of Industrial America.* (New York: Oxford University Press).

McKnight, Tom, L. 2004. *Regional Geography of the United States and Canada, 4th Edition.* (Upper Saddle River: Prentice Hall).

McWilliams, Carey. 1949. *California: The Great Exception.* (Berkeley: University of California Press).

North, Douglas C. 1966. *The Economic Growth of the United States, 1790–1860.* (New York: W.W. Norton).

Rogerson, Peter, A. 2001. *Statistical Methods for Geography.* (London: Sage Publications).

Patterson, J. H. 1994. *North America A Geography of the United States and Canada Ninth Edition.* (New York: Oxford University Press).

U.S. Census Bureau. 2003. *Statistical Abstract of the United States: 2003.* (Washington: GPO).

Wallerstein, Immanuel. 1979. *The Capitalist World-Economy.* (Cambridge: Cambridge University Press).

———. 1991. *The Politics of the World-Economy.* (Cambridge: Cambridge University Press).

Wishart, David. 2004. "Period and Region," *Progress in Human Geography* 28, no. 3:305–319.

Zelinsky, Wilbur. 1973. *The Cultural Geography of the United States.* (Englewood Cliffs: Prentice-Hall, Inc).

———. 1980. "North America's Vernacular Regions," *Annals of the Association of American Geographers* 70:1–16.

———. 1994. *Exploring the beloved country: geographical forays into American Society and Culture.* (Iowa City: University of Iowa Press).

Chapter Nine

Pre-Industrial, Industrial, and Post-Industrial Electoral Alignments in Ohio

Emily J. Duda and Fred M. Shelley

In the 2004 U.S. Presidential election, Ohio was a critical state. Democratic nominee John Kerry and Republican nominee George W. Bush made numerous visits to Ohio, and millions of dollars were spent by both sides in campaign advertising in the state. On Election Day, Bush won the electoral votes of Ohio by a margin of approximately 120,000 votes. Bush's victory in Ohio assured him of a national majority in the Electoral College.

The 2004 election was by no means the first in which Ohio played a pivotal role in determining the nationwide outcome. In 1948, Democrat Harry Truman won Ohio by 7,000 votes in his defeat of Republican Thomas Dewey. In 1976, Democrat Jimmy Carter won Ohio by only 11,000 votes in his win over Republican Gerald Ford. In both cases, a victory in Ohio was critical to national victory in the Electoral College. Dewey and Ford would have been elected to the Presidency had they won the electoral votes of Ohio. Indeed, since the Civil War only three Republican candidates—James G. Blaine in 1884 against Democrat Grover Cleveland, Benjamin Harrison in 1892 against Cleveland, and Richard M. Nixon in 1960 against John F. Kennedy—have won the electoral votes of Ohio while losing the election nationwide. No Republican has ever been elected President without carrying Ohio.

The importance of Ohio to electoral outcomes illustrates that the state holds a unique place in America's political and economic history. Ohio has been called the "Mother of Presidents," because more U.S. presidents have come from Ohio than any other state. This distinction is not a coincidence; because of Ohio's importance in determining the outcomes of elections nationwide, candidates from Ohio have frequently been selected by the major political parties to run for national office. Ohio is one of the country's leading agricultural states, a major industrial state, and the home of three major cities and many smaller metropolitan areas. Historically, Ohio has represented the

United States in microcosm, with its demographic, economic, cultural and political trends closely paralleling that of the country as a whole.

While Ohio as a whole is divided evenly, there is often substantial regional disparity within the state. For example, in 2004 Kerry carried Cuyahoga County, including the city of Cleveland, by a 2-1 popular vote margin. Bush achieved a statewide popular vote majority by winning seventy-two of the state's eighty-eight counties. Western and Southern Ohio are predominantly Republican, while Northeast Ohio is a Democratic stronghold. This pattern has typified most presidential elections in Ohio over the past several decades. The Democratic Party held sway over northeastern Ohio during the heyday of the steel industry, when labor unions were strong. However, the decline of steel and other industries in northeastern Ohio over the past three decades has not dramatically altered the voting patterns of the residents, even between generations.

Since Ohio is of such fundamental importance to both parties, understanding the nature of the voting patterns in this crucial state is of fundamental importance. The past few presidential elections have seen large amounts spent on extensive Ohio campaigns. Given the general pattern of presidential voting in Ohio, Democrats attempt to mobilize enough support in the northeastern part of the state to offset Republican strength elsewhere. For Republicans, it is a matter of eroding this mobilization to limit its effects, and increasing Republican turnout in the South and the West. Examining the politics of political division within Ohio can also offer insight into post-industrial political geography that could be applied to other areas as well. These factors of political and academic importance make it an area worth studying in detail. The analysis also provides support for Carville Earle's arguments about regime changes in the American political economy during the twentieth century.

In this paper, we trace the economic and political history of Ohio from the Civil War through the present. We then present the results of statistical and cartographic analysis of presidential election data on a county level from Ohio since 1860.

HISTORICAL SETTING

Ohio in 1860 was already recognized one of the country's leading industrial and agricultural states. Ohio's size, location, and even division among supporters of both major parties meant that the Buckeye State would play an important role in determining the outcomes of presidential elections throughout the late nineteenth and early twentieth centuries. So critical was Ohio to the outcome of Presidential elections that both parties often placed Ohioans on their national tickets. In fact, six of the ten men elected President in the fourteen Presidential elections between 1868 and 1920—Ulysses S. Grant, Rutherford B. Hayes, James A. Garfield, William McKinley, William Howard Taft, and Warren G. Harding—were from Ohio.

During these years, however, the electoral geography of Ohio was much different than is the case today. Northeastern Ohio is known as the "Western Reserve." The Western Reserve is located directly west of Connecticut and was claimed by Connecticut until the original Thirteen Colonies agreed to relinquish their western land claims in the 1780s. Nevertheless, northeastern Ohio was settled predominantly by migrants from Connecticut and elsewhere in New England. Many residents of northeastern Ohio, like their distant relatives in New England, were strong supporters of abolitionism. One of the leaders of the Underground Railroad was Owen Brown, who was a leading citizen of the Western Reserve community of Hudson, Ohio and the father of the famous abolitionist John Brown (DeCaro 2007). Many residents of the Western Reserve supported the new Republican Party after it came into existence in the 1850s, and they continued to support the Republicans during and after the Civil War.

Much of southern and western Ohio, on the other hand, was settled originally by migrants from Virginia and Kentucky moving northward across the Ohio River. These settlers, with their attitudes shaped by their Southern origins, tended to support Democrats before and after the Civil War. Moreover, some rural counties in Ohio had attracted substantial populations of immigrants from Germany and other parts of northwestern Europe. Ethnicity played a critical role in their votes as well; generally speaking, Protestant immigrants supported the Republicans, while Catholics supported the Democrats.

These considerations of ethnicity and ancestry played a critical role in Ohio's politics throughout the second half of the nineteenth century. Historian Frederick Jackson Turner (1908) noted the importance of these considerations in examining the persistence of sectional voting patterns in Ohio, Indiana, and Illinois. Turner developed choropleth maps showing the county-level distribution of Presidential popular votes in these states in the elections of 1856, 1868, 1888, and 1904. Their maps indicated high degrees of similarity in county-level outcomes in all four elections.

Of course, the major issues debated by political leaders changed dramatically during the last half of the nineteenth century. Even the identity of the voters themselves changed. Only those men who in their seventies, or older, in 1904 had been old enough to have cast ballots in 1856. Given that life expectancy in the United States in 1900 was roughly forty-seven years, the very large majority of those voters who cast ballots in the 1856 election had died before 1904. Yet Turner pointed out that most counties that had been Democratic in 1856 remained Democratic in 1904, and that most counties that had been Republican in 1856 remained Democratic in 1904.

Turner attributed this continuity to the persistence of ethnic and cultural influences on election outcomes. The electoral pattern observed by Turner across Ohio, Indiana, and Illinois was analyzed quantitatively by Shelley and Archer (1989). As Shelley and Archer demonstrated, the traditional voting breakdown observed by Turner broke down during and after the Great Depression. By the 1940s, northeastern Ohio, which was heavily Republican in the nineteenth century, had become strongly Democratic. Meanwhile, rural areas of Ohio become more and more aligned with the Republicans, regardless of the ethnic or cultural origins of their inhabitants.

The political realignment of Ohio is associated with the transition of Ohio's economy from an agricultural to an industrial economy. By the early twentieth century, industrial workers began to outnumber farmers in Ohio. Areas that were once predominantly agricultural evolved into manufacturing centers. Labor unions became active in organizing workers in Ohio, as elsewhere across the United States, especially in the 1930s. The percentage of American workers who were labor union members increased from 8 percent of the labor force in 1920 to more than 25 percent by 1944 (Barone 1990). Within industrializing communities, politics became conceptualized in terms of conflict between management and labor. Many union members and their leaders supported the Democrats, who were regarded generally as more friendly to labor relative to the Republicans, who were considered more oriented to big business.

Immigration also played a role in Ohio's political transition. Between 1890 and World War I, thousands of immigrants from southern and eastern Europe moved to Ohio. Most immigrants who moved to Ohio migrated to industrial cities such as Cleveland, Akron, Youngstown, and Toledo, where many took jobs in steel mills or factories. As they became naturalized U.S. citizens, many of these immigrants, and their children, identified with labor unions and with the Democratic Party.

The steel industry played a fundamental role in Ohio's industrialization, particularly in the northeastern part of the state. The earliest steel companies were in place by the beginning of the century and by World War II, many were confident in the strength of the industry. The unions grew in power and maintained much influence over politics within the area. Thus, after the Depression, the surge of Democratic strength was seen throughout the area, stretching from Cleveland to Pittsburgh in neighboring Pennsylvania. The 1940s also stimulated the perception of steel as a source of pride for the area. Because steel was inherently fundamental to the development of equipment for the war, the industry was connected with patriotism and the sense that the steel workers helped to 'win the war' via their industrial efforts. This also enabled the unions to make significant demands of the industrial corporation leaders since the necessity of steel gave them great clout.

Other heavy industries were prevalent in other Ohio communities. For example, Akron, which called itself "The Rubber Capital of the World," has long been known as a center for rubber production (Love et al. 1998). Companies such as Firestone, Goodyear, and General Tire employed thousands of workers at their plants in Akron, manufacturing rubber tires that were also critical to the war effort during World War II. Toledo was historically the major U.S. center for manufacturing auto safety glass used in windshields (Floyd 2004). Toledo was also a major automobile center. Willys-Overland, which first developed the Jeep, maintained its only production facility in Toledo until the much larger Ford Motor Company was authorized by the U.S. government to make Jeeps during World War II. Tires, windshields, and Jeeps were essential to the U.S. war effort, just as steel was, and their importance gave labor considerable clout during and immediately after the war.

THE DECLINE OF HEAVY INDUSTRY AND ITS POLITICAL IMPLICATIONS

The prevalence of steel and other major heavy industries made many towns highly dependent economically on the plants around which these communities grew up. Steel and other industries brought many immigrants to the areas and populations multiplied as the need for workers expanded. Industry was not diversified in many places and therefore the fate of the city was tied to that of the mill. This made such "steel towns" economically precarious, since any change or impact on the industry directly impacted the population. However, it also created a factor of unification among those who lived in such areas. People could not afford to be apathetic about the fate of the mills, since their fate affected all those who lived in the town. Those employed in service industries depended on revenue from wages paid to industrial workers. Therefore, economic dependence also served to unite people who were concerned about the security of their jobs.

Labor unions achieved their peak levels of influence between the 1930s and the 1950s. Steel factories in Youngstown, rubber plants in Akron, and many other industries unionized in the 1930s following often acrimonious and occasionally violent clashes between union organizers and management. After World War II, however, the level of antagonism between management and labor lessened as both sides participated in the general prosperity of mid-twentieth century America. Both labor and management agreed that unionized industrial workers should be paid "family wages" high enough for them to support themselves, their stay-at-home wives, and their children comfortably (Barone 1990; Glickman 1997). These family wages enabled industrial workers to own houses, cars, and other consumer durables, gave them time and money for recreational activities and vacations, and provided them with the opportunity to save for retirement.

Payment of family wages reinforced loyalty between the worker and the company. A young man graduating from high school in an industrial community in the 1940s and 1950s could expect the opportunity to go to work in a factory shortly after graduation, to get married and raise a family, and to remain with the company until he retired with a comfortable pension and security in his old age. During the heyday of industrialization in Ohio and elsewhere, millions of industrial workers earned such family wages and remained with their companies throughout their working lives. However, this system began to break down in the 1970s. Facing increased global competition, many industrial concerns in Ohio and elsewhere closed, relocated to the Sunbelt, or moved overseas. Plant closure forced thousands of industrial workers who had anticipated and planned on the job security associated with the family wage system out of work. Many of these workers found themselves unemployed, with few skills or employment alternatives, after many years on the job.

Why did steel mills and other plants close? There are a variety of reasons, including industrial restructuring at the global level and management issues at the local level. Some of the closures were associated with global economic restructuring. Plants in Ohio and elsewhere in the Rustbelt became less and less competitive with locations elsewhere in the United States or abroad. The U.S. steel industry, for example, became concentrated in places like Ohio and Pennsylvania in part because of proximity to coal from Appalachia, iron ore from Minnesota, and access to shipping through the Great Lakes or the Ohio River. By the 1970s, however, transportation costs had become a less and less significant component of overall production costs, while labor costs increased. Advancements in shipping made it cheaper for coal and other materials to be purchased cheaply from other countries or areas and then shipped elsewhere, causing the area to effectively lose its geographic edge. Labor costs, in contrast, were high relative to those in other countries. Critics of the labor union movement blamed the unions for keeping wages too high, decreasing the competitiveness of the American steel industry internationally.

In addition, markets that were once concentrated in the United States globalized. As countries such as Japan industrialized rapidly, they became important markets for steel and other heavy industrial products. Thus, more and more American steel was marketed overseas. Not only did the decline in domestic consumption of steel reduce the geographic advantage of places such as eastern Ohio over other domestic locations, but it also increased the incentive for steel company owners to develop operations overseas, where labor costs were typically much lower and which were in many cases located closer to foreign markets.

The city of Youngstown in northeastern Ohio represents an informative case study (Linkon and Russo 2003). Between the 1920s and the 1960s, Youngstown served as the headquarters for Youngstown Sheet and Tube, and hosted foundries operated by Republic Steel and U.S. Steel. During World War II, more than 57,000 people were employed in steel mills and factories in and near Youngstown, producing about 11 percent of all steel in the United States (Youngstown Sheet and Tube 1950). Reinforcing the importance of the family wage, in 1950 a company publication pointed out that Youngstown Steel and Tube had 3,591 employees who had been with the company for more than twenty-five years (Youngstown Sheet and Tube 1950). Youngstown was not immune, however, from labor disputes. The Youngstown steel mills were unionized in 1937, following a prolonged and sometimes violent dispute in which several strikers lost their lives (Stolberg 1937; Blake 2001). In 1952, President Harry S Truman responded to the threat of a steelworkers' strike by attempting to seize steel mills and force them to remain open. The Supreme Court declared such action unconstitutional in *Youngstown Sheet and Tube* v. *Sawyer* (343 U.S. 579 (1952)). In 1955, Youngstown Sheet and Tube was ranked seventieth on the *Fortune* 500 list and had more than 25,000 employees in the Youngstown area, Chicago, and elsewhere.

During the 1960s, Youngstown Sheet and Tube was purchased by the Lykes Corporation. The government had been advised against allowing the merger of Lykes, a shipping corporation, with Youngstown Sheet and Tube, but this recommendation was ignored and the merger proceeded. Lykes had no interest in keeping Youngstown Sheet and Tube competitive, and the Youngstown plant deteriorated. The newest machines dated back to the forties and most of them were older than that. The plants were inefficient and could not be 'justified' from a revenue standpoint. Lykes did not reinvest in the plant or updated it with new technologies. Rather, Lykes invested revenues generated from sales at its Youngstown plant elsewhere (Linkon and Russo 2003).

When Lykes and other plants began to close, questions about blame for the closure were inevitably raised. Management sometimes blamed labor unions, arguing that wages, which represented a significant portion of overall operating costs, were too high. Union members and others blamed the closure on questionable management decisions and processes. Many argued that the plants' lack of profitability was not the fault of the workers and the question was raised of why the workers should have to suffer for irresponsible decisions made by upper management executives who were not "steel people" and who in many cases had few if any ties to the local community.

After the closure announcement, many organizations worked to keep the plants open. Groups such as the Ecumenical Council united people across religious differences, also attempting to bring together both the workers and the local management (Fuechtmann 1989). Voters tended to support politicians who were 'for Youngstown' regardless of party affiliation. The idea of a communal buyout of the plants increased this partisan unity even more.

On a national level, the unions did little to help. Once the plants started to close, the local union chapters were seen as potential liabilities to the unions on a national level. The national leaders did not want to interfere for fear that an attempt to save plants in Ohio would have repercussions for unionized plants elsewhere. Local union leaders got little support from their national unions and were left to their own devices.

Initial efforts were focused on the saving of the Lykes plant and others like it in the area. Workers in these other plants felt that if they promised to maintain company-set quotas they could protect their plants from suffering the same fate as the Lykes plant. Union officials met with company leaders to arrange a situation that would be mutually beneficial. However, as with the Lykes Corporation, duplicity was often involved. Plants were closed even after repeated denials and statements to the contrary.

On what became known as "Black Monday," September 19, 1977, Lykes announced that Youngstown Steel and Tube would soon close. When it became clear that the Youngstown Steel and Tube plant was going to close, the community used a strategy to try and buy the mill itself. However, the courts ruled against the community's effort to buy out the plants. This situation was not unique to Youngstown, however. Such rulings reoccurred in the Eighties when a similar attempt was made near Pittsburgh with the Duquesne mill. The problem was not any particular judge or local conflict. Rather, on a national level "courts provide[d] difficult policy terrain for the realization of populist goals" (Portz 1990: 120).

Due to the level of community involvement, politicians were faced with few possibilities. The community response forced them to support measures to benefit the industry or face a failure to get re-elected. However, this was only possible on the local level. The political investment of many such politicians was called "superficial" and electoral threats were only possible on a local level (Buss and Redburn 1987). Attempts to influence politicians beyond the local sphere met with a distinctly higher measure of failure. This suggests that the plight of Youngstown and similar cities was not a priority for either Democrats or Republicans at the state or national level. Rather it was a local issue which only local politicians took up and represented to the larger government.

The strength of local government and the interest towards buyouts presented a challenge on the national level. Because the sense of community was so intense, there was also perception of the area's politics as tending towards populism or socialism. This fundamental incompatibility with the dominant ideology of capitalism in the United States made a national reaction precarious. It also likely decreased the chance of republican support since, despite the fact that a democratic president was in office when the shutdowns occurred, republicans have a long-standing reputation as being the more capital-oriented of the two major parties.

The disinterest and inability of the national government towards reaction to the economic collapse becomes visible when examining the actions taken and even the possibility of action. Essentially, the government could not react effectively, even if it had wanted to, and did little to show support when it could. There were attempts to influence to government on a national level, such as ads taken out by the Ecumenical Council. However, these largely failed since the constituency's problems were not of sufficient magnitude nationally to sway the government at a federal level.

A similar situation prevailed in nearby Akron. Rubber had been the major economic base of Akron since the early twentieth century (Love et al. 1998). Much of the rubber processed in Akron was used to make tires for the millions of cars, trucks, and other vehicles produced in the Great Lakes region. Akron was the headquarters of the Goodyear Tire and Rubber Company and other rubber-manufacturing corporations, which employed thousands of workers. By 1926, Goodyear was the world's largest rubber company. Tire production soared during World War II in order to meet the needs of Allied military forces, and continued to increase after the war as demand for automobiles expanded in America's rapidly growing suburbs.

However, in the 1950s radial tires came into common use. A radial tire lasts about three times as long as previously produced bias-ply tires. Akron's old tire factories, whose machinery was designed to manufacture bias-ply tires, did not have the technology to handle the manufacturing requirements associated with radial tire production. The shift to radial tires helped accelerate the decline of the rubber industry in Akron during the 1970s. During the 1970s alone, tire factory employment in Akron dropped in half. By the 1990s, Goodyear was the only tire manufacturing corporation that remained active in Akron.

What were the political implications of industrial restructuring and its impact on employment in Youngstown, Akron, and other industrialized communities in Ohio? The Youngstown Steel and Tube case was one of many industrial restructuring crises that occurred in the 1970s and 1980s in Ohio and elsewhere in the "Rust Belt." What were the political implications of this crisis? During the late 1970s, the White House was occupied by Democrat Jimmy Carter, and the Democrats controlled both houses of Congress. Many in Youngstown felt that the Carter administration had done nothing to keep Steel and Tube open, despite local efforts, and this created immense dissatisfaction with the Carter administration.

After the closing of the plants in the Valley, significantly negative factors increased throughout the area. Rates of suicide and spousal abuse went up. There was a sense of loss and dissatisfaction coupled with an inability to take action. People were angry, but that anger had little outlet for venting. People felt that there had to be somebody to blame, but there was uncertainty as to whom they should blame and what they could do about the situation.

By the 1980s, it was clear that the steel industry in Youngstown, the rubber industry in Akron, and other industries had been swept into a decline from which they have never recovered. Today, industrial jobs no longer represent a major portion of the area's economic base. An increasing percentage of employment is in services and in quaternary-sector institutions such as Youngstown State University and the University of Akron. Regardless of industry's actual future, they built up a blue-collar culture that is lasting enough to still influence politics over three decades after Black Monday and the initial closings. Public perception of local image still reflects a blue-collar tendency despite the actual economic move away from jobs in the industrial sector.

The political repercussions of the steel closings varied. However, much of the evidence points to the fact that after the initial shock of closure, political affiliations did not change with the economic shift as they had in the past. Since the closings began under a Democratic presidency and since the unions themselves were of little use in the struggle, a political shift would not only be unsurprising but perhaps even expected. After all, pre- and post-New Deal politics were strongly shaped by the economic setting of the community. However, the shift away from Democrats in national-level politics in northeastern Ohio was only temporary; the Democrats remain the dominant party in northeastern Ohio today.

ANALYSIS

In order to examine changes in Ohio's electoral geography quantitatively, we examined Democratic voting percentages by county in Ohio for each Presidential election between 1860 and 2004. The data set consisted of the percentage of the popular vote obtained by the Democratic presidential nominee in each of Ohio's 88 counties for each of the 36 elections comprising the study period. The boundaries of Ohio's counties have remained unchanged throughout the study period, ensuring geographic continuity. Thus, the data set consisted of 3,168 voting percentages.

In order to extract meaningful information from this large data set, we applied time-series or T-mode factor analysis in order to identify time periods associated with similar electoral patterns. The use of factor analysis in examining election results at the subnational level over time was pioneered by Archer and Taylor (1981), who examined election sequences at the state level in the United States from 1828 through 1980. This state-level analysis has been updated on several occasions (Archer and Shelley 1994; Shelley et al. 1996). It has been applied to county-level data in various states and in various subsections of the United States, including the states of Illinois, Indiana, and Ohio together (Shelley and Archer 1989).

The first step in applying the factor-analytic technique, described in detail by Shelley et al. (1996, chapter 9), involves calculation of correlations between pairs of elections. Thus, a 36x36 matrix of correlations, with a correlation coefficient associated with each pair of elections, was calculated. A high correlation coefficient implies that those areas that were highly Democratic in the first election were Democratic in the second election, whereas those that were highly Republican in the first election were Republican in the second election. For example, the 2000 and 2004 elections were highly correlated. In both cases, the Democrats won northeastern Ohio but lost southern Ohio, western Ohio, and most rural areas. The county-level correlation between the two elections at the county level in Ohio was r=.96. This very high correlation illustrates that the geography of Presidential politics in Ohio changed very little between the 2000 and 2004 elections.

From the correlation matrix, the factor-analytic method identifies factors, or groups of elections that are highly correlated with one another but uncorrelated with other factors. To the extent that a factor is associated with a historically meaningful time sequence, the factor can be seen as representative or typical of the electoral geography of the state during that time period. A factor loading, or correlation coefficient between the factor and the election, is calculated for each election. The higher the factor loading, the more typical the election is of the time period with which the factor is associated. Often, electoral geographers identify and map the outcome of an election associated with a high loading associated with each factor in order to illustrate the geographic parameters of that factor.

When the technique was applied to the Ohio data set, three factors were identified. Together, the three factors accounted for more than 85% of the variance in the initial data set. In other words, the information associated with three factors across 36 elections, or 108 loadings, represents nearly five-sixths of the information in the entire data set of 3,168 data points. Moreover, the three factors each identify important periods in Ohio's political and economic history (figure 9.1).

The first factor is associated with the elections from 1864 through 1932—in other words, from the Civil War through the beginning of the Great Depression. We label this factor "pre-industrial," as it represents a period of history in which agriculture was a mainstay of Ohio's political economy. The geography of the pre-industrial factor is illustrated by the county-level map of the election of 1892 (figure 9.2). In this election, as in other elections in the nineteenth and early twentieth century, the Democrats were relatively weak in northeastern Ohio and were stronger in the southern and western portions of the state. Differences between adjacent rural counties were associated with differences in the ethnic and cultural background of settlers in these counties.

The second factor is associated with the transition period associated with the heyday of union activity and the emergence of Ohio as a modern industrial state. The election of 1940 typifies this pattern (figure 9.3). By 1940, the Democrats had emerged as the dominant party in union-oriented, urban communities such as Cleveland, Akron, Youngstown, and Toledo. Although some residual support for the Democrats remained in rural areas, by 1940 the Republicans had begun to make significant inroads in rural areas throughout the state.

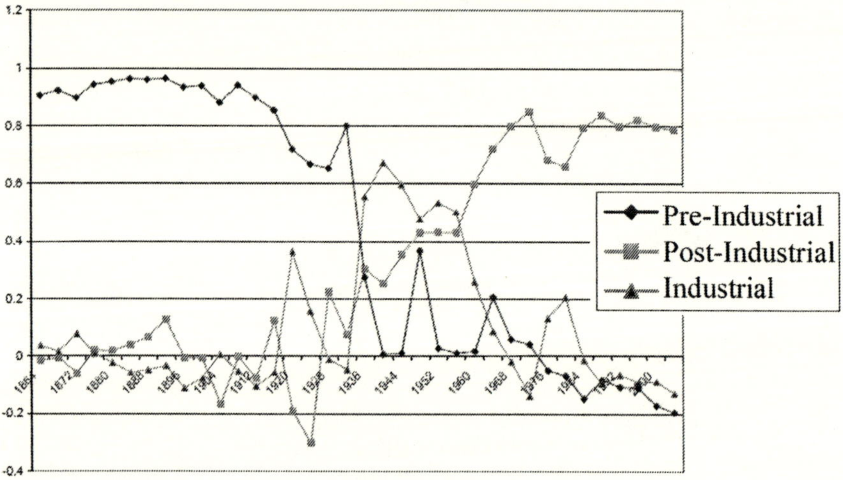

Figure 9.1. Election Year Factor Analysis

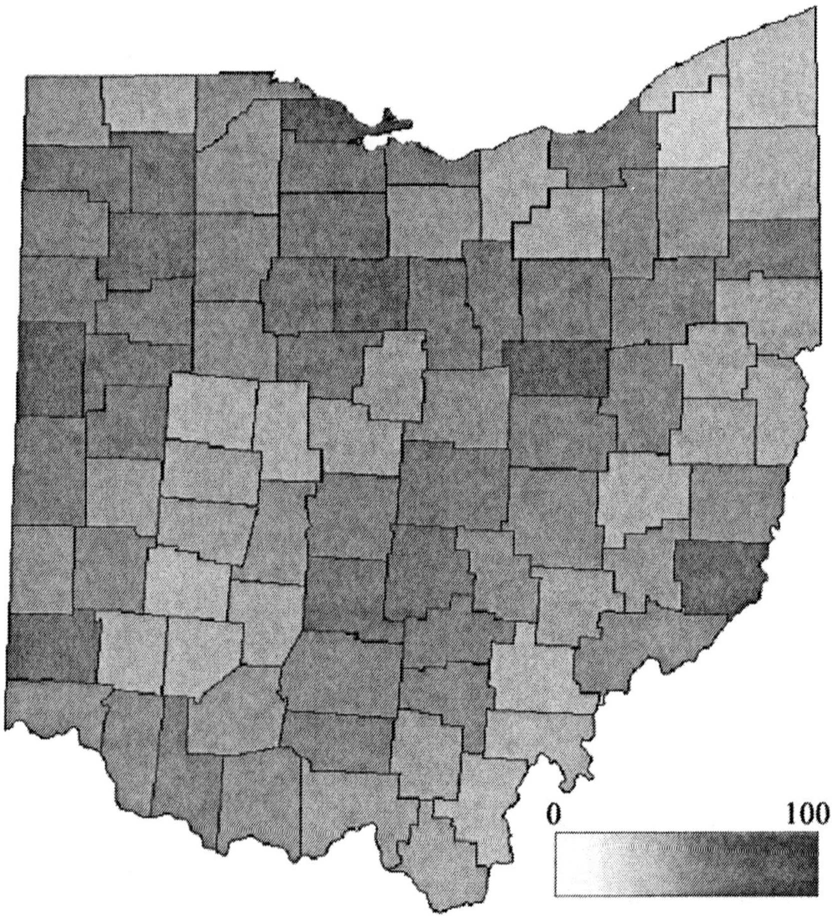

Figure 9.2. Democratic Vote Percentages—1892

The elections since the 1960s, after which industrial employment in Ohio began to decline, are typified by the election of 2004 (figure 9.4). As indicated previously, George W. Bush won 72 of Ohio's counties while John Kerry won only 16. However, Kerry did much better in urban than in rural areas. The average county won by Kerry has more than 350,000 residents; the average county carried by Bush has only 82,000 residents. Bush won the state by sweeping rural and suburban areas across Ohio, particularly in the southern and western portions of the state. This enabled him to overcome Kerry's large margins in Cleveland, Akron, Youngstown, Toledo and other industrial cities and counties.

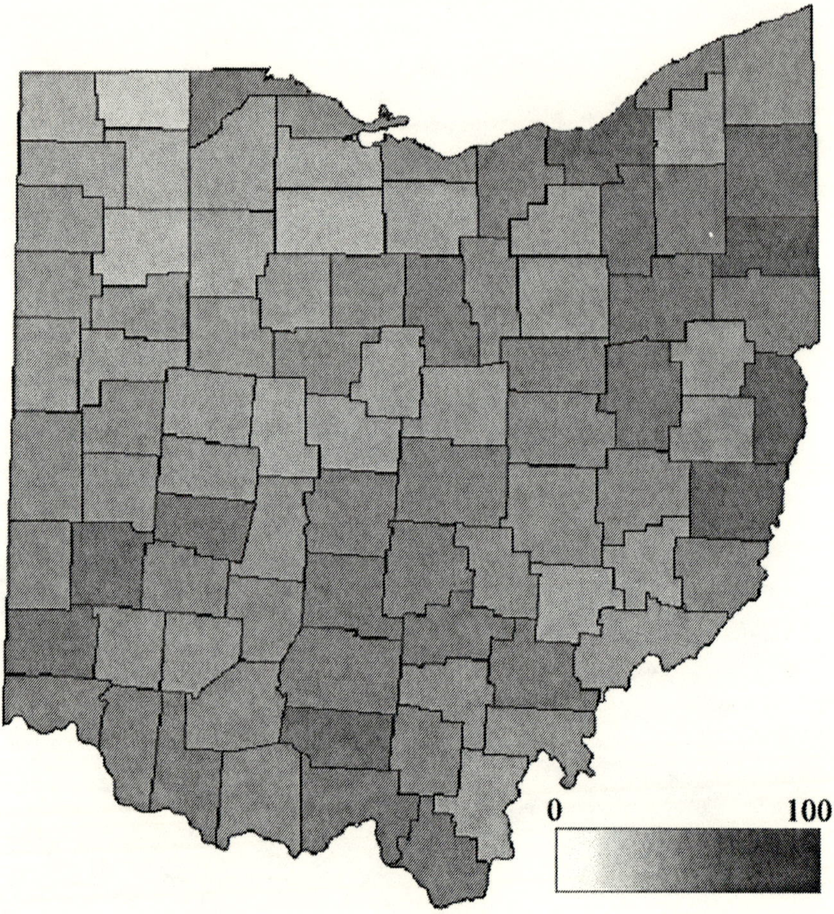

Figure 9.3. Democratic Vote Percentages—1940

Significantly, the transition periods evident in the geography of presidential elections within Ohio coincide with major shifts in the American political economy as described by Earle (2003). Earle argued that American capitalism has shifted between pr "protectionist-elite" cycles and "free trade-masses" cycles at intervals of approximately fifty years. Beginning around 1930, the Depression and the New Deal was a period in which the American political economy cycled from a protectionist-elite regime to a free trade-oriented regime. This transition coincided with transition from the agrarian electoral geography that had characterized Ohio politics since the Civil War to the industrial regime highlighting labor-management disputes that was characteristic of the mid-twentieth century. Another protectionist-elite regime, termed

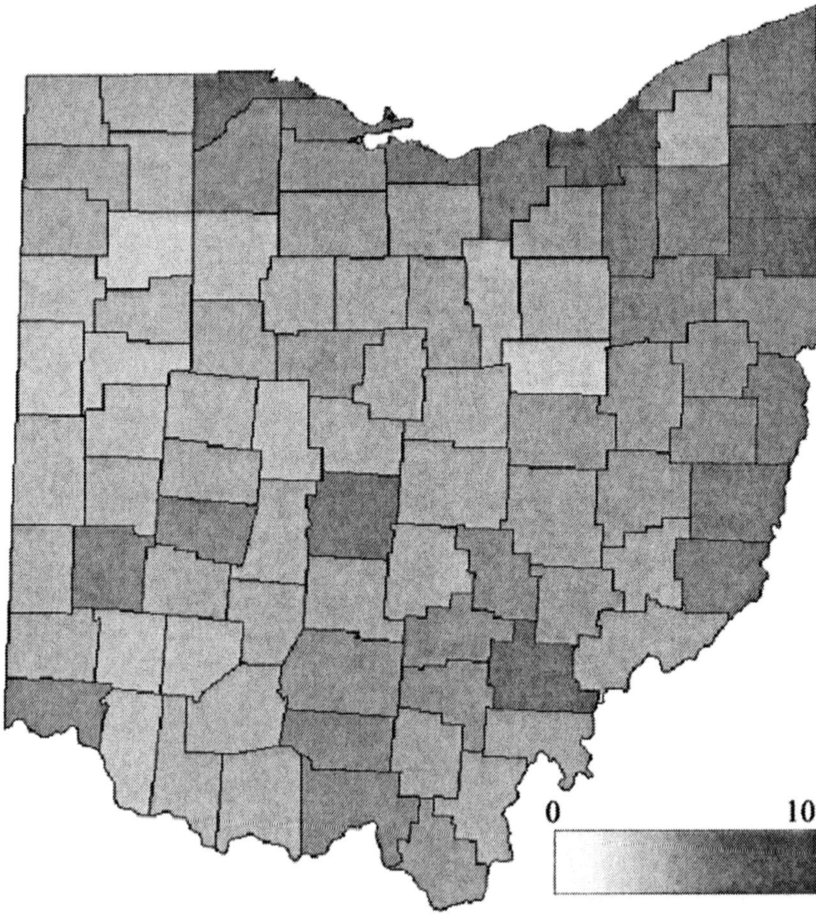

Figure 9.4. Democratic Vote Percentages—2000

the "Third Republic" by Earle, began around 1980. This transition coincided with the large scale closure of steel plants in Youngstown, rubber plants in Akron, and other factories throughout the state. The transition also coincided with the rise of Ohio's current electoral geography.

Overall, the analysis shows clearly how voting patterns in Ohio have changed in response to changes in the state's industrial structure. The elections before the 1930s load most highly on Factor 1. We label this the "pre-industrial" factor in that it represents elections that took place when Ohio was still a predominantly rural and agricultural state. Factor 2, which encompasses the elections of the 1930s, 1940s, and 1950s, is labeled the "industrial" factor in that these elections coincide with the heyday of industrial and labor union activity in Ohio. This factor is associated with Earle's free trade-masses period encompassing the New Deal, World War II, and the postwar period. Factor 3 is labeled the "post-industrial" factor. This factor is associated with the elections that have taken place in recent years. During Earle's "Third Republic," many heavy industries in Ohio and elsewhere have shut down or downsized at a time when continuing prosperity in the state is contingent on post-industrial tertiary or quaternary sector activity.

CONCLUSION

Ohio has played a pivotal role in U.S. presidential politics for the past 150 years. Since the Civil War, only three presidents have been elected without carrying Ohio, and no Republican has ever won the presidency without carrying the state. Yet the state has long been characterized by internal political division. Areas such as the Western Reserve, which were once staunchly Republican, are now solidly Democratic. Parts of southern and western Ohio were Democratic during the late nineteenth and early twentieth centuries, but today they are heavily republican.

Quantitative analysis of election outcomes on a county-by-county basis across Ohio illustrated that geographic changes in the patterns of presidential election outcomes in Ohio were associated closely with political-economic transition. Prior to the 1930s, agriculture remained central to Ohio's economy. At that time, historical ethnic and cultural factors were highly important in determining voting patterns. This period ended abruptly during the 1930s, when the Great Depression and the New Deal nationwide and the unionization of many heavy industries locally resulted in substantial political change. Once heavily Republican, counties of northeastern Ohio shifted toward the Democrats, while historically democratic strongholds gravitated to the Republicans. The decline in heavy industry and the associated transition of Ohio from an industrial to a post-industrial economy has enhanced these divisions. Today, Ohio presidential politics are highly polarized, with formerly industrial areas heavily Democratic and rural and suburban locations strongly republican. The results of the analysis illustrate strong correspondence between economic and political change in Ohio, and provide a springboard for further analysis elsewhere.

BIBLIOGRAPHY

Archer, J. Clark, and Fred M. Shelley. 1994. "Some Geographical Aspects of the 1992 American Presidential Election." *Political Geography*, 13: 137-159.

Archer, J. Clark, and Peter J. Taylor. 1981. *Section and Party*. (Chichester: Wiley).

Barone, Michael. 1990. *Our Country: The Shaping of America from Roosevelt to Reagan*. (New York: The Free Press).

Blake, Benjamin. 2001. "Ohio's Steel Mill War: The Little Steel Strike of 1937." *Crooked River*. December.

Buss, Terry F., and F. Stevens Redburn, 1987. "Plant Closings: Impacts and Responses," *Economic Development Quarterly*, 1: 170–177.

DeCaro, Louis A., Jr. 2007. *John Brown: The Cost of Freedom*. (New York: International Publishers).

Earle, Carville, 2003. *The American Way*. (Boulder, Colorado: Rowman and Littlefield).

Floyd, Barbara. 2004. *Toledo: The Twentieth Century*. (Chicago: Arcadia).

Fuechtmann, Thomas G. 1989. *Steeples and Stacks: Religion and Steel Crisis in Youngstown*. (New York: Cambridge University Press).

Glickman, Lawrence B. 1997. *A Living Wage: American Workers and the Making ofConsumer Society*. (Ithaca: Cornell University Press).

Linkon, Sherry Lee, and John Russo. 2003. *Steeltown USA: Work and Memory in Youngstown*. (Lawrence: University Press of Kansas).

Love, Steve, David Giffels, and Debbie Van Tassel. 1998. *Wheels of Fortune: The Story of Rubber in Akron*. (Akron, Ohio: University of Akron Press).

Portz, John. 1990. *The Politics of Plant Closings*. (Lawrence: University Press of Kansas).

Shelley, Fred M., and J. Clark Archer. 1989. "Sectionalism and Presidential Politics in America: A Twentieth Century Reinvestigation of Voting Patterns in Illinois, Indiana and Ohio." *Journal of Interdisciplinary History* 20: 227–255.

Shelley, Fred M., J. Clark Archer, Fiona M. Davidson, and Stanley D. Brunn. 1996. *Discovering America's Political Geography*. (New York: Guilford Press).

Stolberg, Benjamin. 1937. "Big Steel, Little Steel, and the CIO," *The Nation*, 145:119–123.

Turner, Frederick Jackson. 1908. "Is Sectionalism in America Dying Away?" *American Journal of Sociology*, 13: 661–75.

Youngstown Sheet and Tube, 2007. "50 Years in Steel: The Story of the Youngstown Sheet and Tube Company." June 26, 2007, <http: youngstownsteel.com>.

Chapter Ten

Globalization Bites Back

A New Type of Crisis for the "American Way"?

John Agnew

In *The American Way* (2003), Carville Earle identified a historical-geographical regularity to crisis-response in US history with alternation between periods of "elite nationalist republic" (1780–1828; 1880–1932; 1980–) and "egalitarian internationalist democracy" (1828–1877; 1932–1970s) each with distinctive geographical features (republics: concentration of population, increased between-region income inequality, regional specialization and stability; democracies: the opposite). This alternation has "enabled Americans to cope with . . . recurrent crises (occurring at half-century intervals), to preserve equilibrium in the American polity, to sustain economic growth, and to maintain an expansive political economy" (Earle 2003: 1). If this logic is correct, then the United States has entered a new republican era even as it has established a "transnational state" since 1980 based largely on seemingly opposite (liberal) principles. In this chapter I want to pick up on and explore this paradox, not to dispute the overall argument of Carville Earle's opus, which I think has much merit, but to suggest that perhaps this time around the crisis is somewhat more problematic than previous ones, not least because increasingly any way out of it is no longer entirely in American hands.

Earle sees the new U.S. transnational state beginning with the Reagan administration in 1980 as fundamentally an elite nationalist republic in the historic mold. Yet in many of its fundamentals, as noted by both "liberal" (Friedman 2005) and "Marxist" (Harvey 2006) authors, this regime is famously "neo-liberal," associated with free flows of capital, volatile patterns of regional economic diversification, consumer-driven demand, and the wit and wisdom of Chicago School economists rather than with the stable regional specialization, protectionism, and producer revolutions of the conventional elite nationalist republic (Agnew and Corbridge 1995; Paul 2005). The theoretical problem is that the geographic scope of the operations of the

U.S. state (economic, political and juridical) has globalized, yet the political constituency of the U.S. government remains territorial. This is the root of the contemporary dilemma and what makes the current crisis different from previous ones (Agnew 2005).

As Earle (2003: 47–48) notes in *The American Way*, "it is clear that globalization is imposing new demands on the American political system and, most explicitly, on the nature of the American state." At one and the same time, therefore, the U.S. economy must respond to new challenges imposed by an open economy yet also nurture a state that is increasingly transnational in geographic scope. The world economy the United States has created beyond its territorial boundaries by means of this transnational state is no longer one in which all of America sees a positive reflection. Though the American economy recovered from the worst negative trends of the 1970s and 1980s, there is nevertheless a widespread unease about what the world economy now delivers to the United States. Since the downturn of 2008 this sense of foreboding has only increased. As this chapter claims, there is good reason for this. The United States now faces a crisis in its relations with the global economy. This is not to say that the United States is uniformly a victim of its own hegemony. But during the 1990s and early 2000s it was mainly the financial sector, housing, wholesale and retail, and a bubble economy associated with Internet services and telecommunications that drove national economic growth. Many other sectors have experienced little other than decline, particularly in relation to job growth and global market share provided from plants in the United States. There is a serious contradiction, therefore, between the new transnational U.S. state, on the one hand, and the consequences of its operations on behalf of powerful actors within an increasingly globalized world economy, on the other hand, for the population of the territorial United States (and between its constituent regions) that will not be as readily resolved as the previous crises for which Carville Earle offers such persuasive explanation. Any attempt at trying to resolve it solely domestically is likely to be unsuccessful. The world economy the United States itself helped to engender since 1980 is no longer readily separable into national parts that can be "managed" independently of one another.

A NOVEL CRISIS FOR THE AMERICAN WAY?

Though the American economy might seem to have done well from 1990 to the mid-2000s, or at least better than in the 1970s and 1980s, many Americans have not done very well at all. At the same time the U.S. macroeconomic position has deteriorated profoundly. The outcome for who has won and who has lost depends, however, on where they live and which industries they work for. Major metropolitan areas have experienced the largest shares of total national economic growth, but they also illustrate most visibly the growing national polarization in incomes and wealth between rich and poor. The 1990s and early 2000s was a good period for America's richest people. It was more problematic for everyone else. The second section of the chapter, therefore, moves from the impasse of the United States in the world economy to examination of the consequences for groups and places within the United States. The main point is that the identity between the U.S. and world economies that is necessary for overall domestic political support of the U.S. transnational state can no longer be taken for granted. Political consequences seem likely to follow.

A common view, I think shared by Carville Earle at the time he was writing *The American Way*, is that since 1980 the United States had experienced something of an economic renaissance. Certainly compared to the "dark years" of 1970–1985 when low economic growth combined with high inflation, and relative to other major industrial countries, the recent general trajectory of the US economy was more favorable. In the late 1990s as the U.S. stock market boomed and new informational technologies promised a seemingly endless era of growth, the so-called "new economy," the United States seemed to reestablish its centrality to innovation in manufacturing and services in the world economy (e.g., Jorgenson, Ho, and Stiroh 2006; Amiti and Stiroh 2007). Overall, however, the idea that the American economy stood on top of the world was questionable even before the economic earthquake of 2008. The tendency of U.S. official statistics to overstate economic performance followed by later downward revisions plus the tendency for estimates of economic performance elsewhere (for example in the Eurozone) to be revised upward is an important element in establishing the misleading picture (*Financial Times*, 1 August 2006). Some signs in 2003–2006 did point towards a significant upturn in U.S. economic growth compared to other countries but much of this was due more to higher rates of population growth, cost cutting and employees working longer hours than to a profound "productivity revolution" (McKinsey Global Institute 2001). Part of the story of American economic growth since the 1980s has been of one false dawn after another, based increasingly on cooperative funding by foreigners, so a measure of skepticism is in order as to the sustainability of the most recent 2003 "turnaround," particularly after the credit crunch and financial meltdown of 2008.

Over the fifteen years from 1989 to 2002, the best measure of economic performance, growth in gross domestic product per capita, averaged 1.6 percent for the United States, much the same as in Japan but much less than in

Germany (1.9 percent). At the same time the main measure of what causes economic growth, change in level of multifactor productivity (efficiency of using capital, labor, and technology), grew more slowly in the United States than in either Japan or Germany (respectively, annual averages of 0.9 percent, 1.3 percent, and 2.6 percent). Its unemployment rate averaged 5.8 percent, lower than Germany's 7.8 percent but higher than Japan's 2.4 percent (Economist 8 April 1999: 10; Mishel et al. 2003, chapter 7). In the recession between 2000 and 2003 the U.S. unemployment rate climbed back above 6 percent as the country lost around 2.7 million jobs. In only one way did the United States outperform either of these other industrial countries during this period: job creation. Even in this respect the recovery from the 2001 recession generated far fewer new jobs than expected. Moreover, many of the new jobs that have replaced the mainly manufacturing sector jobs lost in the United States, in the 1990s as well as between 2000 and 2003, however, also pay much less than the ones they have replaced. In Los Angeles, for example, state payroll records show that of the 300,000 new jobs created between 1993 and 1999 most paid less than the $25,000 average per year of the metropolitan area in 1993 and only one in 10 paid $60,000 or more per year; the number of jobs paying $15,000 or less grew at an annual rate of 4 percent, more than twice the rate for all other income categories (Lee 1999). Working Americans also typically work far longer hours than do workers in other industrial countries. This plus a higher percentage of the population in the labor force account for the higher average GDP per capita in the United States, not simply higher productivity or efficiency in using the factors of production (Mishel et al. 1999: 430–32). People in other industrialized countries typically have more leisure and more and better public goods.

Popular "common sense" relies more on comparisons with the past experience of the United States than with other countries. But, here again, the 1990s and early 2000s were not exceptional. On average, the economy grew no faster than in the 1970s and 1980s and much slower than in the 1960s. Across the key indicators of average productivity growth, unemployment, and even inflation the decade was no match for the 1960s. It looks even less impressive when account is taken of the fact that inflation, productivity, and unemployment are now measured in ways that definitely understate the first and third while raising the latter relative to previous decades (Business Week 24 April 2000: 32). In only two respects did the 1990s shine, reflecting the power of U.S. financial markets and the role of the U.S. dollar as an effective global monetary standard more than the overall performance of the U.S. economy (Blackburn 2006). The first is economic stability. Inflation and economic growth both remained steadier over time than previously, probably as a result of the U.S. central bank's capacity to use interest rates to manipulate relative prices. The second, of course, is the stock market. The 15.9 percent real average annual return posted by the S&P 500-stock index was way up relative to the 1960s and the miserable 1970s. Its relative collapse since 2000, however, illustrates the degree to which its ascent in the 1990s was a bubble without much connection to the true state of the U.S. economy.

Notwithstanding the hoopla over the long expansion of the U.S. economy from 1991 to 2000, the explosion of the stock market, and the recovery of productivity in the mid-2000s, the American economic model, therefore, is no longer a national or global paragon. It must now struggle alongside all of the others, producing somewhat higher growth than in the period 1970–1985 but with wider income inequality than in most industrial countries. It is sometimes asserted that America has traded higher inequality for faster growth. Yet over the period 1989–98, average individual incomes rose by similar amounts in Japan, Germany, and the United States, despite America's much bigger income differentials. In the United States the richest 20 percent earned nine times as much as the poorest 20 percent, compared with ratios of four times in Japan, and six times in Germany. Despite a higher average income in the United States, the poorest 20 percent in Japan were about 50 percent better off than America's poorest 20 percent (Economist 8 April 1999: 10).

A plausible account of the phenomena of median income stagnation and fading promise for most Americans would stress first of all the cutting of the Fordist knot that tied together production and consumption. The globalization of labor markets has meant that businesses without fixed local markets are relatively free to move at will to wherever they can obtain the best "deal." Under such conditions expansionism beyond national borders no longer guarantees a return for most of those people left at home. Only those who earn their livings from investments are beneficiaries. At the same time this also discourages businesses from investing in capital, especially in productivity-enhancing equipment (Wolman and Colamosca, 1997: 76–7). This in turn accounts for the decline in capital/output ratios in the United States (a measure of the relative importance of labor and technology in production measured by how many units of capital have to be invested on average to obtain one unit of output) since the early 1980s through the mid-1990s. This now does seem to have turned around, particularly in the manufacturing sector where technology has increasingly begun to substitute for labor. The rate of growth in the amount of capital available to each worker in the United States fell from its peak in the early 1980s through the mid-1990s. The turnaround suggests, then, that the American economy was now producing its goods and services in a more labor-intensive way than it did in the past. In other words, work was substituted for capital; toil increased as investment in capital equipment declined. While productivity increased starkly in 2003 (and more slowly from 1995 through 2002), it is by no means clear therefore that this is entirely or mostly because of increased returns on investment in technology. It may well also be because people are working harder. The long-term dilemma is that without sufficient capital investment, median incomes will not rise and without rising incomes labor will not be able to purchase the products of globalized production. Yet, as the events of late 2008 revealed, much of the growth in the U.S. economy was due to legerdemain in circulating vast amounts of financial paper in the form of derivatives and credit default swaps based on a massive expansion in mortgage debt and other financial obligations well beyond the financial capacity of those taking them on. Bankers may have walked away with spectacular bonuses but they left behind them institutions that were by then shells of their former selves (e.g., Cohan 2009). The gap between the credit based consumption of Americans (increasingly financed by the savings of foreigners) and the lack of domestic capital investment in long-term productive activities is the great conundrum facing the American way.

At first sight this might sound surprising. For example, has there not been a vast investment in computer technology that has presumably improved productivity and reduced the burden on labor? Will this not feed back into the welfare of American workers? In fact, considerable evidence suggests that computer technology has not yet produced the productivity gains widely predicted, particularly in the service sector where much of the growth in the U.S. economy has been concentrated. Information overload, rapid obsolescence, the lack of impact of information processing in many industries and technical-interface conflicts have conspired to reduce the overall effect of the new technology in the U.S. economy (e.g., Mishel et al. 2003: 203–12, 238–43). Where computerization has had undeniable positive effects, for example in the operations of a firm such as Wal-Mart, it does not seem to be to the long-term benefit of the U.S. labor force in terms of increasing its standard of living. Indeed, it has simply made more efficient the import of goods and the export of jobs.

The increasing breakdown of the geographical matching of production and consumption, as manufacturing jobs succumb to technology or move overseas and are replaced by lower paying service sector ones so that American consumers increasingly purchase goods and, increasingly, services as well, that they do not produce, has been exacerbated by increasing pressures on governments to facilitate "market access" and to make "their" businesses "lean and mean" for the rigors of global competition. There are fewer and fewer "policy buffers" between countries and the global business cycle (Drache 1996: 31–61; Higgins and Klitgaard 2007). Even large and previously "sheltered" economies such as that of the United States find themselves subject to economic shocks that are increasingly beyond the powers of central government to manage. At the same time, in order to conform to the discipline of financial markets, countries must restrict their welfare-state expenditures. Yet, as Rodrik (1997) has persuasively suggested, traditionally more open economies have had bigger relative welfare expenditures than more closed ones. The United States with its minimalist welfare state (by industrial country standards) is faced, therefore, by a prospective massive social problem as welfare cutbacks parallel increased openness of the national economy.

The sense of a more fragile and unstable economic future has given rise to a widespread questioning of the "common sense" of the American commitment to open trade and investment. Free trade and international economic competition are openly criticized in ways that would not have been thought possible thirty years ago. Criticism draws on the sorry condition of the U.S. balance of payments beginning in the 1980s and 1990s. The figures suggest an economy increasingly dependent on imports of goods and capital from elsewhere rather than a powerhouse economy dominating the rest of the world and invulnerable to foreign decision makers. But the setting of wages at the lowest-cost location without attending to the collective consequences for Americans of expanding production overseas and without commensurate increases in the earnings capacity for American consumption is seen as a violation of the American promise to its own population. Interestingly, criticism comes from both left and right ends of the political spectrum, as seen most dramatically in the protests against the World Trade Organization Meeting in Seattle in 1999. Labor unions, environmental activists and far-right militia groups all take exception to the idea that the United States and its regions are just locations for investment and disinvestment rather than parts of the abstract space of economic promise bequeathed to them by the "American way." This attitude is manifested in the increase in isolationist positions on both economic and military issues. These question such core U.S. commitments as global diplomatic activism, leadership of liberal international organizations, such as the World Trade Organization, membership in the UN system, and various alliance structures, such as NATO. Though there is a range of "isolationisms," giving priority to different issues—from protecting existing jobs and environmental regulations to worrying about foreign cultural influences—all share a basic antipathy to the globalist status quo (Dumbrell 1999: 24–43). Lurking within all of them is the imperative to squeeze the genie of globalization unleashed by U.S. expansionism back into the territorial bottle of the United States.

One dimension of globalization is particularly in question. This is the faith in the benefits of free trade. Increasingly heard are criticisms of a free-trade regime in which wages are set at the lowest cost location without attention to the collective consequences of expanding production without commensurate increases in the earnings capacity for global consumption. Now, this is a global as much as it is an American problem. It is just that Americans are no longer sheltered from its effects. Even though the United States is less open to and less dependent on foreign trade than any other major industrial country its relative position has changed significantly in the years since 1960. Particularly, less skilled and lower income workers tend to oppose liberalization of trade, immigration, and foreign direct investment and increasingly so, between the 1960s and the 1990s. This reflects the reality of their situation. As of 1998, however, two-thirds of Americans, not just low-wage earners, thought that trade has been a "principal cause" of lower U.S. living standards (Scheve and Slaughter 2001: 90). Obviously, the negative perception of globalization, therefore, extends well beyond those immediately affected by it. The numbers are likely to have increased after 2008.

The most basic issue in the overall status of the U.S. economy is that of its relative autonomy compared to its relative capability. On the one hand, an indicator of interdependence or susceptibility to external shocks (the ratio of U.S. trade and exports to GNP or GDP) has increased dramatically since 1970. On the other hand, an indicator of capability within the world economy (the ratio of U.S. GNP or GDP to total core [industrial world] GNP or GDP) declined almost linearly between 1950 and 1980 but since then has fluctuated with marked increases in the early 1980s and, following a significant drop from 1985 to 1995, in the late 1990s. With the U.S. economy as the "motor" of the world economy in both the early 1980s and again in the late 1990s these results are not surprising. The sustainability of the late 1990s "bounce," however, now depends more on the recovery of other industrialized economies as much as it does on overall U.S. economic performance. The United States has been spending way beyond what it produces and saves. A drop like that after the 1980s is very much on the cards. Fred Bergsten (1982: 13) has used the term "scissors effect" to describe the joint consequences for the U.S. economy of increased economic interdependence and declining, if more recently, somewhat resilient capability:

> The United States has simultaneously become much more dependent on the world economy and much less able to dictate the course of international events. The global economic environment is more critical for the United States and is less susceptible to its influence.

In the late 1980s I provided a detailed analysis of why U.S. economic autonomy and capability had declined (Agnew 1987: Chapter 4). With respect to autonomy today, the massive and ever-widening U.S. current account and trade deficits show the country as the world's largest debtor and importer relative to exports and the central banks of Japan and China as its single largest creditors. But beyond this, the increased interdependence and velocity of world financial markets affect the United States as they do other countries. The United States does still have some obvious advantages. The most important of these is that the country's major traders hold their reserves largely in U.S. dollars and thus help to finance the U.S. deficits given that the savings rate in the United States is too low to do so domestically. Controlling the world's major transnational currency, the one in which much of the world's trade is denominated, also gives the United States the capacity to allow the dollar to fall in order to boost exports and affect the relative real prices of its rivals' products. These advantages, however, are by no means absolute (Gray 2004). For one thing, losing foreign cooperation could lead to a dramatic fall in the value of the dollar because at least one-third of U.S. Treasury debt is owned by official foreign agencies. For another, "talking down the dollar" can lead to a crash rather than a managed decline in value. The idea that the U.S. economy has "empire-like power," therefore, as alleged by numerous writers, needs relating to the actual performance of the U.S. economy rather than to abstract accounts of the powers the United States potentially has available to it (e.g., Gowan 1999). While these powers may have aided financial institutions, multinationals investing outside the United States, and the monetary position of the United States, they have not translated into an automatic superior general economic performance for the U.S. economy or most of the U.S. population.

With respect to capability, the main problem lies with the relative decline in GNP potential or the capacity to produce. This is partly a function of the changing labor force (more dependents, lower skills), but it is largely a product of declining national productivity. In 1990 this was indexed at 1.4 compared to 4.3 in 1965. By 2000 it had improved somewhat to 1.9. As a consequence, real GNP or GDP growth has slumped from 4.4 percent in the 1960s, to 3.3 percent in the 1970s to 3.1 percent in the 1980s and 3.1 percent in the 1990s. Part of the answer to this pattern is that the service industries whose share of total GDP and in which employment is growing most in the United States show much lower increases in productivity than do those manufacturing industries whose share in total GDP and in employment is shrinking dramatically (Rowthorn and Ramaswamy 1999). But globalizing capital and labor markets are also undoubtedly part of the answer. On the one hand, the increasing uniformity of regulations and accessibility across different national economies makes it easier for businesses to move investment from one to another. On the other hand, labor is now increasingly available on a global basis. In particular, skilled labor can be imported if a local economy provides insufficient qualified workers. Competition from lower paid (often overseas) labor and legal restrictions have jointly affected the ability of labor unions to organize the workforce. As a result, not just average wages but also average benefits (such as pensions and health insurance), which tend to be considerably higher for union members, have gone down. This makes production more flexible as it also makes it less dependent on relatively immobile local populations. The net effect is to turn wages from the source of demand they were under Fordism to the cost of production they have become in a more globalized economy (Jessop 2002: 105). As a result there is a potential global "leveling" of incomes. That the "golden age" of middle-class incomes and lifestyles for American workers correlated with relatively high-levels of membership in labor unions and limited global capital mobility is no mere coincidence (Mishel et al. 2003: 189–96).

The expansionism inherent in the American experience, and according to Earle supposedly central to elite nationalist republic periods in particular, has recently come into question in the United States. Elsewhere the benevolence of American omnipotence has long been openly problematic. What has focused minds has been the seemingly negative impact that the globalization brought by American global hegemony is now having at home. On one side the dramatically increased polarization of incomes and wealth between the rich and everyone else has been attributed by many commentators and some politicians to the effects of globalization, particularly the loss of the relatively high-paying assembly line jobs that characterized Fordist America (e.g., O'Loughlin 1997). It seems somewhat more than a coincidence of timing that U.S. median male earnings peaked in 1973 and have stagnated ever since with a massive earnings gap opening up during the same period between the richest 1 percent of the population (who garner their incomes largely from stocks and commercial real estate) and everyone else (whose incomes come from work). Now, it is the case that the real-wage slowdown is concentrated in the less-traded services, but given that jobs in this sector are the only ones on offer with the shrinkage of higher-paying manufacturing jobs, globalization is working through this displacement to affect average earnings. A more skilled but "leaner" manufacturing workforce now shares the proceeds of productivity growth (though hardly proportionately!) with a tiny number of people at the top of the income distribution, leaving the rest of the population (particularly the huge number of non-citizens mainly at the bottom of the income distribution with limited political and labor-market influence) lagging far behind (Deitz and Orr 2006; Dew-Becker and Gordon 2005; Economist 17 June 2006; Piketty and Saez 2006; McCarty et al. 2006). Though unemployment in the United States has been consistently lower than in Europe over most of this period, this difference is largely accounted for by the growth of part-time employment and the proliferation of low-paid consumer service jobs in the United States relative to the old continent. For example, between 1965 and 1998, jobs in retail and service sectors—the two lowest paying sectors—rose from 30 percent to 48 percent of all production and non-supervisory jobs in the United States (*Business Week*, 7 February 2000: 34). Wal-Mart is not only where much of America shops, mainly for imported goods, but also where much of it may soon be working—at poverty wages. As Paul Krugman (2006: A19) puts it: "It's a great economy if you're a high-level corporate executive or someone who owns a lot of stock. For most other Americans, economic growth is a spectator sport."

This represents an unstable economic and political situation. From the late nineteenth century through until the 1980s, the massive economies of scale in American manufacturing production allowed the country to profit from a virtuous circle of expanding production, expanding median incomes, and expanding consumption. In the contemporary global economy, the United States serves as the giant purchasing machine for products increasingly made elsewhere. US economic growth in the recent past (2000–2008) has been almost entirely consumption driven (Brenner 2004). As incomes rise elsewhere for those who make these products, however, alternative mass markets to the United States will inevitably emerge. The United States will then lose much of its leverage in relation to the world economy as the "buyer of last resort." In other words, the productivity that results from larger economies of scale in places actually producing goods—that is, rising output per worker—will give rise to increasing revenues that can pay higher wages and fatten profits that, in turn, can be plowed into research and marketing of new products. From this viewpoint, just being the world's biggest consumer is unsustainable. It is no longer possible in such a situation for the United States to retain access to the profits and incomes that its mass market once made possible.

From a different angle of vision, the point has been made that there is increasing pessimism on the part of Americans about achieving one of the fundamental "promises" of the American historical experience: the high likelihood that one's children will have a higher standard of living than one does. The generations coming to maturity after the Second World War and employed in the burgeoning Fordist industries of the epoch enjoyed continuing real growth in their incomes. From 1973 to 1999 and again since 2003, however, this pattern was replaced by net declines in real weekly earnings for U.S. workers. Now, this is not to suggest that this promise is necessarily a good thing in the context of growing concern about the sustainability of high levels of economic growth under conditions of environmental degradation, but only that the promise of increasing incomes is very much a part of the American popular capitalist ethos. Its potential loss is of major cultural and political significance (e.g., Reich 2008). It is this "compact" between populace and expanding economy that has bonded so many Americans to the norms of the "American way."

Yet, it would be mistaken to presume that the myth of American exceptionalism is simply fading away as a result of the excesses of globalization. Far from it. Shopping is still not only the major national pastime in the United States but also absolutely central to national economic growth. "Consumers in America spend because they feel they must spend. More than in the past, the necessities of life, real and perceived, eat up their incomes" (Uchitelle 2003). This spending is huge, roughly $7.6 trillion a year in goods and services; around two-thirds of total national economic activity. Increasingly, however, it is less and less discretionary and relatively more of it is financed by non-wage income, such as that from mortgage refinancing, or by credit. Writing of the period 2000–2003, Robert Brenner (2004: 77) notes: "U.S. economic growth in the past three years has been driven by increases in demand generated by borrowing against the speculative appreciation of on-paper wealth, far more than in demand generated by increased investment and employment, driven by increasing profits." He is referring specifically to the financing of current consumption from the cash released by mortgage refinancing and house-price inflation. The economic unsustainability of this credit based consumption is apparent from the massive financial crisis in 2007–2008 brought on by the mismatch between credit extended and assets financed (Wolf 2007). A major force also keeping up spending comes from the fact that the average household now has two adults at work compared to the early 1970s when a single earner could provide what now takes two. In other words, more people are working harder and harder to stay in the same place.

Even as doubts about the returns on the old consumption ethos spread, the rhetoric of techno-capitalism is combining with that of American exceptionalism to suggest new frontiers that lie in cyberspace rather than in geographical space. The belief is that "technology"—now the Internet and its progeny—will once again rescue Americans from economic peril, this time that produced by their own profligacy. At the same time, many Americans seem to accept, and even to relish, the social inequalities that the economic boom of the 1990s and early 2000s has entailed. Increasingly, as huge inequalities in wealth are taken as natural measures of market-based demonstration of success and worth, the federal government, journalism, academia, and Hollywood are excoriated by conservative politicians and pundits as populated by a motley "new class" systematically engaged in undermining faith in the "American way." Relationships to this "market populism," to use Thomas Frank's term, were at the center of the 2000 and 2004 American presidential elections with its amazing geographical polarization of the country between the largely skeptical coasts and the true believers in a God-given natural social inequality in the American "heartland" in between (Frank 2000; 2004; McCarty et al., 2006). Political polarization and economic inequality have long gone hand-in-hand in US history, as Earle (2003) argues and McCarty et al. (2006) have shown empirically, but this time around the fruits of economic inequality are even more concentrated in the hands of fewer people than previously and in a historical context in which the U.S. government has favored the winners and has lessened capacity to help the losers. Given that greater social egalitarianism has historically encouraged greater personal investment in education and subsequent enhancement of technological innovation in the economy in question, the consequences of recent economic and political polarization in the United States extend well beyond social inequality per se (Cohen 2006; 126–29). Neither the frontiers of cyberspace nor the satisfactions of market idolatry, therefore, completely offsets the depredations of globalization and the image of an America now on the receiving, rather than on the delivering, end of powerful forces from beyond as well as inside its borders.

THE NEW GEOGRAPHY OF WINNERS AND LOSERS

It is misleading to portray the United States and its population as simply one more set of "victims" of globalization. In the first place, many Americans and some American localities have benefited mightily from the growth of trade and foreign investment. This is particularly the case for those workers and places with successful export firms and those benefiting from flows of foreign direct investment. Critically, for example, the growth of trade with the Asian Pacific Rim has particularly benefited the western states of the United States with respect to transportation, finance, resource and food exports, and strategic alliances as the Asian countries have inserted themselves in the circuits of globalized production. Second, and well worth reiterating, the contemporary world economy is largely a product of U.S. design and ideology. From its origins as a new state in the late eighteenth century political-economic expansionism has lain at the heart of the American experience. This is a key insight of Earle's *The American Way*. In a position to realize its old ambitions globally after the Second World War, U.S. government and business became enthusiastic supporters of a shrinking world in which capital would know no boundaries. Americans now also live with the consequences: a world much more open to trade, investment and cultural influences but also one of increased economic competition and insecurity.

What happened in the 1990s is that established manufacturing industries were largely sacrificed as service and financial sectors came to dominate the United States economically and politically in the new global economy (Fligstein and Shin 2004). So, the relative well-being of different groups and localities has much to do with the domestic sectors that now lose in global competition and those that have a continuing or growing competitive advantage.

From the late nineteenth century until the years after the Second World War the United States had a regionally structured national economy. The bulk of manufacturing and related employment was located within a belt running from Long Island in the east to Illinois in the west and bounded on the south by the Ohio River and to the north by the Canadian border (with an extension into Ontario). In their classic work, Perloff et al. (1960) showed that this geographical pattern, with the exception of new industrial investment in California and the textile industry in the piedmont South, lasted from the 1890s into the 1950s. Most of the classic manufacturing industries located in the industrial core had all stages of production on site or nearby. In other words, there was a low level of separation of functions within production and a low level of variation in locational requirements between functions. This was based upon technological conditions (high transport costs, poor long-distance communication, and so on) and the lack of international competition in U.S. markets. The spatial division of labor was thus based on sectoral specialization such as cars in Detroit, steel in Pittsburgh, paint in Cleveland, beer in Milwaukee, and so on. The other regions specialized in resource extraction and agriculture with "islands" of more specialized economic activity, such as film-making in Los Angeles, scattered according to various rationales relating to climate, local resources, and the serendipity of prior historical development.

Some commentators have argued that by the 1960s an internal rebalancing between core and periphery within the U.S. economy was overdue. In this view, regions go through life-cycles with rising scale economies in their youth and declining scale and external economies as they age. By the 1960s costs were rising in the core, so business turned to the periphery to take advantage of low-cost, non-union labor; growing markets; and low-cost sites on major transport routes. As a result, manufacturing industries began to close down in the industrial core and move their operations southwards and westwards. Interregional competition produced a more dispersed pattern of industrial location and a concomitant diminution in interregional income inequality.

The problem with this interpretation is twofold. It was only when the U.S. position in relation to the world economy changed after the 1960s that the old geographical pattern began to disintegrate (Agnew 1987: Chapter 3). During the 1960s, trade negotiations, particularly the Kennedy Round in the GATT, lowered many tariffs on manufactured goods traded between the world's most industrialized countries. This was to have a dramatic impact in the United States. U.S. companies that had taken their massive national market for granted were now faced with foreign competitors hungry for market share in the United States. Increasing competition from foreign firms was the initial catalyst, therefore, in the geographical restructuring of the U.S. economy by forcing U.S. manufacturing firms into strategies such as relocating to the south and west and abroad in order to meet the competitive challenge. As the Fordist firms of the industrial core started to shift to out-sourcing or externalizing many functions to other smaller firms, they were able to enjoy cost advantages by decentralizing production yet retaining central corporate control. This led to a new uneven development in the United States with the seeming paradox of a delocalization or concentration of control over many firm functions and a localization or decentralization of firm operations to the most "attractive" locations for this or that particular function.

The second point relates to the nature of competition. In the context of increased competition from foreign firms it is localities and cities that have to compete with one another to get more or keep what they have, not large regions or sections (Agnew 1988). As firms become more competitive with one another without the protective cocoon of high tariffs and quotas, places become oriented to retaining and attracting the mobile capital that often primes the pump of local development. As a result, one political consequence of the increased openness of the American economy has been that the American states and various municipalities have embarked on programs to set up their own investment and trade policies without going through Washington, D.C., the national capital (Paul 2005). For example, California, which has the seventh largest economy in the world, has its own health and pension policies and has tried to establish its own immigration policy.

The new uneven development in the distribution of manufacturing industry, beginning in the late 1960s but increasing its pace thereafter, has had a large number of effects not just on the geography of production but on consumption as well. These would include the increased polarization in occupational structure between cities and suburbs as new high tech industries locate in the latter and old plants close down in the former; a deindustrialization of old industrial cities with replacement by jobs in relatively high-paying producer and relatively low-paying consumer services; new branch plants on green field sites in the South and West; a concentration of headquarters functions in the largest cities such as New York, Chicago, and Los Angeles with high-skilled groups provided with services by much lower paid people, often recent (and illegal) immigrants to the United States; the emergence of new centers for certain service industries, such as banking in Charlotte NC and

Miami; and major new high-tech industrial districts such as Silicon Valley in California. In sum, a new spatial division of labor stimulated by foreign competition and made possible by new informational and communications technologies and new non-spatial scale economies created a pattern of localized restructuring.

Not surprisingly, given this process of global competition and localized growth and decline, there is a very localized aspect to the pattern of median income decline and polarization (Kodras 2002). If in the period between 1945 and the early 1970s the major regions of the United States had converged in incomes, reflecting a nationwide process of growth in the middle class, the period since then has seen a trend towards the regional distinctiveness in development and incomes that had characterized earlier epochs in American history. This time around, however, the geographical pattern is much spottier with city-suburban and metropolitan-small city differences more significant than simply regional ones (Wallace 1999; Rigby 2002). Some broader regional trends are apparent, however. As a result of its economic domination by declining heavy manufacturing industries, the Midwest region has experienced the highest levels of job loss in middle-income categories, with only lower-income manufacturing and service sector jobs available as substitutes. At the other extreme, California and New England have benefited most from increased domestic and foreign trade and investment, particularly in high-tech industries and informational technology. The Northeast and West totally dominate with respect to new capital investment, reflecting concentrations of skilled workers, existing clusters of technological innovation, and the presence of capital locally in the hands of those who have profited from previous rounds of investment. Six states—California, Massachusetts, New York, Texas, Washington, and Colorado—accounted for 75 percent of venture capital in 1999, up from their 50 percent share in 1995. Technology advances, as measured by new patents, are overwhelmingly concentrated in these states. Venture capital comes from the wealth accumulated by established high-tech entrepreneurs. These people tend to live in areas such as Silicon Valley, Boston, and Seattle and to favor investing in local companies that they can easily keep watch over (*Business Week* 7 February 2000).

If anything, the picture for many U.S. manufacturing industries, the places they are located in, and the people who work in them has grown more dismal since the late 1990s. After recovering in the late 1980s after a huge fall from the historic high in 1979, U.S. manufacturing employment climbed back to 17.6 million in 1998. Since then it has simply collapsed, shedding almost 3 million of those jobs by 2003. This owes much to United States and other companies relocating operations abroad, particularly to China, to the substitution of technology for labor in U.S.-based operations, and to the overall loss of manufacturing industry from the confines of the United States or as U.S. firms go out of business (Deitz and Orr 2006). Symptomatic of the trend, in 2002–2003 the U.S. economy had a largely "jobless recovery" from the 2000–2001 recession as gains in productivity drastically outpaced increases in employment (Beattie and Swann 2003). This is a structural change. In the past, laid-off workers could expect to be recalled once business picked up. Not today. Many U.S. manufacturing industries have either gone out of business or shrunk permanently in employment terms (Head 2003). So, the likelihood of closing the "job gap" through the revival of high-paying manufacturing jobs looks exceedingly unlikely. Housing and consumption services, now relying heavily on credit imported from abroad, provide an unsustainable alternative economy, as seen from the vantage of 2008.

The emerging geographical structure of the new American economy, reflecting the centrality of service and high-tech sectors as its leading edges, is a heavily city-oriented one. Some writers argue that cities are increasingly part of global networks in which the cities are service centers for multinational companies that have "gone global" (e.g., Taylor 2004). The network flows of information, decisions, personnel, and capital that draw cities together and give them their purposes are channeled to only a limited extent by national boundaries. New York and London, the two cities that sit astride the entire global network for the widest range of functions, are the decision centers for a worldwide hierarchical system of cities. Research by Peter Taylor (2004: 204) shows, however, that beyond New York, Chicago, Los Angeles, San Francisco, and Miami, most U.S. cities are still "relatively separated from world cities in other countries." Taylor suggests that this may be so for two reasons. One is that foreign service firms are typically non-competitive beyond New York and a few other US cities where they locate to serve non-U.S. clients. Another is that many U.S. firms expand to other U.S. cities beyond their home base instead of going transnational because the U.S. market is so large.

What is clear is that U.S. cities are at the heart of the emerging U.S. economy (Florida 2009). The leading industries in terms of contribution to U.S. GDP in the 1990s and early 2000s have been those in information technology, processing and telecommunications, on the one hand, and users of the products of these industries in finance, insurance, and real estate (FIRE), on the other. It is the largest cities that have reaped much of the benefits of this new economy and many of the costs during the downturn of 2001–2003. Collectively these large-city based sectors generated fully 26 percent of U.S. GDP in 1996 (Castells 1996: 148–49). Their concentration in large cities has been matched by their contribution to massive suburban development around these cities, producing the so-called edge cities where office centers and residential developments spill over into countryside as much as fifty miles from the historic cores of such cities as Atlanta, Washington, D.C., Houston, and Los Angeles. The flip side to this trend is the increasing marginality and destitution in those central-city neighborhoods that have lost the old line manufacturing jobs but without the access either spatial or educational to the newer jobs appearing at the urban fringe or in downtown office blocks.

Across U.S. metropolitan areas the net effect of the dual trends towards growth in informational and finance capitalism and the decline of traditional manufacturing industries has been a polarization between two sets of cities. Older, specialized industrial cities in the U.S. Northeast and Midwest have done poorly in economic growth and in retaining population (see table 10.1). The cities that have done better are overwhelmingly smaller and more diversified and located outside the historic industrial core. Some are involved in the new dynamic high tech manufacturing sectors; but many more are

Table 10.1. Top and Bottom Ten Cities in the United States with 100,000+ Population in 2000 Ranked by Percent Increase or Decrease in Population 1990–2000 and Type of Economy

City (State)	*Population in 2000*	*Percent Change since 1990*	*Economy*
Highest Growth			
Gilbert (AZ)	109,697	265.6	R&R*
Henderson (NV)	175,381	169.4	Suburb
North Las Vegas (NV)	115,930	140.8	Suburb
Peoria (AZ)	108,364	111.8	R&R
Pembroke Pines (FL)	137,427	110.0	R&R
Chandler (AZ)	176,581	94.7	R&R
Las Vegas (NV)	478,434	84.1	Recreation
Plano (TX)	222,030	72.8	Services
Corona (CA)	124,966	64.0	Suburb
Scottsdale (AZ)	202,705	55.8	R&R
Highest Loss			
St. Louis (MO)	348,189	–12.2	Industrial
Gary (IN)	102,746	–11.9	Industrial
Flint (MI)	124,943	–11.6	Industrial
Baltimore (MD)	650,100	–11.5	Industrial
Hartford (CT)	121,578	–11.4	Industrial
Buffalo (NY)	292,648	–10.8	Industrial
Norfolk (VA)	234,403	–10.3	Port/Military
Syracuse (NY)	147,306	–10.1	Industrial
Pittsburgh (PA)	334,563	–9.6	Industrial
Cincinnati (OH)	331,285	–9.1	Industrial

*Recreation and Retirement

Source: US Census, *City and County Data Book*, 2000, Table C-1.

recreational, retirement or government centers or suburbs for such places. Real estate is their most important industry. The range in population growth or loss rates over the period 1990–2000 was tremendous, suggesting a definite geography of winners and losers in the new U.S. economy, although the extremes had weakened in the 1990s as rates of growth dampened (except for Las Vegas and some other cities) and rates of decline slowed throughout the Northeast and Midwest (compare Bourne 1999). Regional and local patterns solidified, however, suggesting limited prospect of any ready reversal in urban fortunes.

The new openness of the U.S. economy to external pressures since the 1970s has had radically different political impacts in different parts of the country depending on economic mix and vulnerability to foreign competition. It is not surprising that the most fervent proponents of free trade tend to be from California and New England with those counseling greater degrees of protectionism and opposing the development of more free trade accords with other countries tending to come from the Midwest and those parts of the South with the most to lose from a further globalization of labor markets by mobile capital (Phillips 1991). The pattern is likely to be much more variegated than this, however, because the interests at stake are typically more localized today than was the case in the past. The consequences of localized economic restructuring might be expected to show up, therefore, in a relatively motley geographical pattern of votes by congressional representatives on trade and investment legislation. That this is in fact the case is shown, for example, in the votes for two pieces of legislation that were introduced in the U.S. Congress in 1985 relating to trade and investment issues: the Textile Import Quotas Bill (HR1562) of 10 October 1985, a bill imposing quotas on textile imports, and the Plant Closings Notification Bill (HR1616) of 21 November 1985, a bill requiring employers of fifty or more employees to give workers at least ninety days notice of any plant shutdown or layoff involving at least 100 employees or 30 percent of the workforce (Agnew 1988). The first bill, which passed the House of Representatives 252-159 (Republicans 75-97; Democrats 187-62) has no apparent regional pattern in the votes for and against. Because of the scatter of textile-related industries there is also no sectional or regional "position" to vote for or against. A three-region (Northeast, West, South) analysis of variance does not support a sectional interpretation. The second bill, rejected by the House 203-208 (Republicans 20-154; Democrats 183-54), does have a sectional effect. Here the northeastern congressional delegations tended to support the bill and others voted against. The fact that this bill was strongly supported by labor unions which have had their greatest strength in the old industrial core of the Northeast and Midwest probably has much to do with this result.

The changed pattern of geographic concentration of much economic activity, from the greater clustering of vertically integrated firms under Fordism to the much more decentralized pattern evident today, however, makes the sectional vote something of an anomaly. Much more variegated votes on trade and investment issues are now the norm. This is important for the making of national policy. The first 1985 bill with its localized support passed, the second, sectionally based one failed. As Ronald Rogowski (2002: 204) shows more generally, "Deconcentration increases protectionist influence; it means increased pressure-group activity, more district-level contests among pressure groups, a shift of power to interests that were formerly more concentrated, and increased volatility of policy." Rogowski demonstrates that "moderately dispersed" interests are the ones that win most congressional support over concentrated and highly dispersed ones. Consequently, as the number of districts with moderate vulnerability to foreign trade has increased, the traditional U.S. support for free trade comes under greater pressure than when industrial activity was geographically concentrated and representatives from elsewhere could outvote those from the heavily industrial areas.

CONCLUSION

In 1950 the United States territorial economy dominated the world in terms of its shares of manufactured output, merchandise trade, and foreign investment. Of course, this was in the shadow of the Second World War when most of the world's major industrial economies other than the United States remained devastated. Many Americans in the years following, however, assumed that this was the "natural" state of affairs. But by 2000 the relative share of the U.S. economy in world manufacturing had declined by around 50 percent from its postwar peak, its trade position had weakened enormously, and from providing almost one half of the world's FDI in 1960 the United States now provides under 25 percent. In large part these changes are the result of the globalization of the world economy with its increasing fragmentation of production and the geographical separation of different stages of processing. In this global context, the U.S. national economy has experienced a number of profound realignments, from the increased "global shift" of U.S.-based businesses through the relative decline of the manufacturing sector as a source of jobs and GDP and the rise of the service sector, to the geographical restructuring of population and jobs in new economic spaces, generally in terms of a movement from the Northeast and Midwest to the South and the West. The explosion of flows between the largest metropolitan areas has boosted the role of cities in the overall economy of the country but with increasingly polarized incomes and wealth between those in rising sectors such as informational technology and FIRE and those trapped in personal service jobs. Indeed, in this context, writing of the United States as a separable national economy makes little sense compared to times past.

Nevertheless, these trends have occurred in a macroeconomic context in which the United States has acquired an increasingly asymmetric position in the world economy: borrowing from foreign creditors to fund domestic spending in excess of what could be financed internally. The U.S. can do so because of the dominant position of the U.S. dollar as a transnational currency. This position is probably unsustainable, however, unless American demand declines and that of other key economies increases. Allowing that to happen would require abandonment by the U.S. government of its strategy of propping up the transnational state by manipulation of the U.S. dollar and a unilateralist foreign policy. Yet, for many people and places inside the United States this no longer suffices. They do not benefit. In the past there was no such dilemma. America's national economic well being and its global status were mutually reinforcing. Serving one now no longer guarantees the other. Globalization and the new geography of power have cut the connection between them. As the country begins a new century, that is the root of America's crisis. No adequate response of whatever combination of liberal and republican principles—Carville Earle's "recovery phase"—is yet in sight. The outcome of the U.S. presidential election of 2008 will be fateful in more ways than one. As fallout from the economic crisis beginning in 2008, the boundaries between government and market, state and individual are more fluid than they have been at any time since 1980. As a result, President Obama has the best opportunity to remake American capitalism than any president since Ronald Reagan. Whether this will simply be a reiteration of Earle's "egalitarian internationalist democracy" or something new entirely, as I have argued, remains very much to be seen.

BIBLIOGRAPHY

Agnew, J. 1987. *The United States in the World Economy: A Regional Geography.* (Cambridge: Cambridge University Press).

———. 1988. "Beyond Core and Periphery: The Myth of Regional Political-Economic Restructuring and Sectionalism in Contemporary American Politics," *Political Geography Quarterly*, 7: 129–141.

———. 1995. *Hegemony: The New Shape of Global Power.* "Philadelphia: Temple University Press).

Agnew, J. and S. Corbridge. 1995. *Mastering Space: Hegemony, Territory, and International Political Economy.* (London: Routledge).

Amiti, M. and K. Stiroh. September 2007. "Is the United States Losing its Productivity Advantage?" *Current Issues in Economics and Finance* (Federal Reserve Bank of New York 13, 8).

Beattie, A. and C. Swann. 2003. "Gains in Productivity Leave Jobs Market Lagging Behind Recovery," *Financial Times* October 2, 2003: 2.

Bergsten, C. F. 1982. "The United States and the World Economy," *Annals of the American Academy of Arts and Sciences* 460: 13.

Blackburn, R. 2006. "Finance's Fourth Dimension," *New Left Review*, 39: 39–70.

Bourne, L. S. 1999. "The North American Urban System: The Macrogeography of Uneven Development," *North America: A Geographical Mosaic*, edited by F. W. Boal and S. A. Royle. (London: Arnold).

Brenner, R. 2004. "New Boom or New Bubble? The Trajectory of the US Economy," *New Left Review*, 25: 57–100.

Business Week. February 7, 2000. "Where Venture Capital Ventures: To Just a Few States and Industries," *Business Week*: 30.

———. April 24, 2000. "Yes, the '90s were Unusual but not because of Economic Growth," *Business Week*: 32.

Castells, M. 1996. *The Rise of Network Society*. (Oxford: Blackwell).

Cohan, W. D. 2009. *House of Cards: A Tale of Hubris and Wretched Excess on Wall Street*. (New York: Doubleday).

Cohen, D. 2006. *Globalization and Its Enemies*. (Cambridge MA: MIT Press).

Deitz, R. and J. Orr. A Leaner, 2006. "More Skilled U.S. Manufacturing Workforce," *Current Issues in Economics and Finance* (Federal Reserve Bank of New York 12, 2, February/March 2006).

Dew-Becker, I. and R. J. Gordon. 2005. "Where did the Productivity Growth Go? Inflation Dynamics and the Distribution of Income," *NBER Working Paper,* Number 11842.

Drache, D. 1996. "From Keynes to K-mart: Competitiveness in a Corporate Age," *States Against Markets: The Limits of Globalization,* edited by R. Boyer and D. Drache. (London: Routledge).

Dumbrell, J. 1999. "Varieties of Post-Cold War American Isolationism," *Government and Opposition* 34: 24–43

Earle, C. 2003. *The American Way: A Geographical History of Crisis and Recovery*. (Lanham MD: Rowman & Littlefield).

Economist. 1999. "Desperately Seeking a Perfect Model," *Economist* April 8, 1999: 10.

———. 2006. "The Rich, the Poor and the Growing Gap Between Them," *Economist* June 17, 2006:28–30.

Financial Times. 2006. "Revisionist Version of History," *Financial Times* August 1, 2006: 12.

Fligstein, N. and T. Shin. 2004. "The Shareholder Value Society: A Review of Changes in Working Conditions in the U.S., 1976–2000," *The New Inequalities*, edited by K. Neckerman. (New York: Russell Sage Foundation).

Florida, R. 2009. "How the Crash will reshape America," *The Atlantic*, March 2009: 44–56.

Frank, T. 2000. *One Market under God: Extreme Capitalism, Market Populism and the End of Economic Democracy*. (New York: Random House).
———. 2004. "Lie Down for America: How the Republican Party Sows Ruin on the Great Plains," *Harper's*, (April 2004): 33–46.
Friedman, T. 2005. *The World is Flat: A Brief History of the Twenty-First Century*. (New York: Farrar, Straus and Giroux).
Gowan, P. 1999. *The Global Gamble: Washington's Faustian Bid for Global Dominance*. (London: Verso).
Gray, H. P. 2004. *The Exhaustion of the Dollar: Its Implications for Global Prosperity*. (Basingstoke: Palgrave Macmillan).
Harvey, D. 2006. *Spaces of Global Capitalism. Towards a Theory of Uneven Geographical Development*. (London: Verso).
Head, S. 2003. *The New Ruthless Economy: Work and Power in the Digital Age*. (New York: Oxford University Press).
Higgins, M. and T. Klitgaard. 2007. "Financial Globalization and the US Current Account Deficit," *Current Issues in Economics and Finance* (Federal Reserve Bank of New York 13, 11, December 2007).
Jessop, B. 2002. *The Future of the Capitalist State*. (Cambridge: Polity Press).
Jorgenson, D., M. Ho, and K. J. Stiroh. 2006. "Potential Growth of the US Economy: Will the US Productivity Resurgence Continue?" *Business Economics*, 41 (January 2006): 1–10.
Kodras, J. E. 2002. "With Liberty and Justice for All: Negotiating Freedom and Fairness in the American Income Distribution," *American Space/American Place: Geographies of the Contemporary United States*, edited by J. Agnew and J. Smith. (Edinburgh: Edinburgh University Press).
Krugman, P. 2006. "Left Behind Economics," *New York Times*, July 14, 2006, A19.
Lee, D. L.A. 1999. "County Jobs Surge since '93, but not Wages," *Los Angeles Times*, July 26, 1999, A1, A10.
McKinsey Global Institute. 2001. *US Productivity Growth, 1995–2000*. (New York: McKinsey and Company).
McCarty, N., K. T. Poole, and H. Rosenthal. 2006. *Polarized America: The Dance of Ideology and Unequal Riches*. (Cambridge MA: MIT Press).
Mishel, L. et al. 2003. *The State of Working America*. (Ithaca NY: ILR Press).
O'Loughlin, J. 1997. "Economic Globalization and Income Inequality in the United States," *State Restructuring in America: Implications for a Diverse Society*, edited by Lynn Staeheli, Janet Kodras and Colin Flint. (Thousand Oaks CA: Sage).
Paul, D. 2005. *Rescaling International Political Economy: Subnational States and the Regulation of the Global Political Economy*. (New York: Routledge).
Perloff, H. S. et al. 1960. *Regions, Resources, and Economic Growth*. (Lincoln NE: University of Nebraska Press).
Phillips, K. 1991. *The Politics of Rich and Poor*. (New York: Random House).
Piketty, T. and E. Saez. 2006. "The Evolution of Top Incomes: a Historical and International Perspective," *American Economic Review*, 96, 2 (May 2006): 200–205.
Reich, R. 2008. "America's Middle Classes are no Longer Coping," *Financial Times*, January 30, 2008.

Rigby, D. L. 2002. "Urban and Regional Restructuring in the Second Half of the Twentieth Century," In *American Space/American Place: Geographies of the Contemporary United States*, edited by J. Agnew and J. Smith. (Edinburgh: Edinburgh University Press).

Rodrik, D. 1997. *Has Globalization Gone Too Far?* (Washington DC: Institute for International Economics).

Rogowski, R. 2002. "Trade and Representation: How Diminishing Geographic Concentration Augments Protectionist Pressure in the U.S. House of Representatives," *Shaped by War and Trade: International Influences on American Political Development,* edited by I. Katznelson and M. Shefter. (Princeton NJ: Princeton University Press).

Rowthorn, B. and R. Ramaswamy. 1999. "Growth, Trade and Deindustrialization," *IMF Staff Working Papers* 46: 18–41.

Scheve, K. F. and M. J. Slaughter. 2001. *Globalization and the Perceptions of American Workers.* "Washington DC: Institute for International Economics".

Taylor, P. J. 2004. *World City Network: A Global Urban Analysis*. (London: Routledge).

Uchitelle, L. 2003. "Why Americans Must Keep Spending," *New York Times,* December 1, 2003, A1, A4.

Wallace, I. 1999. "Manufacturing in North America," In *North America: A Geographical Mosaic*, edited by F. W. Boal and S. A. Royle. (London: Arnold).

Wolf, M. 2007. "Why the Credit Squeeze is a Turning Point for the World," *Financial Times*, December 12, 2007.

Wolman, W. and A. Colamosca. 1997. *The Judas Economy: The Triumph of Capital and the Betrayal of Work.* (Reading MA: Addison-Wesley).

Chapter Eleven

Conclusion: The Rhythms of America's Geographical Past

Samuel M. Otterstrom and John Heppen

In this collection of essays we have endeavored to show the wide variety of ways that the American historical landscape has been shaped by individual forces and large-scale processes. Each chapter has taken the challenge to apply a theoretical framework based on a fifty-year cycle of crisis and recovery of the American political economy to at least one fundamental issue in the historical geography of the United States. Together they provide a picture of spatial economic and political restructuring across a wide swath of American history. The questions raised also invite future empirical analysis and exploration so our evolving understanding of the geographic restructuring of the American political economy can continue to be refined.

RECAPITULATION

This book has revealed how the political economy of the United States has experienced constantly reconfiguring spatial geographies. This evolution has spanned the entire period since European contact. Each succeeding generation has seen changes in settlement patterns, political systems, and economic control. This process has not followed a smooth trajectory. Instead it has been one of fits and starts, where changes in the American landscape have been impacted by political and economic policies and practices both in the continent and by foreign powers during the colonial period. This volume has sought to interconnect the world of America's past using examples that span nearly three hundred years of history while ranging in geographic scale from the very local to the global. Together they illustrate the power of taking an expressly geographic approach in order to answer significant historical and geographic questions.

M. J. Morgan's chapter refers us back to the beginning of North American colonization similar to Earle's (1979) study of Jamestown, where a strong geographically based argument formed the crux for the success or failure of the colony. While the historical record provided only sketchy evidence regarding sources and possibilities, this more geographic approach gives plausible credence to combining space-based historical geographies with the archival data sources in developing a sound explanation of past events. Morgan's analysis successfully pulls out tidbits of information to expose how subtle environmental differences could have caused conflict between the Cahokia Indians and the French. These geographical elements are crucial to understanding the reasons why one particular area experienced friction between Indian and European while surrounding settlements seemed to have no such trouble. Thus, in this example, Morgan makes a strong argument that localized geography such as river flood levels had a key role in explaining why even neighboring localities with outwardly similar circumstances experienced different historical outcomes.

As America gained independence, it was also on the cusp of rapid growth propelled by the Industrial Revolution. In the United States the Northeast had particular advantages that led to the rise of industry and tertiary economic activities. Kristen Keegan's chapter emphasizes this growth in Connecticut and shows how its various communities experienced varying levels of employment in the different economic sectors. The fact that population growth related to increases in services is logical but the uneven pattern of city growth points once again to some important underlying geographic factors that may have affected the success of certain urban areas over others. The time period of Keegan's study falls within both the first American Republic and first American Democracy. Therefore, the uneven development of cities within Connecticut was affected by regional specialization initially followed by regional diversification during the first American Democracy after approximately 1828. These larger spatial processes can help explain the development that occurred within the state during its early growth.

Keumsoo Hong took a different approach to evaluating settlement change by illustrating how the Red River valley evolved during its early growth using post office data as an indicator of city importance in the urban system. The movement of mail through the postal system of the region showed how this transfer of information indicated the development of the regional settlement system. Keumsoo tied this process nicely into the larger national picture. He found that Antebellum Louisiana, following Earle's (2003) paradigm, had passed through the Republican regime prior to 1830 and the Democracy regime after that year. During the Republican regime, the postal settlement increased in number and size as frontier regions were established and settled consistent with Republican ideology. Afterward, the earlier expansion phase of postal settlement was replaced by the consolidation during and after the 1840s, which was consistent with Democratic regimes. In summary, the alternating regimes were related to the crisis from cotton monoculture and the subsequent recovery that occurred by adopting environmentally sound agrarian wisdom of crop rotation combining corn, cotton and cowpeas.

We next consider the success of Anne Mosher's attempt to illuminate how political issues revolving around the Erie Canal were scale dependent. In this case, the state level must be considered rather than just the national one, because the canal lost its high level of local economic impact very quickly as distance from its route increased. Mosher's political index that compared the party affiliation of New York State elected officials with that of national leaders was an innovative method to show how both state and national scales have experienced their related but distinct political cycles. This realization drives home the point that both scale and place matter when one develops an historical explanation for political change. Mosher's efforts to apply Earle's cyclical historical thinking to her research provided important insights that can come to others studying a wide range of questions concerning America's past.

Similar to Anne Mosher, Samuel Otterstrom's chapter is an example where clear spatial patterns of alternating concentration and dispersion occurred. Once again, scale seems key to understanding these differences. In his analysis of manufacturing employment concentration in the United States since 1840, Otterstrom showed the presence of some long-term cycles in concentration change that correspond to Earle's model, while other findings are not so easy to fit into that theoretical structure. Generally, at the city-system level manufacturing concentration was higher than population concentration during most periods, but as population concentrated and manufacturing dispersed throughout each region the distribution of each became more similar. The timing of this convergence of relative population and manufacturing distributions appears to be related to larger scalar shifts tied to the change of America from a sectional state to a national state after the 1880s.

John Heppen's chapter examined the argument that income levels among states were affected by the policies extending from alternating politico-economic regimes. By dividing the country into classes of states ranging from core to periphery, Heppen illustrated how particular states either remained within one income category or moved between groups as changing regional economic fortunes impacted their incomes. The convergence of income during the Democracy of the mid-twentieth century and the subsequent increase of states in the peripheral income categories during the present protectionist-elite

Republic are evidences of the measurable influence that the regime- related policies have had on the American economy.

The work of Emily Duda and Fred Shelley was similar to Heppen's given that their study partially overlapped in twentieth century decades and it examined the transition between policy regimes. However, Shelley and Duda's concern was voting behavior and economic evolution in just one state, Ohio, rather than income conditions across the United States as Heppen emphasized. This chapter gives a fine example of the interlocking interaction between politics and local and regional economic realities. As Ohio has made the transition first, from a rural agrarian society to one very reliant on heavy manufacturing activities, and second, to one that has relinquished much of its industrial strength in the present post-industrial age, the political geography of presidential elections has shifted as well. The timing of these political and economic changes fits nicely within the policy regime rubric. The agrarian period up until 1932 mostly fell under a Protectionist Elite Republic, while the industrial heyday of Ohio from the mid-1930s to the late 1970s was in the midst of a pronounced Democracy. Ohio's latest move into post-industrialism corresponds with the current Republic that the United States is in. Shelley and Duda illustrated how the geography of presidential elections within individual Ohio counties was integrally connected with long-term economic trends that cannot be ignored and which, incidentally, supports the theory that one cannot disassociate a place from its geographical, political and economic histories without the risk of bypassing the actual explanation for the behavior of its people, which is the original purpose of the study.

John Agnew brought us to the present by arguing how the shift to globalization has fundamentally changed the economic standing of the United States. As America's manufacturing sector has declined over the past several decades and its jobs have been outsourced to more competitive locations, the country is now more affected by global influences. Its reliance on a consumer economy purchasing products increasingly not produced at home, translates into trade deficits supported by foreigners (especially China and Japan), using more and more consumer credit or loans backed by the paper value of real estate equity. This practice has put the country in an increasingly dangerous fiscal state. In explaining how foreign countries are gaining the advantage as they produce the goods that countries such as the United States consume, Agnew states "the productivity that results from larger economies of scale in places actually producing goods—that is, rising output per worker—will give rise to increasing revenues that can pay higher wages and fatten profits that, in turn, can be plowed into research and marketing of new products. From this viewpoint, just being the world's biggest consumer is unsustainable. It is no longer possible in such a situation for the United States to retain access to the profits and incomes that its mass market once made possible" (p. 211). Agnew points out that the winners and losers of this new economy have an unequal spatial distribution. Middle class manufacturing workers in the traditional industrial regions have lost jobs by the millions. These jobs have been replaced by generally lower paying retail and other service jobs. On the other hand, the highly skilled technological, financial, and international trade workers have prospered in this environment with large concentrations found in the Western and Northeastern metropolitan centers. Greater income inequality has also been a result. In summary, the United States has lost much of its ability to independently control its economic and political destiny precisely because it has moved beyond the National State into the realm of the Transnational State. Thus, Agnew sees this brewing economic turbulence as creating a serious crisis much earlier than Earle's paradigm predicts, which begs for a very innovative solution that has yet to arise.

AMERICA'S FUTURES

What is the future trajectory of the United States in terms of its political economy? For the sake of argument we will assume that the crisis outlined by John Agnew or another predicament will come at approximately fifty-year intervals. Accordingly, the current macro-historical period began in 1980 with a shift to an elite protectionist (PE) strategy. If our cycle is to last similar to previous cycles, then it should continue until about 2030. In accordance with this view, we speculate that there will be an important geographic reconfiguration coming before 2030 precipitated by a crisis in capitalism spurred by under-consumption or the implosion of consumption levels because of the lack of consumer purchasing power (with the current world economic crisis this change may come much earlier than 2030). This will require new geographic restructuring. The latest free-trade (FTM) configuration, we believe, will include regional volatility in incomes, especially in urban and rural areas and a return to more productive activities in cities since technological advances available will be diffused to urban and rural areas in an attempt to increase aggregate demand.

In other words, tied to Agnew's insights on widening income disparity, we believe that increasing income unevenness between highly dense and populated urban areas and rural areas will result in new and important regional changes. With millions of Americans underemployed or unemployed in the cities, because people have exited to suburban and exurban areas, there will be a huge pool of cheap labor and untapped markets. Just as in previous FTM regimes, under-consumption will need to be addressed. For example, hundreds of thousands of underemployed and unemployed Detroiters could be seen as a way out of a current economic crisis providing untapped consumers and low-cost labor. Transportation linkages seen as shuttling people out of the cities will be looked at as ways of getting raw material into and finished product out of cities. Programs to rebuild urban infrastructure, much like the TVA, WPA, and other New Deal programs, will be started to create greater aggregate demand and solve this distinct economic crisis. Educational funding will be increased as well and a renewed national attention to the sciences and technology will be sought in response to the scientific gains made by India and China.

As of this writing (March 2009), the U.S. political economy is moving farther and further into foreign territory. Not only is the country attempting to extract itself from an extended conflict in Iraq, it also has a very strained relationship with neighboring Iran and a military presence in Afghanistan that remains firmly in place while tensions and troubles continue. Geopolitically, America's military is seeking to keep its nation's interests intact even during the transition from the Bush to the Obama presidencies. Economically, the United States is experiencing one of the most distressing periods it has had over the past century. It is faced with increasing unemployment, significant stock markets declines, the collapse of the housing market in many areas, tremendous failures among the nation's top financial institutions, disintegration of consumer confidence, and a manufacturing sector that is on life support. With fluctuating demand at home and economic turmoil abroad, oil has shifted from being extremely high priced in the summer of 2008 when the dollar was quite weak followed by a spectacular dive in prices as demand slowed and the dollar strengthened as currencies such as the British Pound, the Euro, and the Japanese Yen have lost their luster. The U.S. housing boom that added trillions of dollars to the value of the country's housing stock between 2002 and 2006 has unwound with surprising fury. With an economic crisis in full swing during the fall of 2008, the nation chose a new president from the Democrats, Barack Obama, who is now implementing a huge stimulus plan in hopes that it will stave off an even more difficult situation. This appears to be a major transitional period for the country, the trajectory of which cannot be predicted.

After the Republicans enjoyed years of dominance in the House and Senate, congressional power shifted to the Democrats with the 2006 elections, and increased even more with the election of Barack Obama as president in 2008. What will happen next in the political economy of the United States is anyone's guess, but what does occur will surely impact its spatial structure both internally in its economic, settlement, and political reconfigurations, and externally with its projection of geopolitical influence in the international realm. Where is the United States in its current macro-historical period outlined by Earle, which began in 1980? Are we near the end of the diffusion phase of the creative changes instituted by the "Third Republic" or have we moved to dissent in the midst of the controversies revolving around America's military involvement in the Middle East and an economic dissolution at home?

THE CHALLENGE

We end with a challenge to scholars of the American past. This book has been an attempt to underscore the utility of a theoretically based political, historical, and spatial construct to understand and explain how the actions of Americans past and present have been interwoven with the long-term cycles of history and the opportunities and limitations of an evolving geographic base. We have shown that political regimes and their policies are not only explainable in terms of historical cyclical context, but they also manifest themselves in their impact on the organization of settled and unsettled territory.

It is crucial that researchers intent on discovering the nuances of America's past continue exploring American history using geographically-informed theory. To each of us the challenge is offered to give insight to the unfolding geographic patterns of economic growth and change in America. If we can take these opportunities and apply focused effort and expanding bases of knowledge to their best use, we will be able to more accurately portray the intricate workings of this exceptionally dynamic American landscape.

BIBLIOGRAPHY

Earle, C. 1979. *Environment, Disease, and Mortality in Early Virginia: The Chesapeake in the Seventeenth Century*. Chapel Hill: University of North Carolina.

———. 2003. *The American Way: A Geographical History of Crisis and Recovery*. Lanham, MD: Rowman & Littlefield.

Index

About the Contributors

John Agnew is professor of geography at the University of California–Los Angeles.

Emily Duda is a Ph.D. student in geography at the University of Texas.

John Heppen is associate professor of geography at the University of Wisconsin–River Falls.

Keumsoo Hong is associate professor at the Geography Education Department at Korea University.

Kristin Keegan is a Ph.D. student in geography at the University of Connecticut.

M. J. Morgan is adjunct professor of history at Kansas State University.

Anne Mosher is associate professor of geography at Syracuse University.

Samuel Otterstrom is associate professor in geography at Brigham Young University.

Fred Shelley is professor of geography at the University of Oklahoma.